Homeric Speech and
the Origins of Rhetoric

Homeric Speech and the Origins of Rhetoric

RACHEL AHERN KNUDSEN

Johns Hopkins University Press
Baltimore

Johns Hopkins University Press
2715 North Charles Street
Baltimore, Maryland 21218-4363
www.press.jhu.edu

Library of Congress Cataloging-in-Publication Data

Knudsen, Rachel Ahern.
    Homeric speech and the origins of rhetoric / Rachel Ahern Knudsen.
      pages cm
    Includes bibliographical references and index.
    ISBN-13: 978-1-4214-1226-9 (hardcover : alk. paper)
    ISBN-13: 978-1-4214-1227-6 (electronic)
    ISBN-10: 1-4214-1226-8 (hardcover : alk. paper)
    ISBN-10: 1-4214-1227-6 (electronic)
    1. Homer. Iliad.   2. Rhetoric, Ancient.   3. Aristotle—Criticism and
interpretation.   I. Title.
    PA4037.K575   2014
    883'.01—dc23

                                                          2013020204

A catalog record for this book is available from the British Library.

*Special discounts are available for bulk purchases of this book. For
more information, please contact Special Sales at 410-516-6936 or
specialsales@press.jhu.edu.*

Johns Hopkins University Press uses environmentally friendly
book materials, including recycled text paper that is composed of at
least 30 percent post-consumer waste, whenever possible.

For Margaret Ahern
My first and best teacher

Contents

Acknowledgments

This book would not have come into being without the influence and assistance of numerous individuals. First among them are the teachers whose guidance set me on the path to this endeavor: Margaret Ahern, who provided a home/school bursting at the seams with books; Fritz Hinrichs, who introduced me to the Great Books, including Homer; and Bruce McMenomy, who taught me the delights of grammar, rhetoric, and literary criticism. Special thanks must go to Richard Martin: no one could ask for a better teacher or dissertation advisor. His advice from the very earliest stages of this project to the very last has been invaluable. I am also grateful to Andrea Nightingale and Anastasia-Erasmia Peponi, whose comments on early versions of this manuscript refined its focus and improved its argument.

Several friends and colleagues have contributed advice at various stages along the way to publication. At Stanford, Eirene Visvardi, Lela Urquhart, Jason Aftosmis, and Vincent Tomasso engaged with these ideas when they were still in gestational form, asking astute questions that I had not thought to ask. My colleagues at the University of Oklahoma have supported me admirably through the latter stages of the publication process. In particular, I have benefitted from the comments and suggestions of Ellen Greene, who read parts of the manuscript; I would also like to thank Sam Huskey and Kyle Harper for providing advice, encouragement, and fruitful discussion of the ideas contained in this book. I am grateful to the University of Oklahoma for the generous award of Junior Faculty Summer Research Fellowships in 2010 and 2011, which allowed me to complete much of the writing and revision.

The critiques provided by an anonymous reader at Johns Hopkins University Press were thoughtful and incisive, and have very much improved the finished product. I must also thank Matthew McAdam, the Classics and Humanities editor at JHU Press, for expertly shepherding this work to its completion. Any remaining faults are entirely my own.

Final thanks are owed to my husband, Ed, who has listened, exhorted, and expanded my perspective during this process. I dedicate this book to my mother, Margaret Ahern, who homeschooled me and my siblings from kindergarten through high school. She read me stories from Greek myth and the Trojan war before I read them myself; she infected me with the joy of learning and reading and writing; she set me loose in the wonderland of literature, which has not yet ceased to amaze.

Homeric Speech and
the Origins of Rhetoric

Introduction

From ancient times to the present, rhetoric has been recognized as essential to the discourses of politics, advertising, law, education, and interpersonal relations. Definitions of rhetoric from the ancient Greek and Roman world attest to its deep significance. According to Plato, rhetoric is "a way of directing the soul by means of speech"; to Aristotle, it is "an ability, in each particular case, to see the available means of persuasion"; to Quintilian, "the science of speaking well."[1] In modern-day parlance, by contrast, the term "rhetoric" tends to have one of three connotations: it may refer disparagingly to the polished, superficial appeal of the diction of set speeches (such as those of a politician or lecturer), implying that this appeal masks vacuous or deceitful content; it may refer to a narrow, ossified set of stylistic tropes found in literature, bearing little relevance beyond the high-school English or composition classroom; or it may be broadly applied, particularly in academic contexts, to the type of discourse peculiar to a subject or author—"the rhetoric of freedom," "the rhetoric of Milton," or "the rhetoric of corporate social responsibility," for example. None of these connotations, however, reflects the robust and far-reaching presence of rhetoric in everyday modern life, if we understand the term as it has been understood and used for most of its history. As Brian Vickers has observed, modern usage "has reduced rhetoric not just from a primary to secondary role—from oral to written communication—but to *elocutio* alone, now detached from its expressive and persuasive functions, and brought down finally to a handful of tropes."[2]

Although it may be impossible to posit a universal definition of rhetoric due to the numerous and context-dependent ways that it can be (and historically has been) defined, it is safe to say that rhetoric in its earliest formulation in ancient Greece was credited with much broader significance and power than it carries today.[3] Namely, it was conceived of as the power to achieve change in a listener's actions or attitudes through words—particularly through persuasive techniques and argumentation. Rhetoric was thus a "technical" discipline in the ancient Greek world, a craft (*technê*) that was rule-governed, learned, and taught. This technical understanding of rhetoric can be traced back to the works of Plato and Aristotle, which provide the earliest formal explanations of rhetoric; Plato, indeed, is thought to have coined the term, which appears for the first time in his *Gorgias* (c. 385 BCE). But do such formal explanations constitute the origins of rhetoric as an identifiable, systematic practice? If not, where does a technique-driven rhetoric first appear in literary and social history?

The answer proposed by this book is that the Homeric epics are the locus for the origins of rhetoric. This claim has implications for the fields of Homeric poetry and the history of rhetoric. In the former field, it refines and extends previous scholarship on direct speech in Homer by identifying a new dimension within Homeric speech: namely, the consistent deployment of well-defined rhetorical arguments and techniques, including sensitivity to individual audiences. In the latter field, it challenges the traditional account of the development of rhetoric, probing the boundaries that currently demarcate its origins, history, and relationship to poetry. I do not aim to rewrite wholesale the history of rhetoric. I do aim, however, to suggest that there might be a different starting point than the ones generally identified by historians of rhetoric, and to examine the implications of that different starting point. I will therefore begin by summarizing both the traditional account of rhetoric's beginnings and the more recent scholarly debate over the precise dating and definition of rhetoric within this traditional account.

According to the traditional account, best articulated in modern rhetorical scholarship by George Kennedy (1963, 1994), the Syracusans Corax and Tisias invented the discipline of rhetoric in the mid-fifth century by identifying the parts of a speech and the argument from probability.[4] These two shadowy figures (possibly one and the same person, according to both Kennedy and Thomas Cole) are known to us only through the references of other authors; Plato and Aristotle both speak of them as inventors of rhetoric.[5] The craft of persuasive speaking through instruction and performance of set speeches was popularized by another Syracusan, Gorgias, who came to Athens in 427 BCE. Handbooks with instruction in persuasive techniques (the so-called *technai logôn*) began to circulate around or after 400 BCE, later to be subsumed under the exhaustive Aristotelian treatise on the subject.[6] But there has been considerable debate in recent years about the exact point at which rhetoric emerged as a theoretically grounded system. This debate centers on whether to locate the origins of rhetoric in the fifth or the fourth century. According to several recent works, it is only with the emergence of a technical vocabulary for rhetoric in the fourth century that we can speak of the true invention of rhetoric. Thomas Cole, in *The Origins of Rhetoric in Ancient Greece* (1991), proposes an alternative to the widely held notion that rhetoric originated with Corax, Tisias, Protagoras, and Gorgias in the fifth century. He argues that Plato and Aristotle are the true founders of rhetoric because of the "radical clarity" with which they established the philosophical and theoretical underpinnings of the discipline.[7] Edward Schiappa, in *The Beginnings of Rhetorical Theory in Classical Greece* (1999), takes a somewhat similar view, but makes his case on the basis of technical terminology: until the term *rhêtorikê* appears in Plato's *Gorgias*, Schiappa argues, we cannot speak of the historical occurrence of rhetoric or even rhetorical pedagogy.[8]

This book argues that both accounts of the origins of rhetoric—the traditional account, which locates the origins in the fifth century with Corax, Tisias, and Gorgias; and the more recent movement, which places them in the fourth century with Plato and Aristotle—are missing something. This is because both are operating from the same fundamental framework—namely, they restrict their parameters for "rhetoric" to the same narrow range of fifth- and fourth-century prose texts. This modern reconstruction of the discipline neglects what is in fact a richer ancient tradition that does not so strictly demarcate boundaries between the literary and the critical, or even between poetry and prose. In fact, many ancients saw poetry and rhetoric as having symbiotic relationship. Peter Struck discusses this reality in his work on ancient literary criticism, noting that "many in the ancient world thought rhetoric and poetry share a great deal"; the prime example of this, according to Struck, is Quintilian, who "produces literary commentary nearly always within the context of rhetorical investigation."[9] The ancient assumption of a close relationship between the *technê* of rhetoric and Homeric poetry, which I will examine in greater length in chapter 1, is captured in the assertion of the late second-century CE critic Pseudo-Plutarch: "no reasonable person will deny that Homer was an artificer of discourse (τεχνίτης λόγων)"[10] (*Essay on the Life and Poetry of Homer* 171). But this assumption is one that has been gradually lost since antiquity—a tendency that, I will argue in chapter 6, can be attributed particularly to Aristotle, with his fondness for division and categorization.

That Homer was the father or inventor of rhetoric is not an original claim, though it is now considered an outdated one. The contention of this book is more pointed: that Homer not only demonstrates rhetorical practice in the speech of his characters, but that the patterns of persuasion that he depicts embody, in very specific ways, the rhetoric identified in theoretical treatises from the fifth and fourth centuries BCE, and that reached its fullest expression in Aristotle's *Rhetoric*. Contrary to the characterization of Homeric speech found in modern histories of rhetoric—that it consists of "native eloquence" or inspiration—I contend that the Homeric narrator presents speaking as a technical skill, one that must be taught and learned, and one that varies according to speaker, situation, and audience. While much scholarly work has analyzed the phenomenon of direct speech in Homer, this work has tended to focus not on the internal rhetoric of the speeches but on the way that speech reflects either the characters' personalities or the poet's powers of characterization (see, among others, A. Parry 1956; Friedrich and Redfield 1978; Griffin 1986; and Mackie 1996). Somewhat closer to the topic of "Homeric rhetoric" are works on formal aspects of Homeric speech, such as speech type (Fingerle 1939) and structure (Lohmann 1970); on Homeric speech analyzed through the lens of discourse analysis (Martin 1989); and on speech presentation in Homer from a narratological perspective (de Jong 1987 and Beck 2012).[11] Generally, though, where the term "rhetoric" has been attributed to Homeric speakers, it has referred to the surface-level rhetoric of stylistic devices: James Redfield, for example, speaks of Achilles' great Book 9 speech as "full of rhetorical virtuosity, with its use of simile, analogy, and irony, its repeated series, its mixture of long and short sentences."[12] Such stylistic features are certainly worth noting, but they are not particularly uncommon within Archaic poetry, nor are they comparable to the deeper level of argumentative strategies that constitute formal rhetoric on the Aristotelian model. Few scholars have examined Homeric direct speech in light of the later development of formal rhetoric.[13] In a sense, then, this book seeks to revive the ancient interest in Homer's relationship to rhetoric; but it takes a comprehensive analytical approach rather than a doxographical one. I am aware of the pitfalls of such an undertaking. As Laurent Pernot cautions when dismissing the ancients' opinion on this subject, "We must be wary of a retrospective interpretation, overlaying *a posteriori* the art of rhetoric onto texts still unaware of it."[14] I believe that the way to avoid such anachronism is to approach the issue with a comprehensive look at speeches throughout the whole text of a Homeric epic, and to analyze them according to a consistent standard for ancient rhetoric.

There are many indications in the *Iliad* that the Homeric composer—and the Homeric heroes themselves, as depicted by the composer—conceive of speech as a craft (*technê*), something that can be taught, learned, and improved upon.

The most basic evidence for this is the frequent comparison made between two different heroes in terms of their speaking prowess. The character of Antenor, in conversation with Helen during the *teikhoskopia*, compares the speech styles of Menelaus and Odysseus in the famous passage in Book 3.203–24.[15] The narrator, in 18.252, contrasts the abilities of two Trojan heroes thus: "But he [Pouly-damas] was better in words (μύθοισιν . . . ἐνίκα), the other [Hector] with the spear (ἔγχεϊ) far better."[16] The embassy to Achilles in Book 9 presents the widely divergent styles and strategies of three characters trying to achieve the same goal, inviting the hearer or reader to compare the persuasive power of Odysseus, Phoenix, and Ajax. Phoenix himself claims that he has taught Achilles to be a "speaker of words" (μύθων ῥητῆρ) as well as a "doer of deeds" (9.443)—the passage most often quoted by ancient critics as evidence of rhetoric in Homer. A fuller accounting of such "meta-rhetorical" passages appears at the end of this chapter.

In establishing my claim that the composer(s) of the *Iliad* was representing a rule-governed practice that might fairly be called "rhetoric," I will not present the entirety of the Homeric corpus as evidence. This is because I do not consider the poetic / narrative voice to be rhetorical in the robust, technical sense of the word that I am using in this study. It is the narrative voice, not character speech, which has inspired many of the comments about Homer's rhetorical genius from ancient enthusiasts; likewise, the narrative voice is almost exclusively the focus of any modern scholarship referring to the "rhetoric" of Homer.[17] In contrast, my argument focuses on *direct speeches* in the *Iliad* that are *intended to persuade*, since direct speeches bear the closest correspondence to later oratory and thus provide the most relevant examples for my contention. My definition of "speeches that are intended to persuade" does not include those speeches that consist simply of commands in the imperative, but rather those that bring some type of argument to bear on the desired outcome: logical reasoning, shaming, the offering of incentives, etc.

As the primary textual data for my investigation of Homeric rhetoric, I have chosen speeches in the *Iliad*, which I hold up to the rhetorical standards codified in Aristotle's *Rhetoric*. Why the *Iliad*, it may be asked—not other works of Archaic poetry, and not also (or instead) the *Odyssey*? First of all, direct speeches in the Homeric epics provide the largest data set from Archaic literature for the phenomenon that is most analogous to Classical oratory, and hence to rhetoric. Homeric speeches are longer and much more numerous than the speeches found in other Archaic texts (although represented speech in other Archaic texts— Hesiod, the Homeric Hymns, and Pindar, for example—will be examined for its role in the development of rhetoric in chapter 5), and thus are uniquely able to constitute a significant sample size for testing my claim that there is a systematic employment of rhetorical techniques prior to the so-called "invention" of rhetoric. That Homeric speeches are embedded into a narrative framework also makes them a fruitful subject for analysis because such a presentation creates "critical distancing," in the words of Pernot. "Sometimes it is another character who judges the speech that has just been delivered; sometimes the action itself, by the course of events, is responsible for showing if a speech was accurate or not, appropriate or not."[18]

The reason for my choice to focus on speeches in the *Iliad*, and refer to the *Odyssey* only incidentally, is because the former provides a sufficiently large body of evidence for my claims about rhetoric in Homer, while the latter adds comparatively little to this evidence. It is clear from even a cursory reading of the *Odyssey* that its speeches are generally of a different nature than those of the *Iliad*, due to the difference in subject matter. There is very little "public" speaking in the *Odyssey*—that is, speeches made for the benefit of an audience, in the setting of an assembly or a battlefield—aside from the obvious set-piece of Odysseus' four-book travel narration at the center of the poem, which, in both form and function, bears more resemblance to narrative than to direct speech. Instead, speech in the *Odyssey* tends to occur in the context of private, conversational interactions, most often between two individuals;[19] such interactions provide fewer occasions for the kind of formal persuasive speeches that are found in the *Iliad*. Deborah Beck notes that whereas the *Odyssey* makes extensive use of one-on-one conversation, "the *Iliad* depicts its characters engaged in a wide range of speech exchange systems other than one-on-one conversation. These systems, which include vaunts, challenges, assemblies, athletic games, and laments, either do not appear in the *Odyssey* or appear in a very limited way."[20] Finally, the *Iliad* is a poem filled with opportunities for and attempts at persuasion by virtue of its setting in war; the military struggle is mirrored in a constant dialectical exchange between the warring sides, as well as among them. While my rubric for identifying and analyzing rhetorical speeches in the *Iliad* could certainly be extended to include speeches in the *Odyssey*, that will be the work of another project.

This book is divided into two separate but related parts. Part I aims to demonstrate the presence of a theoretical conception of rhetoric in the *Iliad*. Part II explores the implications of part I by asking, first, how we might account for the phenomenon of rhetoric in Homer; and second, how might the Homeric system of rhetoric have influenced the Classical-era development of formal rhetoric, crossing lines of time, genre, and societal / performance contexts?[21] Chapter 1 sets the stage for my primary investigation by considering a diverse body of ancient testimony on the subject of rhetoric in Homer. This testimony stands in stark contrast to modern scholars' dismissal of such a notion in favor of the view that Homer merely operates from a vague conception of "eloquence." Chapter 2 contains the textual analysis central to my contention, an examination of persuasive direct speeches from the *Iliad* that reveals consistent, detailed similarities between ancient rhetorical theory and Homeric poetry. Chapter 3 summarizes the findings of chapter 2 with the aid of figures, tracing patterns both in the rhetorical techniques used across the 58 "rhetorical" speeches that I have identified in the *Iliad*, and in the speakers most likely to employ rhetoric generally and to use specific techniques in particular. In chapter 4, I consider possible explanations for the correspondences between Homeric rhetoric and Aristotelian rhetorical theory, and use comparative evidence from several ancient societies to shed light on whether such correspondences are due to the universality of rhetoric. In chapter 5, I look diachronically at the awareness and use of rhetoric in Archaic Greek poetry. The book's final chapter considers the relationship of Homeric rhetoric to the Classical-era developments of tragedy, sophistry, and rhetorical theory. It challenges the conceptual boundaries that have been erected—beginning with Aristotle and continuing into the present— between poetry and prose, and between genre categories such as "poetry" and "rhetoric."

Before proceeding, it is important to establish the way in which I am defining the term "rhetoric" for this study. There are myriad ways in which rhetoric can be (and has been) defined, from Kennedy's sweepingly general notion of rhetoric as "a form of mental and emotional energy" prior to and more basic than speech[22] to Pernot's relatively specific definition as "a way to produce persuasive speech based upon a certain know-how and even on recipes," grounded in "a profound and systematic reflection on the nature and functioning of the spoken word."[23] Pernot's definition gets at a basic distinction within the usage of the term "rhetoric": in the ancient world, as well as in our own, "rhetoric" can describe both practice ("a way to produce persuasive speech based upon a certain know-how") and theory ("a profound and systematic reflection on the nature and functioning of the spoken word"). This distinction is important to my argument, for while I rely heavily on Aristotle's *Rhetoric* as a comparandum for the techniques of persuasive speech found in Homer, and claim that Homeric characters employ highly developed rhetoric, I recognize that the two authors embody different sides of the practice / theory distinction. Homer presents rhetoric in practice, while

Aristotle presents rhetoric in theory. The operational definition of rhetoric for this study draws on Aristotle's *Rhetoric*, since it both provides a highly detailed and structured explanation of rhetoric, and represents the most wide-ranging ancient treatment of the subject, having collected and codified the various *technai* that preceded it. Aristotle's short definition of rhetoric, provided at the beginning of his treatise, is "the faculty (δύναμις) of discovering the possible means of persuasion in reference to any subject whatever" (*Rhetoric* 1.2.1); the remainder of the *Rhetoric* provides the technical and practical expansion of this definition.[24] The definition from which I will operate is a condensation of Aristotle's ideas: *Rhetoric is a learned and deliberately practiced skill, involving the deployment of tropes and techniques according to a rule-based system, and aimed at winning an audience's approval or assent.*

—◦ ◦—

To conclude this introduction, I present a collection of passages from the *Iliad* that suggest an awareness, on the part of both the narrator and the characters, of strategies of persuasive speech. In his discussion of the *teikhoscopia* in *Iliad* 3, Richard Martin has noted that "the speeches embody an assumption, often overlooked: that heroes themselves can evaluate one another's 'style,' particularly in the act of speaking."[25] I would extend this observation by saying that such internal evaluations treat not only speaking style, but other aspects of persuasive speech as well: argumentative content, argumentative completeness, and the suitability of persuasive techniques to the particular listener, to name a few. The following "meta-rhetorical" passages from the *Iliad* all exhibit this kind of reflective analysis. Some of them have long been used to support the argument that Homer knew and employed rhetoric; others have gone previously unremarked in connection with this topic, to my knowledge.[26]

1. Odysseus' use of different exhortation strategies based upon the particular audience, 2.188–206:

> Whenever he encountered **some king, or man of influence** (τινα μὲν βασιλῆα καὶ ἔξοχον ἄνδρα), he would stand beside him and **with soft words** (ἀγανοῖς ἐπέεσσιν) try to restrain him: "Excellency! It does not become you to be frightened like any coward. Rather hold fast and check the rest of the people. . . ." When he saw **some man of the people** (δήμου τ' ἄνδρα) who was shouting, he would strike at him with his staff, and **reprove him** (ὁμοκλήσασκέ τε μύθῳ) also: "Excellency! Sit still and listen to what others tell you, to those who are better men than you, you skulker and coward."

Odysseus tailors his approach to persuasion according to the social class of the addressee, both verbally—using soft words and reasoned arguments ("it does not become you") for the kings, but imperative commands and insults for the common soldiers—and also physically. He literally stands on equal footing (παραστάς, 189) with the kings, but beats the soldiers into action. The narrator's characterization of the speech-act involved in each rhetorical approach reinforces the status hierarchy at play: Martin's work has shown that "the word muthos implies authority and power; epos implies nothing about these values."[27] It is no surprise, then, that Odysseus is depicted as using *epos* to address the kings and *muthos* to command the commoners.

2. Antenor's description of the contrast between Menelaus' and Odysseus' speech, 3.212–224:

> Now before all when **both of them spun their speech and their counsels** (μύθους καὶ μήδεα πᾶσιν ὕφαινον), Menelaos indeed spoke rapidly, in few words but exceedingly lucid, since he was no long speaker nor one who wasted his words, though he was only a young man. But when that other drove to his feet, resourceful Odysseus, he would just stand and stare down, eyes fixed on the ground beneath him, nor would he gesture with the staff backward and forward, but hold it clutched hard in front of him, like any man who knows nothing. Yes, you would call him a sullen man, and a fool likewise. But when he let the great voice go from his chest, and the words came drifting down like the winter snows, then no other mortal man beside could stand up against Odysseus. Then we wondered less beholding Odysseus' outward appearance.

More a eulogy for the forcefulness and eloquence of these two speakers than a detailed analysis, Antenor's observations nevertheless bespeak an attentiveness to differences in speech qualities and the effect produced by speakers on an audience. In addition, his use of the verb ὑφαίνειν ("to weave," "to contrive") with regard to speech suggests calculation and craft on the part of the speaker.

3. Nestor's commentary on Diomedes' speaking and persuasive ability, 9.53–62:

> Son of Tydeus, beyond others you are strong in battle, and in counsel also are noblest among all men of your own age. Not one man of all the Achaians will belittle your words nor speak against them. Yet **you have not made complete your argument** (οὐ τέλος ἵκεο μύθων), since you are a young man still and could even be my own son and my youngest born of all; yet still **you argue in wisdom** (πεπνυμένα βάζεις) with the Argive kings, since **all you have spoken was spoken fairly** (κατὰ

μοῖραν ἔειπες). But let me speak, since I can call myself older than you are, and **go through the whole matter** (πάντα διίξομαι), since there is none who can dishonor the thing I say, not even powerful Agamemnon.

Nestor critiques Diomedes' failure to achieve a τέλος μύθων and contrasts this with his own ability to "go through the whole matter" (that is, both encouraging the disheartened Achaean army and at the same time humoring the cowardly Agamemnon) in his speech. I will discuss the significance of this speech in greater depth in chapter 2; in the present context it is simply worth noting that Nestor applies qualitative and comparative judgments to speech (as Antenor had done in the previous passage). Nestor's words indicate an *awareness* of what elements are successful and unsuccessful for persuasion, and a conception of speech as a skill—a skill that, according to Nestor, increases with practice and experience.

4. The wary introductory comments of Achilles in response to Odysseus' embassy speech, 9.309–14:

> **Without consideration** for you (ἀπηλεγέως, "forthrightly"[28]) I must make my answer . . . [so] that you may not come one after another, and sit by me, and **speak softly** (τρύζητε). For as I detest the doorways of Death, I detest that man who hides one thing in the depths of his heart, and speaks forth another. But I will speak to you the way it seems best to me.

The use of speech for deceit and manipulation is one of Plato's major complaints against rhetoric in the *Gorgias*; but Achilles recognized this as a problem long before the rise of the sophists. The distinction between open, forthright speech and guileful, manipulative speech is one that recurs in both the *Iliad* and the *Odyssey*, and the latter type is especially associated with Odysseus. Antenor's Book 3 observations had pitted the "exceedingly lucid" Menelaus against the πολύμητις Odysseus, with his snowstorm-shower of words; the Book 9 embassy draws an implicit contrast between the three speakers (crafty Odysseus, rambling Phoenix, and straightforward Ajax); and the prominent Odyssean epithet πολύτροπος can refer to, among other things, his wily, "twisting" speech.

5. Phoenix's words to Achilles, 9.442–43:

> Therefore he sent me along with you to teach you of all these matters, **to make you a speaker of words and one accomplished in action** (μύθων τε ῥητῆρ' ἔμεναι πρηκτῆρά τε ἔργων).

This is the most commonly cited statement for ancient commentators making the argument for rhetoric in Homer, as it provides a tidy summation of evidence.

There is the vocabulary of oratory / rhetoric, seen in the term ῥητῆρ; and there is indication that Homeric characters viewed speaking as a matter for *didaxis*, and therefore as a *technê*.

6. Nestor urging Patroclus to convince Achilles to rejoin the battle, 11.792–93 (repeated by Patroclus to Eurypylos, 15.403–4):

> Who knows if, with God helping, **you might trouble his spirit with entreaty** (θυμὸν ὀρίναις παρειπών), since the **persuasion** (παραίφασις) of a friend is a strong thing.

Nestor's gnomic statement about the persuasion of a friend (παραίφασις carries the connotations of "encouragement" as well as "beguilement," according to the *Greek-English Lexicon* of Liddell, Scott, and Jones) again points to a conception among the Iliadic characters of the power of speech. In addition, it acknowledges that the relationship between speaker and addressee is of critical importance to persuasion—something that Aristotle establishes at length in his *Rhetoric* when discussing the orator's *êthos*.

7. The exchange between Polydamas and Hector, 12.211–250: Polydamas begins his speech by saying "Hektor, somehow in assembly you move ever against me **though I speak excellently** (ἐσθλὰ φραζομένῳ)" (211–12). Hector begins his response with the words, "Your mind knows how to contrive a saying better than this one (οἶσθα καὶ ἄλλον μῦθον ἀμείνονα τοῦδε νοῆσαι)" (232); and ends it with a threat of death if Polydamas turns any soldier away from fighting by "beguiling him with your arguments (παρφάμενος ἐπέεσσιν)" (249). This exchange, with its dynamics of power and persuasion, will receive fuller treatment in the appendix. Of interest here is the two Trojans' clash over the use of speech. Polydamas cites his own excellence in speaking as reason for Hector to assent to his plans; Hector keeps the quarrel centered on speaking prowess, but finds fault with Polydamas on two somewhat contradictory counts: at the beginning, he decries the poor quality of Polydamas' speech (because he had criticized Hector's plan); at the end, he accuses Polydamas of abusing his persuasive power by "beguiling" the soldiers to cowardly action. Persuasive speech, in this exchange, is a locus for debate among the characters, an abstract concept about which qualitative (if disputed) judgments can be made.

8. Odysseus' rebuke to Agamemnon after the latter's third speech urging the Greek army to sail home (following his "test" speech at 2.110–41 and his speech at 9.17–28), 14.90–93:

> Silence, for fear some other Achaian might hear this **word** (μῦθος), which could never at all get past the lips of **any man who understood inside his heart how to**

speak soundly (ὅς τις ἐπίσταιτο ᾗσι φρεσὶν ἄρτια βάζειν), who was a sceptered king, and **whom the people obeyed / were persuaded by** (οἱ πειθοίατο λαοί).

This criticism demonstrates that speaking skill was for the Homeric characters a matter of knowledge and understanding, not simply a matter of natural eloquence. It also provides another example of speech being assessed and judged; Agamemnon's speech, according to Odysseus, displays a lack of "soundness," which is incompatible with the authoritative persuasion of a leader. Indeed, Odysseus and Diomedes must take over from Agamemnon the duty of persuading the army to stay and fight.

9. The Homeric narrator's comments on the respective strengths of Polydamas and Hector, 18.252:

> But he [Polydamas] was better in words, the other [Hector] with the spear far better (ἀλλ' ὁ μὲν ἄρ μύθοισιν, ὁ δ' ἔγχεϊ πόλλον ἐνίκα).

This statement reinforces what we have already seen, namely that standards of speech (good, bad; better, worse; persuasive, unpersuasive) exist in the minds of both characters and narrator.

10. A legal dispute occurring in a marketplace, depicted in one of the scenes on the shield of Achilles, 18.498–508:

> Two men were disputing over the blood price for a man who had been killed. . . .
> **[They] took turns speaking their cases** (ἀμοιβηδὶς δὲ δίκαζον), and between them lay on the ground two talents of gold, to be given to that judge who in this case **spoke the straightest opinion** (δίκην ἰθύντατα εἴποι).

This case is complete with arguments from both sides and a decision (δίκη) by a judge. Notably, the verb δικάζειν is the same one that Aristotle uses to speak of forensic oratory in the *Rhetoric*.

11. Agamemnon's approval of Odysseus' proposal to rest before battle (a sensible alternative to the reckless approach of Achilles), 19.185–86:

> Hearing **what you have said** (τὸν μῦθον), son of Laertes, I am pleased with you. **Fairly have you gone through everything and explained it** (ἐν μοίρῃ γὰρ πάντα διίκεο καὶ κατέλεξας).

This is yet another example of the internal evaluation of speech in the *Iliad*. Agamemnon's praise is reminiscent of Nestor's speech to Diomedes in Book 9 (cited above), where he had said that the young man "spoke fairly" (κατὰ μοῖραν ἔειπες 9.59). In addition, Agamemnon uses the same verb (διϊκνέομαι) for the act of "going through" or "covering" everything in speech that Nestor had applied to himself (πάντα διίξομαι 9.61).

12. Aeneas' battlefield challenge to Achilles, 20.201–2 (repeated by Hector to Achilles, 20.432–33):

> I myself understand well enough how to speak in vituperation and how to make insults (σάφα οἶδα καὶ αὐτὸς / ἠμὲν κερτομίας ἠδ' αἴσυλα μυθήσασθαι).

This assertion, coming in response to Achilles' taunts, indicates that Aeneas views speech (μυθήσασθαι) as something that must be understood (σάφα οἶδα)—that is, apprehended or learned. His use of αὐτὸς emphasizes the notion that an ability to wield *muthoi* is not simply a universal practice; it is a skill that he (like Achilles) has mastered.

13. Again from Aeneas' battlefield challenge to Achilles, 20.248–56:

> **The tongue of man is a twisty thing** (στρεπτὴ δὲ γλῶσσ' ἐστὶ βροτῶν), **there are plenty of words there of every kind** (πολέες δ' ἔνι μῦθοι παντοῖοι), **the range of words is wide, and their variance** (ἐπέων δὲ πολὺς νομὸς ἔνθα καὶ ἔνθα). The sort of thing you say is the thing that will be said to you. But what have you and I to do with the need for squabbling and hurling insults at each other. . . . You will not **by talking turn me back** (ἐπέεσσιν ἀποτρέψεις) from the strain of my warcraft.

Aeneas makes several observations about the nature of speech: he characterizes the tongue as "twisty" or "flexible" (other metaphorical uses of this adjective in Homer describe the gods (*Iliad* 9.497) and "good men" (*Iliad* 15.203) to refer to their capacity for adaptation and compromise); and he describes words as abundant, diverse, and able to provide the material for wide-ranging expression. The choice of the phrase νομὸς ἐπέων, "range of words," indicates a recognition of speech as having an enclosed area, with boundaries and rules, but also as being broad (πολύς) and variable (ἔνθα καὶ ἔνθα).[29] This *sententia*, and particularly the word νομός ("range, district"), attributes qualities of delimitation, order, and thus calculation to speech. According to the scholia on this passage, the activities denoted by the phrase πολὺς νομός are "to distribute and to scan many things; to blame and to praise" (πολλὰ νεμηθῆναι καὶ ἐπιδραμεῖν, καὶ ψέξαι καὶ ἐπαινέσαι)[30]—a description which looks strikingly similar to later descriptions of the functions of rhetoric. Finally, Aeneas also acknowledges the limitations of persuasive speech; in this particular situation—a duel with Achilles—words will be of no avail.

In summary, the meta-rhetorical features contained in this list include: (1) evaluation of speech quality according to standards such as completeness of argument, adherence to order or propriety, forthrightness / authenticity of voice, and ability to persuade (a capability viewed in both positive and negative terms); (2) discrimination between speakers with regard to their ability (e.g., the comparisons made between Menelaus and Odysseus, Nestor and Diomedes, Hector and Polydamas); (3) discrimination between audiences with regard to the rhetorical approach taken (e.g., Odysseus' exhortations to the Greek chiefs and the common soldiers); and (4) references to instruction in speaking (e.g., Phoenix to Achilles) and practical knowledge about speaking (e.g., Hector to Polydamas, Aeneas to Achilles). The cumulative force of this list suggests that the Homeric composer possesses an overarching awareness of what constitutes persuasively effective speech. But this list alone is only a fraction of the argument; a greater body of evidence is to be found in the *Iliad*'s persuasive speeches themselves. As I examine these speeches in the coming chapters, it will be useful to keep in mind the framework provided by the meta-rhetorical passages above. They support the notion that persuasive speech in the *Iliad* is a regulated system, undergirded by reflection, assessment, and learned technique.

PART ONE

Rhetoric in Homer

CHAPTER ONE

Reconsidering the Origins of Rhetoric

I. HOMER AND RHETORIC: MODERN OPINIONS

Although modern accounts of the history of rhetoric (Kennedy 1963, 1994; Cole 1991; Schiappa 1999; and Pernot 2005 being primary examples) vary in emphasis and approach, all of them generally agree on the role of Homeric poetry in their histories. In their view, Homer is innocent of any systematic craft of rhetoric, a perspective summed up by Cole's use of the phrase "native eloquence" to account for the sophisticated patterns of speech that occur in Homer.[1] Kennedy and Pernot, whose works represent a fairly traditional account of the origins of rhetoric, both mention Homer in their introductory chapters. These chapters cover Greek history and literature up to the fifth century BCE—before the "invention" of rhetoric, by their calculation: Kennedy's (1963) first chapter is entitled "Persuasion in Greek Literature before 400 B.C.E.," and Pernot's is "Rhetoric before 'Rhetoric.'" A few representative passages can convey the attitude taken by these scholars toward the presence of rhetoric in Homer. In describing speech within the Homeric epics, Pernot draws upon Marcel Detienne's notions of "parole magico-religieuse" ("magico-religious speech") and "parole-dialogue" ("dialogue-speech"):

> Certain passages are related to the notion of an empowered speech, in the full sense of the term, a speech endowed with an intrinsic efficaciousness, the speech of the "masters of truth," who are also masters of deceit. Yet Homer uses speech more often as a means of exchange between individuals or within a group. . . . This dialogue-speech is fraught with thought, but also with emotion or trickery,

making use of arguments and stylistic and structural effects. It does not have, however, codified forms (in the way that the forms of rhetorical discourse will be codified later).[2]

Pernot does no more than speak in vague terms about Homer's depiction of speech; he goes on to say that "Homer did not anticipate the laws of rhetoric, but he established, in accord with the ideas of his own time, the importance of the spoken word."[3] While the Homeric epics may have prized "eloquence," they do not, according to Pernot, betray any knowledge of formal elements of persuasive speech ("codified forms"). Any persuasion effected by Homer's characters is due to the mysterious quality of "intrinsic efficaciousness," or by "emotion and trickery" rather than by systematic deployment of rhetorical techniques. Kennedy is slightly more open than is Pernot to the notion of a Homeric awareness of rhetoric on some level:

> When study of rhetoric began in the fifth century B.C.E. much of what was said was merely a theorizing of conventional practice. Techniques of rhetorical theory are already evident in the speeches of the Homeric poems to such a degree that later antiquity found formal rhetoric everywhere in Homer and on the basis of *Iliad*, 15.283f., even conjured up a picture of practice declamations among the Homeric heroes. Speech in epic is generally treated as an irrational power, seen in the ability to move an audience and in its effect on a speaker himself, and is thus inspiration, a gift of the gods. But it is difficult to believe that there did not exist in all periods certain critical principles, generally, if tacitly, accepted.[4]

However, he seems to be attributing Homeric use of "techniques of rhetorical theory" to a universal consciousness of "certain critical principles." Any notion of Homeric speech as technical or calculated is effaced by Kennedy's assertion that it was depicted as an irrational, divinely inspired power (a notion that, if anything, is more Hesiodic than Homeric).[5] Kennedy's attitude toward Homer shows a tendency typical among modern scholars of rhetoric, namely to characterize him as the unsophisticated but artistically gifted bard. The attitude can be summarized by Kennedy's claim that "the most interesting aspects of Homeric rhetoric are its native vigor and its relation to the concept of the orator which was later to develop."[6]

Cole and Schiappa diverge somewhat from the traditional account of the origins of rhetoric as articulated by Kennedy and Pernot. Cole claims that the "true founders" of the discipline were Plato and Aristotle, not their fifth-century predecessors Corax, Tisias, Gorgias, and the writers of technical handbooks on the subject. He sees literacy as essential for producing analytical thinking about rhetoric,[7] and consequently posits the "basically 'arhetorical' character of early Greek views of artistic discourse," given the oral nature of that discourse.[8] Speech in Archaic poetry, according to Cole, has no connection to or knowledge of technique. He draws a strong distinction between the "eloquence" that occurs in Homer, and the rhetoric of the Classical era:

> What does come out in Homeric speech is eloquence: a combination of volubility, native gift for holding the attention of an audience, and a mind well stocked with accurate memories and sound counsels. . . . Possession of "a tongue that speaks sweetly" (Tyrtaeus 12.8) is simply another instance . . . of a natural quality or external possession that is not worth having unless accompanied by bravery in battle.[9]

The theories of Plato and Aristotle, for Cole, represent a clear break with the past because it is in their work that a "meta-language" for analyzing rhetoric first comes into play. According to the definitional parameters that Cole has set for rhetoric—that it involves written, explicit theory with its own technical terminology—Plato and Aristotle may indeed be the first practitioners. Whether this definition is sufficient to describe rhetoric in ancient Greece is a question that I will take up in the following chapters.

Like Cole, Schiappa advocates a rethinking of current notions about the emergence of rhetorical theory. Though using a different approach and emphasis, Schiappa makes an argument similar to Cole's: that "meta-rhetoric," that is, a theory of rhetoric, did not arise until explicit terminology and treatises describing it arose, namely in the works of Plato and Aristotle. Central to Schiappa's contention is that the term *rhêtorikê* was not coined until the fourth century, in Plato's *Gorgias*. He argues that this coinage imposed a radical change on the notion of persuasive speaking, reflecting his belief that the shift from oral to literate culture was critical to the development of a theorized understanding of disciplines in fourth-century Greece:[10]

> A distinction needs to be made between the use of the word *rhetoric* to denote the practice of oratory and the use of the word to denote a specific domain of theorizing. The first sense, rhetoric as persuasive speaking or oratory . . . obviously occurred long before Plato, but is distinct from the second sense, the history of rhetorical theory. Since traditional rhetoric is as old as civilization, rhetoric as a practice is coextensive with the history of society (Kennedy 1980, 8). . . . This book is concerned with the status of conceptual or meta-rhetoric that attempts to theorize about oratory.[11]

Although Schiappa's distinction between "rhetoric" and "meta-rhetoric" mirrors the distinction I have made between "rhetoric in practice" and "rhetoric in theory," I find it problematic that this formulation still treats "rhetoric" as a universal practice, "coextensive with the history of society." This flattens any distinctions between societies' or individuals' understanding and use of persuasive speech ("rhetoric"), and would seem to deny the possibility that speech uttered or represented before the advent of explicit rhetorical theory could employ technical devices according to a conceptualization of their efficacy for persuasion.

With these accounts of the origins of rhetoric in Greece giving almost exclusive attention to the developments of fifth- and fourth-century Athens, it seems to me that an important foundational element is missing from the story. The remainder of this book will highlight the representation of a systematic and strategic practice of rhetoric occurring much earlier than the fifth century—a practice that forms an important first stage in the history of Greek rhetoric. Although this book does not claim that the Homeric epics express any sort of explicit theory of rhetoric, it does argue that they depict a learned, taught, technique-based craft (and as such, a *technê*) of rhetoric. The term rhetoric as I use it—and as Homer represents it—does not denote something "coextensive with the history of society," but rather something robust and distinctive, a "marked" category even within the speech-act category of directives (described by John Searle as "attempts . . . by the speaker to get the hearer to do something").[12] My contention is that many Homeric direct speeches are analogous to (for example) the fifth-century model speeches of Gorgias, Antiphon, Antisthenes, and other sophists as exemplars of a highly developed system of rhetorical argumentation that provided the basis from which explicit theory was derived. As such, Homeric speech is the earliest instantiation of Greek rhetoric.

My contention has affinities with the work of Jeffrey Walker, whose *Rhetoric and Poetics in Antiquity* also challenges the traditional placement of rhetoric's origins in Classical Athens. Walker puts forward "a revised account of the history of rhetoric in antiquity, one that understands 'rhetoric' in more or less sophistic terms as centrally and fundamentally an art of epideictic argumentation / persuasion that *derives originally from the poetic tradition* and that extends, in 'applied' versions of itself, to the practical discourses of public and private life."[13] This approach allows Walker to trace continuities between archaic poetry and rhetoric from the fifth century through the Second Sophistic, particularly as embodied in what he calls "epideictic discourse" (that is, discourse that employs "ancestral / archival authority" and "rhythmic eloquence" as "suasory means . . . by which skillful speakers, chanters, and singers may promote traditional, untraditional, or even antitraditional values and beliefs").[14] Walker's project is more sweeping than my own, and his discussion leaves aside Homer for the most part; but his insights into the inseparability of poetry and rhetoric in ancient Greece seem to me to point to a productive direction for research on both of these subjects. The notion of a "rhetorical poetics" that Walker finds embodied in Archaic poetry—in which argumentative propositions were a natural feature of the authorial (particularly lyric) voice—has undergone a "gradual occlusion . . . in the grammatical tradition and the 'grammaticalized' rhetoric and poetics transmitted from the Middle Ages to early modernity."[15] It is this long tradition of disciplinary compartmentalization that I, like Walker, hope to combat.

II. HOMER AND RHETORIC: ANCIENT OPINIONS

In a project that reconsiders the origins of rhetoric as posited by modern scholars, it would be remiss to overlook the diverse body of ancient testimony on this subject. Among the many ancient philosophers and critics who attribute rhetoric to Homer are Plato, Philodemus, Strabo, Pseudo-Plutarch, Hermogenes, Cicero, and Quintilian. With differing degrees of detail, these authors identify and analyze rhetoric in Homer, labeling Homeric speakers as sophists or rhetoricians and attributing to them the deployment of argumentative techniques and various oratorical styles. It may be tempting to brush aside such a notion as romantic or anachronistic. Indeed, this is what most modern scholars have done: Kennedy, for example, remarks dismissively that "grammarians and scholiasts were the first to note the existence of formal rhetoric in Homer, since they would have training in rhetorical systems and quite likely would be lacking the historical sense which might have told them that Homer was innocent of the rules which he seems to illustrate."[16] But these ancient authors have made some of the same claims (on a much smaller and less analytical scale) that I make and seek to demonstrate in chapter 2. The following survey thus provides a supplement to my own claims, a contrast to current conventional views on rhetoric in Homer, and a glimpse into the intersection of Homeric and rhetorical criticism in the ancient world.

Of the following passages, several are gleaned from Radermacher's edition of the *Artium Scriptores*, a collection of ancient accounts of the foundations of rhetoric, many of them dating to before Aristotle; others come from the *Prolegomenon Sylloge* of Rabe, which focuses on the works of Greek grammarians and rhetorical commentators primarily from the fourth and fifth centuries CE. All other sources are individually noted.

Pseudo-Plutarch

The most extensive and detailed ancient claims about the existence of rhetoric in Homer come from the *Essay on the Life and Poetry of Homer*, a work erroneously attributed to Plutarch by manuscript tradition. This well-preserved text has only recently received scholarly attention, primarily through the editions of Kindstrand (1990) and Keaney and Lamberton (1996). It was preserved as part of "a large body of ancient Homer interpretation that has defied analysis and is largely impossible to date," according to Keaney and Lamberton, who postulate a composition in the late second century CE.[17] Pseudo-Plutarch argues for Homer's priority in the discovery and practice of various philosophical notions and literary devices (the latter including "tropes," τρόποι and "figures," σχήματα). Among the claims of the *Essay* are that Homeric characters display irony and sarcasm in their speeches (for example, Achilles in his response to the embassy at *Iliad* 9.335–37, 346–47, and 391–92), as well as allegory and hyperbole (*Essay* sections 68–71). Most pertinently, a considerable portion of the *Essay* is devoted to demonstrating Homer's awareness and employment of rhetoric:

> ὁ δὲ πολιτικὸς λόγος ἐστὶν ἐν τῇ ῥητορικῇ τέχνῃ, ἧς ἐντὸς Ὅμηρος πρῶτος γέγονεν, ὡς φαίνεται. εἰ γάρ ἐστιν ἡ ῥητορικὴ δύναμις τοῦ πιθανῶς λέγειν, τίς μᾶλλον Ὁμήρου ἐν τῇ δυνάμει ταύτῃ καθέστηκεν, ὃς τῇ τε μεγαλοφωνίᾳ πάντας ὑπεραίρει **ἔν τε τοῖς διανοήμασι τὴν ἴσην τοῖς λόγοις ἰσχὺν ἐπιδείκνυται;**

> Political discourse is a function of the craft (τέχνη) of rhetoric, which Homer seems to have been the first to understand, for if rhetoric is the power to speak persuasively, who more than Homer has established his preeminence in this? He surpasses all others in grandiloquence and **his thought displays the same power as his diction.**[18] (*Essay* 161)

Significant here is the author's recognition of a connection between Homer's "thought" (διανόημα) and "diction" (λόγος). Homer is credited with not merely eloquent diction, but also intention—suggesting a systematic understanding of the "power to speak persuasively." This notion receives further support by Pseudo-Plutarch's use of the term ῥητορικὴ τέχνη to describe the craft understood by Homer. From the level of general praise for Homer's rhetorical abilities, Pseudo-Plutarch quickly moves to the specific, and in particular highlights his ability to adapt speech patterns to the individual character speaking:

> πολλὰ δὲ τῶν εἰσαγομένων ὑπ᾽ αὐτοῦ προσώπων λέγοντα ποιῶν ἢ πρὸς οἰκείους ἢ φίλους ἢ ἐχθροὺς ἢ δήμους **ἑκάστῳ τὸ πρέπον εἶδος τῶν λόγων ἀποδίδωσιν.**

Many of the characters he introduces he causes to speak, whether to relatives or friends or enemies or to the people, and **he gives to each the appropriate form of speech.**[19] (*Essay* 164)

He follows this observation with an analysis of the speeches of Chryses, Achilles, and Agamemnon in *Iliad* 1 according to their calculated effect on the audience: Achilles, he says, affiliates himself with the rest of the Greek soldiers in his diatribe against Agamemnon "in order to make the others feel well disposed (εὐνουστέρους) toward him as they listened" (164). Such an attempt to put the audience in a favorable frame of mind is one of the three primary techniques identified by Aristotle as the "proofs" of persuasive speech in his treatise on rhetoric:

Of the **proofs** (πίστεις) provided through speech there are three species; for some are in the character of the speaker, and **some in disposing the listener in some way** (τὸν ἀκροατὴν διαθεῖναί πως), and some in the speech itself, by showing or seeming to show something. (*Rhetoric* 1.2.3)

The act of "disposing the listener in some way"—achievable through a variety of means, but hinging on a knowledge of and sensitivity to the particular audience addressed—is a key rhetorical technique for both the Homeric characters (as Pseudo-Plutarch recognized) and Aristotle. I will henceforth refer to it as *diathesis*, a term derived from the verb that Aristotle uses in this passage; the concept and its deployment will be discussed at greater length at the beginning of chapter 2.

In addition to claiming that Homer is an expert in all manner of rhetorical devices, Pseudo-Plutarch credits him with creating nuanced characterization through speech, even borrowing the term "prosopopoeia" from oratorical terminology to describe this phenomenon:

ἔστι παρ᾽ αὐτῷ πολὺ καὶ ποικίλον τὸ τῆς προσωποποιίας. πολλὰ μὲν γὰρ καὶ διάφορα πρόσωπα εἰσάγει διαλεγόμενα, οἷς καὶ ἤθη παντοῖα περιτίθησιν.

The figure prosopopoeia ("character-making") is abundant and varied in Homer, for he brings in many different characters to whom he gives all sorts of qualities. (*Essay* 66)

Keaney and Lamberton observe that Pseudo-Plutarch makes a characteristically idiosyncratic critical move by attributing this technique—"one of the most broadly exploited ornaments in oratory"—to Homeric poetry. "That the *Iliad* and *Odyssey* should be thought of in these terms underlines the oddness of this presentation of Homer-as-rhetor," they note.[20] However "odd" such a presentation may be, though, Pseudo-Plutarch supports it with examples from the text. He does not elaborate further on Homer's prosopopoeia at this point in the *Essay*, in the midst of a section (7–73) that summarily lists the rhetorical tropes to be found in Homer's "diction" (λέξις), such as neologism, metonymy, pleonasm, paronomasia, etc. But he returns to the concept later, in the more analytical and example-based section (161–74) on rhetorical "discourse" (λόγος) in Homer, from which I have drawn most of the passages cited above. In 172, Pseudo-Plutarch provides further insight into his earlier claim about Homer's prosopopeia:

> οὐκ ἠμέλησε δὲ οὐδὲ **χαρακτηρίσαι τοὺς ῥήτορας**. τὸν μὲν γὰρ Νέστορα ἡδὺν καὶ προσηνῆ τοῖς ἀκούουσιν εἰσάγει, τὸν δὲ Μενέλαον βραχυλόγον καὶ εὔχαριν καὶ τοῦ προκειμένου τυγχάνοντα, τὸν δὲ Ὀδυσσέα πολλῇ καὶ πυκνῇ <καὶ> πληκτικῇ τῇ δεινότητι τῶν λόγων κεχρημένον.

> He was concerned **to give each orator a particular character** and makes Nestor sweet and saying things pleasing to the listeners, Menelaus brief and winning, coming right to the point, and Odysseus using many complex ingenuities of language. (*Essay* 172)

This trio of characters is commonly cited among ancient critics as representing the three registers or styles of rhetorical speech, with Odysseus traditionally illustrating the grand and complex style, Nestor the middle and balanced style, and Menelaus the plain style.[21] This sort of retrojection of Hellenistic and Imperial rhetorical categories onto Homeric speakers is certainly anachronistic; but Pseudo-Plutarch avoids such terminology, merely observing that Homer creates and distinguishes his characters, at least in part, according to their modes of speaking. What is of more import is the way he fits this observation into his larger matrix of argumentation for Homer's awareness and implicit articulation of rhetorical theory. To this end, Pseudo-Plutarch devotes sections 167–70 of the *Essay* to characterizing and analyzing the speech of Nestor, Diomedes, and the three members of the *Iliad* 9 embassy to Achilles. "[Homer] shows the orators (τοὺς ῥήτορας) in the embassy itself using various techniques (ποικίλαις τέχναις)," he claims (169). He then identifies these techniques: Odysseus aims to evoke pity in Achilles for the suffering Greek army (169)—a clear instance of Aristotle's notion of *pathos* as rhetorical device, though Pseudo-Plutarch never mentions Aristotle in connection with his *Rhetoric*, here or elsewhere. Additionally, Odysseus appeals to the authority of Peleus (recalling Aristotle's argument from *êthos*); and in general he tries to downplay Agamemnon's role in the negotiations in order to placate Achilles, displaying mindfulness of his audience's disposition (Aristotle's notion of *diathesis*). Phoenix, in Pseudo-Plutarch's analysis, takes the "kitchen-sink" approach: "as he proceeds he leaves out nothing that might persuade him, rhetorically summarizing all the main points" (169), including appeal to his own fatherly relationship to Achilles, argument for the nobility of yielding to persuasion, and presentation of the cautionary example of Meleager. Ajax takes the route of directness, employing "tactful rebukes (εὐκαίρως ἐπιπλήττων) mixed with polite requests (εὐγενῶς παρακαλῶν) . . . appropriate to one who had military prowess" (169). Having made his case for Homer's prosopopoeia, Pseudo-Plutarch caps his larger argument that Homer had a conception of rhetoric by appealing to the passage most commonly cited for this purpose among ancient critics, namely *Iliad* 9.440–43 (in which Phoenix claims to have taught Achilles to be a μύθων ῥητῆρ): ἐν δὲ τοῖς τοῦ Φοίνικος λόγοις κἀκεῖνο **παρίστησιν, ὅτι τέχνη ἐστὶν ἡ ῥητορική** ("In Phoenix' speech **Homer** also **indicates that rhetoric is an art**" 170).[22]

The *Essay on the Life and Poetry of Homer* is admittedly a biased source, one that doggedly pursues its project of tracing all contemporary intellectual pursuits (philosophy, rhetoric, politics) to Homeric origins.[23] As such, it does not propound a coherent ideology, but rather presents a litany of examples and arguments for an encomiastic purpose—it is a highly didactic instantiation of the epideictic tradition. There is little evidence that Pseudo-Plutarch favors any of the competing philosophical schools of thought prominent in the Imperial milieu; as Buffiere puts it, "la *Vie* est presque une doxographie: on y résume à larges traits l'opinion d'une école ou d'un philosophe sur une question, pour montrer aussitôt l'accord avec Homère. Or, le style doxographique ne permet guère à un auteur d'affirmer sa personnalité."[24] Its value to modern scholarship, I would argue, is not in its broad, doxographic project (which is common enough in this and later eras), but in the flashes of idiosyncratic insight that it provides in the course of analyzing certain Homeric phenomena—in particular, its astute observation of the aspects of τέχνη present in Homeric characters' speech. The *Essay* is remarkable for the range and detail of its presentation of rhetoric in Homer, in close reliance on the text of the *Iliad* (very few of its examples come from the *Odyssey*). Pseudo-Plutarch's assertions on the subject can be summarized by this characteristically enthusiastic statement:

καὶ ὅτι μὲν **τεχνίτης λόγων** Ὅμηρος οὐκ ἂν ἄλλως τις εἴποι εὖ φρονῶν· δῆλα γὰρ καὶ τὰ ἄλλα ἐξ αὐτῆς τῆς ἀναγνώσεως.

No reasonable person will deny that **Homer was an artificer of discourse**, for this much and more is clear simply from reading him. (*Essay* 171)

Classical and Hellenistic Greece

The *Essay on the Life and Poetry of Homer* is not unique in its claims; it is merely the most sustained treatment of rhetoric in the Homeric poems that survives from the ancient world. As early as the fourth century BCE, ancient critics of Homer had been making similar arguments. Several of Plato's works contain the suggestion that Homeric characters practiced oratory equivalent to the sophistic speeches of his own day. In the *Cratylus*, for example, Socrates comments on the subject in the course of framing his speculative etymology of the term "hero":

> ὅτι σοφοὶ ἦσαν καὶ ῥήτορες δεινοὶ καὶ διαλεκτικοί, ἐρωτᾶν ἱκανοὶ ὄντες· τὸ γὰρ "εἴρειν" λέγειν ἐστίν. ὅπερ οὖν ἄρτι ἐλέγομεν, ἐν τῇ Ἀττικῇ φωνῇ λεγόμενοι οἱ ἥρωες ῥήτορές τινες καὶ ἐρωτητικοὶ συμβαίνουσιν, ὥστε ῥητόρων καὶ σοφιστῶν γένος γίγνεται τὸ ἡρωικὸν φῦλον.

> [It is] because they were sophists, clever speech-makers and dialecticians, skilled questioners—for *"eirein"* is the same as *"legein"* ("to speak"). And therefore, as we were saying just now, in the Attic dialect, the heroes turn out to be speech-makers and questioners. Hence the noble breed of heroes turns out to be a race of speech-makers and sophists.[25] (*Cratylus* 398d–e)

Although he does not specifically name any Homeric characters, Socrates surely has in mind the Homeric epics as he asserts that the name "hero" may derive from the heroes' evident skill in speaking. Plato leaves this tantalizing suggestion unelaborated in the remainder of the *Cratylus*, but a similar claim occurs in the *Phaedrus*, this time attesting the influence of Homeric characters' speech on the rhetorical handbooks that were popular in fifth- and fourth-century Athens. In response to Phaedrus' assertion that artful speaking is found primarily in the law courts, Socrates asks,

> ἀλλ᾽ ἦ τὰς Νέστορος καὶ Ὀδυσσέως τέχνας μόνον περὶ λόγων ἀκήκοας, ἃς ἐν Ἰλίῳ σχολάζοντες συνεγραψάτην, τῶν δὲ Παλαμήδους ἀνήκοος γέγονας;

> Well, have you only heard of the rhetorical treatises of Nestor and Odysseus— those they wrote in their spare time in Troy? Haven't you also heard of the works of Palamedes?[26] (*Phaedrus* 261b)

Once again, it is Nestor and Odysseus who serve as the prototypical representatives of rhetorical speech (along with the noncanonical figure of Palamedes, renowned in legend for his linguistic cleverness as well as his inventiveness).[27] Plato even characterizes their supposed "rhetorical treatises" as τέχναι περὶ λόγων, which in the terminology of the time denoted instructional handbooks on rhetoric (Aristotle also makes reference to τέχναι τῶν λόγων, *Rhetoric* 1.1.3).[28] Although Socrates quickly abandons this line of questioning and moves on to further analysis of rhetoric, David White sees significance in Socrates' seemingly offhand reference to the Homeric characters:

> Why then did he name Nestor and Odysseus as producing such treatises when there is no evidence in Homer that they ever contemplated doing such a thing? Recall, however, that both Nestor and Odysseus were extremely eloquent. Thus, their treatises on rhetoric are their speeches. Socrates is pointing to the fact that skilled rhetoricians—even mythic ones—must have some sort of theoretical glimmer of what they are doing before they speak. So in their idle moments, i.e., when not actually speaking, Nestor and Odysseus are envisioned as reflecting on, and writing about, how to be eloquent. Whether or not they were ever depicted as actually doing so is irrelevant. . . . Nestor and Odysseus are no less theoretical for being only expert rhetoricians than those rhetoricians who have studied, and written about, this art.[29]

Plato's references (via Socrates) to the Homeric heroes as "rhetoricians" and to their speeches as "rhetorical treatises" represent a perspective that can be found throughout antiquity.

This perspective is evident in the Homeric commentary of Philodemus, a first-century BCE poet, critic, and Epicurean philosopher whose work on a broad range of literary and philosophical subjects survives only in fragments.[30] The first two books of his work *On Rhetoric* focus primarily on the question of whether rhetoric is an art (τέχνη).[31] In a fragmentary discussion on whether rhetoric is possible without the existence of formal training, Philodemus invokes the heroes of the past and refers to an "account" (λόγος) of their grasp of this skill:

> οὐ κρείνω δὲ παλινλογεῖν ἀναγκαῖον εἶναι τῆς ἀποδείξεως κατά γε τὴν δύναμιν οὐθὲν διαφερούσης τοῦ διδάσκοντος λόγου **ἥρωας** ἤτοι [ἰδιώτ]ας, μὴ μαθόντας τὴν ῥητορικήν, **δυν[α]το[ὺς ῥητορεύειν γεγονέν]αι.**

> I do not judge it to be necessary to deny the proof, differing not at all in its force from the account teaching that **the heroes**—although they were nonprofessionals,

not having learned rhetoric—**became capable of speaking rhetorically.**[32] (Περὶ 'Ρητορικῆς II fr. VIII Sudh.)

The contention that Homer was the inventor of rhetoric was evidently much debated by scholars of Philodemus' time, and in the following fragment Philodemus calls "unintelligent" those who would deny that contention:

ἀλλ' οὕτως ἀσύνετοί τινές ἐσμεν, ὥστε φιλοσοφίας μὲν αὐτὸν εὑρετὴν λεγόμενον ἀκούειν, οὐχί τε τῶν κριτικῶν μόνον ἀλλὰ καὶ τῶν φιλοσόφων αὐτῶν, οὐδὲ μιᾶς μόνον αἱρέσεως ἀλλὰ πασῶν· τὸ δὲ **ῥητορικῆς εὑρ[ετὴν** νομί]ζεσθαι τέρας [ὑπολαμβάνειν].

But some of us are so unintelligent that we hear this man being called the inventor of philosophy—not only by the critics but by the philosophers themselves, and not of one school only but of all—and yet assume that it is a monstrosity for him to be considered **the inventor of rhetoric.** (Περὶ 'Ρητορικῆς II fr. XXI Sudh.)

Although the logic of this passage is convoluted, Philodemus seems to be taking a position similar to that adopted by Pseudo-Plutarch: that Homer is the source of both philosophy and rhetoric. At the very least, he argues that critics cannot claim to find a philosophical foundation in Homer's works without acknowledging the presence of a rhetorical foundation as well.

The Roman World and Late Antiquity

Authors in the Roman world and late antiquity who take up the subject of rhetoric in Homer tend to focus on the stylistic aspects of Homeric speech, in keeping with the interest in style among poets, orators, and grammarians alike that had begun in the Hellenistic period.[33] Cicero authored several works of rhetorical theory, treating practical rules for oratory (*De Inventione*), the philosophy of rhetoric (*De Oratore*), and the history of oratory (*Brutus*). Composed in 46 BCE, the *Brutus* addresses "when they [orators] first made their appearance, and who, and of what sort they were" (*quando esse coepissent, qui etiam et quales fuissent*, 20).[34] Curiously, Cicero seems to give two accounts of the origins of rhetoric in Greece in quick succession. In the first, sections 26–39, he claims that orators and written records of oratory first appeared in Athens, with Pericles and Themistocles being the first practitioners. Having completed a brief history of Greek oratory, however, Cicero returns the discussion of origins to an earlier point with the statement, "And yet I do not doubt that oratory always exercised great influence" (*nec tamen dubito quin habuerit vim magnam semper oratio*, 39). He continues:

neque enim iam Troicis temporibus tantum laudis in dicendo Ulixi tribuisset Homerus et Nestori, quorum alterum vim habere voluit, alterum suavitatem, nisi iam tum esset honos eloquentiae; neque ipse poeta hic tam [idem] ornatus in dicendo ac plane orator fuisset.

Surely even in Trojan times Homer would not have allotted such praise to Ulysses and Nestor for their speech unless even then eloquence had enjoyed honour—to the one, you will recall, he attributed force, to the other charm—nor indeed otherwise had the poet himself been so accomplished in utterance and so completely the orator. (*Brutus* 40)

Cicero identifies the same exemplars of eloquence—Odysseus and Nestor—as do many of his Greek counterparts. He locates *eloquentia* in "Trojan times," and labels Homer an *orator*. But it is not clear that Cicero views this Homeric instantiation of "eloquence" on a par with the historical orators and written handbooks that he had cited in his first account of Greek oratory. By providing these two parallel histories, Cicero may indeed represent the beginnings of an opinion that is now well-entrenched in modern histories of rhetoric: that Homer and his characters were capable of *eloquence*, but possessed no understanding or practice of *rhetoric* as a technique-based discipline.

Strabo, a geographer and historian from Amaseia in Asia Minor, composed the *Geographica* in the early part of the first century CE. This work contains a polemic against the Hellenistic scholar Eratosthenes (who also wrote a *Geographica*, mostly lost) because the latter had dismissed Homer as a source of knowledge about practical and scientific matters. One of the practical matters that Homer contributed to, according to Strabo, is rhetoric; like other ancient critics, Strabo finds evidence for rhetoric particularly in the diction of Odysseus:

Ἡ δὲ ῥητορικὴ φρόνησίς ἐστι δήπου περὶ λόγους, ἣν ἐπιδείκνυται παρ' ὅλην τὴν ποίησιν Ὀδυσσεὺς ἐν τῇ διαπείρᾳ, ἐν ταῖς λιταῖς, ἐν τῇ πρεσβείᾳ, ἐν ᾗ φησιν "ἀλλ' ὅτε δὴ ὄπα τε μεγάλην ἐκ στήθεος εἴη καὶ ἔπεα νιφάδεσσιν ἐοικότα χειμερίῃσιν, οὐκ ἂν ἔπειτ' Ὀδυσῆί γ' ἐρίσσειε βροτὸς ἄλλος."

Rhetoric is knowledge concerning speech, which Odysseus demonstrated through the whole poem in the trial, in supplications, and in the embassy, in which [Homer] says: "But when indeed there was a great voice from his chest and words like wintery snowflakes, then no other mortal would quarrel with Odysseus [*Iliad* 3.221–23]."[35] (*Geographica* 1.2.5)

Strabo's argument is notable for its assertion that Homeric characters were intentional and knowledgeable about speech—that they possessed knowledge or practical wisdom (φρόνησις) about the craft. Such knowledge was specialized enough to serve Odysseus in a variety of different rhetorical contexts: trial, supplications, and embassy.

Quintilian, writing his *Institutio Oratoria* at the end of the first century CE, notes that the *Iliad* depicts both instruction in rhetoric and different registers of rhetorical style:

> apud Homerum et praeceptorem Phoenicem cum agendi tum etiam loquendi, et oratores plures, et omne in tribus ducibus orationis genus, et certamina quoque proposita eloquentiae inter iuvenes invenimus, quin in caelatura clipei Achillis et lites sunt et actores.

> Even in Homer we find Phoenix as an instructor not only of conduct but of speaking, while a number of orators are mentioned, the various styles are represented by the speeches of three of the chiefs and the young men are set to contend among themselves in contests of eloquence: moreover lawsuits and pleaders are represented on the shield of Achilles.[36] (*Institutio Oratoria* 2.17.8)

"The speeches of three of the chiefs" refers to Odysseus, Nestor, and Menelaus, who came to be oft-cited representatives of the three *genera dicendi* (grand, middle, and plain styles). Later in his treatise, Quintilian makes one of the strongest statements from an ancient author concerning rhetoric in Homer, claiming that Homer displays "every department of eloquence" and "all the rules of art" for the different genres of rhetoric:

> omnibus eloquentiae partibus exemplum et ortum dedit . . . tum copia tum brevitate mirabilis, nec poetica modo sed oratoria virtute eminentissimus. nam ut de laudibus exhortationibus consolationibus taceam, nonne vel nonus liber, quo missa ad Achillem legatio continetur, vel in primo inter duces illa contentio vel dictae in secundo sententiae omnis litium atque consiliorum explicant artes? . . . iam similitudines, amplificationes, exempla, digressus, signa rerum et argumenta †ceteraque quae probandi ac refutandi sunt† ita multa ut etiam qui de artibus scripserunt plurima earum rerum testimonia ab hoc poeta petant.

> [Homer] has given us a model and an inspiration for every department of eloquence . . . remarkable at once for his fullness and his brevity, and supreme not merely for poetic, but for oratorical power as well. For, to say nothing of his eloquence, which he shows in praise, exhortation, and consolation, do not the ninth

book containing the embassy to Achilles, the first describing the quarrel between the chiefs, or the speeches delivered by the counselors in the second, display all the rules of art to be followed in forensic or deliberative oratory? . . . Then consider his similes, his amplifications, his illustrations, digressions, indications of fact, inferences, and all the other methods of proof and refutation which he employs. They are so numerous that the majority of writers on the principles of rhetoric have gone to his works for examples of all these things. (*Inst. Orat.* 10.1.46–49)

This litany of rhetorical devices allegedly employed by Homer is impressive, though Quintilian's analysis is perhaps less illuminating than is Pseudo-Plutarch's similar treatment, as he fails to provide a close reading of his cited examples. It is left to the reader to infer which parts of the Homeric speeches mentioned display the "rules of art to be followed in forensic or deliberative oratory." Clearly, however, examples (*testimonia*) drawn from Homer were common in the rhetorical commentaries of Quintilian's day. Quintilian returns to Homer's primacy in the history of rhetoric at several points in his work, citing Priam's supplication to Achilles in Book 24 as an example of the use of an epilogue-speech (*epilogus*) at 10.1.50, and the familiar threesome of Odysseus, Nestor, and Menelaus to illustrate the different registers of oratorical style at 12.10.64.

The tradition of attributing rhetoric to Homer continued during the Roman Imperial period, with Pseudo-Plutarch as the most prominent example. But other rhetoricians and literary critics touched on the subject as well.[37] The rhetorical theory of Hermogenes, a critic of the late second century CE, points to Homeric speech as a prototype for orators, and his influential work attracted commentaries that provide further elaboration of this idea. In *On Types of Style*, Hermogenes identifies Homer and Demosthenes as leading their respective genres in rhetorical ability (1.260). While acknowledging the differences between poetic and prose categories in the following passage, he nevertheless articulates the transcendence of formal distinctions that Homer achieves with his speech-craft:

ὅπερ γὰρ ἦν ὁ Δημοσθένης ἡμῖν κατὰ τὸν πολιτικὸν λόγον ἔν τε τῷ συμβουλευτικῷ καὶ δικανικῷ καὶ ὁ Πλάτων ἐν τῷ πεζῷ πανηγυρικῷ, τοῦτ᾽ ἂν Ὅμηρος εἴη κατὰ τὴν ποίησιν . . . ἀρίστη τε γὰρ ποιήσεων ἡ Ὁμήρου, καὶ **Ὅμηρος** ποιητῶν **ἄριστος, φαίην δ᾽ ἂν ὅτι καὶ ῥητόρων καὶ λογογράφων**, λέγω δ᾽ ἴσως ταὐτόν· ἐπεὶ γάρ ἐστιν ἡ ποίησις μίμησις ἁπάντων, ὁ δὲ μετὰ τῆς περὶ τὴν λέξιν κατασκευῆς ἄριστα μιμούμενος καὶ ῥήτορας δημηγοροῦντας καὶ κιθαρῳδοὺς πανηγυρίζοντας ὥσπερ τὸν Φήμιον καὶ τὸν Δημόδοκον καὶ τὰ ἄλλα πρόσωπά τε καὶ πράγματα ἅπαντα, οὗτος ἄριστός ἐστι ποιητής, ἐπειδὴ οὖν ταῦθ᾽ οὕτως ἔχει, τάχ᾽ ἂν ταὐτὸν εἰρηκὼς εἴην, εἰπὼν εἶναι ποιητῶν ἄριστον, ὡς εἰ καὶ ῥητόρων ἄριστον καὶ λογογράφων ἔλεγον. στρατηγῶν μὲν γὰρ ἢ τεκτόνων ἢ τῶν τοιούτων ἴσως οὐκ ἄριστος ... οὐ λόγος ἐκείνοις ἡ τέχνη οὐδὲ ἐν λόγοις· **οἷς δ᾽ ἔστιν ἐν λόγῳ τὸ ἔργον, οἷον ῥήτορσι λέγω καὶ λογογράφοις, ὁ τούτους ἄριστα μιμούμενος καὶ λέγων, ὥσπερ ἂν ὁ ἐκείνων ἄριστος εἴποι, πάντως ἂν εἴη καὶ αὐτὸς ἐκείνων ἄριστος.** ἄριστος οὖν κατὰ πάντα λόγων εἴδη καὶ ποιητῶν ἁπάντων καὶ ῥητόρων καὶ λογογράφων Ὅμηρος.

What, in our opinion, Demosthenes is to practical oratory, both deliberative and judicial, and Plato is to panegyric oratory in prose, Homer is to poetry. . . . The best poetry is that of Homer, and Homer is the best of poets. **I would say that he is also the best of orators and speech-writers**, although perhaps this is implicit in what I have already said. Poetry is an imitation of all things. The man who best imitates, in a suitable style, both orators delivering speeches and singers singing panegyrics, such as Phemius and Demodocus and other characters engaged in every pursuit, this man is the best poet. Since this is the case, perhaps by saying that Homer is the best of poets I have made a statement that is tantamount to saying that he is also the best of orators and the best of speech-writers. He is perhaps not the best general or craftsman or other such professional. . . . Their skill does not reside in the use of speech and words. **But as for those whose business is with the use of speech, such as orators and speech-writers, the one who represents them best and describes how the best of them would speak, is surely himself the best of them.** Thus of all poets and orators and speech-writers Homer is the best at using every kind of style.[38] (Περὶ Ἰδεῶν Λόγου 2.374–75)

Hermogenes does not glibly call Homer the most knowledgeable figure in every field of expertise: he admits that the poet is no general or craftsman. But he does identify Homer's representation of speech as the supreme paradigm for oratory, citing Homer's diversity of styles. For Hermogenes, Homer puts rhetoric into practice as a ῥήτωρ and λογόγραφος.

The commentators on Hermogenes contribute more specific analysis to this rhetorical reading of Homer. Sopatros, writing in the fourth century CE, declares in his commentary that

φαίνεται δὲ καὶ ὁ ποιητὴς παντοῖα εἰδὼς ῥητορικῆς παραδείγματα. τὸν μὲν γὰρ ταχὺν καὶ σύντομον καὶ ἀποδεικτικὸν ῥήτορά φησι λέγειν νιφάδεσσιν ὅμοια, καὶ τὸν πυκνὸν καὶ σύντομον, οὐδὲν δὲ ἧττον ἀποδεικτικὸν παῦρα μὲν, ἀλλὰ μάλα λιγέως. οἶδεν δὲ τὴν ἀταξίαν τῆς δημαγωγίας καὶ τοὺς ἀδιακρίτως καὶ ἐντέχνως λέγοντας, ὁποῖοί ποτέ εἰσιν, ὥσπερ τὸν Θερσίτην, ὅς ῥ᾽ ἔπεα φρεσὶν ᾗσιν ἄκοσμά τε πολλά τε ᾔδει.

The poet [Homer] reveals that he knows all sorts of *paradeigmata* of rhetoric. For he says that the one [Odysseus], a swift and concise and demonstrative speaker, says things like snowflakes, and the other [Menelaus] is both compact and concise, and says few things no less demonstratively, but with great fluency. But he knew the disorder of demagoguery and those speaking with artifice and indiscriminately, what sort they are—such as Thersites, "who knew many and disorderly words in his mind" [*Iliad* 2.213].³⁹ (*Sopatros in Hermogenem comm.* Walz V 6, 3)

Again we see certain Homeric speakers being singled out as exemplary, and as is often the case, Odysseus and Menelaus are primary exemplars. Sopatros draws on the vocabulary of rhetorical theory when he describes Odysseus and Menelaus as "demonstrative" (ἀποδεικτικός) speakers.⁴⁰ His addition of Thersites as an example of unappealing rhetorical qualities is more unusual; not even Pseudo-Plutarch's *Essay* discusses Thersites in this capacity. Although Walz amends the manuscript reading of ἐντέχνως ("artistically") to ἀτέχνως ("unskillfully") in describing Thersites' speech, I join Radermacher in printing the rarer adverb ἐντέχνως. I find the manuscript reading, however jarring, to give a more provocative, and indeed more Homeric, reading of Thersites: in *Iliad* 2, Homer characterizes him as a speaker with unharnessed (ἄκοσμα) artifice, but a degree of artifice nonetheless:

Θερσίτης δ' ἔτι μοῦνος ἀμετροεπὴς ἐκολῴα,
ὃς ἔπεα φρεσὶ ᾗσιν ἄκοσμά τε πολλά τε ᾔδη. . . .
    τῷ δ' ὦκα παρίστατο δῖος Ὀδυσσεύς,
καί μιν ὑπόδρα ἰδὼν χαλεπῷ ἠνίπαπε μύθῳ·
"Θερσῖτ' ἀκριτόμυθε, **λιγύς περ ἐὼν ἀγορητής**. . . . "

But one man, Thersites of the endless speech, still scolded, who knew within his head many words, but disorderly. . . . But brilliant Odysseus swiftly came beside him scowling and laid a harsh word upon him: "**Fluent orator though you be,** Thersites, your words are ill-considered. . . ." (*Iliad* 2.212–13, 244–46)

As Hanna Roisman observes, Thersites' speech is "an example of verbal dexterity put to wrong purposes."⁴¹ The adjective / adverb cluster ἥντεχνος / -ως also comes up on numerous occasions in Aristotle's *Rhetoric* in his effort to distinguish the rhetorical argumentation with which he is concerned—which he describes as ἥντεχνος—from "inartistic" means of persuasion such as witnesses, documents, and the like. Sopatros' use of the word to describe Thersites' speech (if indeed ἐντέχνως is the correct reading, which I believe is interpretively plausible and is the *lectio difficilior*) is then another example of vocabulary from rhetorical analysis being applied to the speech of Homeric figures.

Finally, at the late end of antiquity, we find the following discussion by an anonymous author. It appears in Rabe's *Prolegomenon Sylloge*, a collection of "introductions" to rhetoric (many of them drawn from Walz's earlier collection *Rhetores Graeci*), which Kennedy places in the fourth and fifth centuries CE.[42] Its presentation of rhetoric among the Homeric heroes touches some by-now familiar themes, but it fleshes out these themes in explicit and vehement fashion, thus providing a fair summation of this particular strand of ancient opinion:

Δεύτερον δέ ἐστι κεφάλαιον, ἐν ᾧ ἐλέγχομεν, εἰ καὶ ἐν ἥρωσιν ἡ ῥητορική. ἔδει γὰρ καὶ καλῶς ἔδει τὰ τῶν θεῶν δημιουργήματα τοὺς ἐκ θεῶν φανέντας πρώτους καρπώσασθαι. ἔστω τοίνυν τούτων ἁπάντων μάρτυς ὁ θεσπέσιος ἡμῖν καὶ ἱεροφάντης Ὅμηρος, ὃς εἰς φανερόν τε καὶ σαφὲς ἤγαγε τὰς περὶ τούτων ζητήσεις ἡμῖν. **οὗτος γὰρ βουλόμενος σημᾶναι ἡμῖν, ὅτι ἐν τοῖς ἥρωσιν ἑκάτερα ποιότης τῆς ῥητορικῆς εὕρηται, εἰσάγει τὸν Νέστορα σύμβουλον ὄντα,** περὶ οὗ λέγει

"τοῖσι δὲ Νέστωρ
ἡδυεπὴς ἀνόρουσε, λιγὺς Πυλίων ἀγορητής,
τοῦ καὶ ἀπὸ γλώσσης μέλιτος γλυκίων ῥέεν αὐδή."

καὶ τὸ μὲν γλυκὺ καὶ προσηνὲς τῆς ῥητορικῆς ἔχειν τὸν Νέστορα ἐξέφηνεν ὁ ποιητής· τὸ δὲ σύντονον καὶ ἐπίχαρι διὰ τοῦ Μενελάου ἐνδείκνυται, εἰπὼν περὶ αὐτοῦ

"ἀλλ' ἤτοι Μενέλαος ἐπιτροχάδην ἀγόρευε
παῦρα μέν, ἀλλὰ μάλα λιγέως."

εἰσφέρει δὲ καὶ τὸν Ὀδυσσέα τὸ τροχαλὸν καὶ ὀξὺ καὶ τὸ σφοδρὸν καὶ τὸ λαμπρὸν τῆς ῥητορικῆς δι' αὐτοῦ εἰκονίσαι βουλόμενος, λέγων περὶ αὐτοῦ

"ἀλλ' ὅτε δὴ ὄπα τε μεγάλην ἐκ στήθεος εἴη
καὶ ἔπεα νιφάδεσσιν ἐοικότα χειμερίῃσιν,
οὐκ ἂν ἔπειτ' Ὀδυσῆι γ' ἐρίσσειε βροτὸς ἄλλος."

ὅτι δὲ καὶ τὸ ὄνομα τῆς ῥητορικῆς ἦν ἐγνωσμένον τοῖς ἥρωσι, φέρει τὸν Φοίνικα πρὸς τὸν Ἀχιλλέα λέγοντα

"τοὔνεκά με προέηκε διδασκέμεναι τάδε πάντα,
μύθων τε ῥητῆρ' ἔμεναι πρηκτῆρά τε ἔργων."

But there is a second main point on which we argue: whether in fact there was rhetoric among the heroes. For it was necessary, and rightly necessary, that they, having appeared first from the gods, should make use of the crafts of the gods. Let Homer therefore be the divine witness to us of all these things, since he led the investigations for us concerning these things both into evidence and into clarity. **For he, wishing to mark for us that among the heroes was found each individual [type] of the quality of rhetoric, presented Nestor as a counselor,** about whom he says:

> "But Nestor the sweet-speaker rose up among them, the fluent assembly-speaker of the Pylians, from whose tongue poured a voice sweeter than honey" [*Iliad* 1.247–49].

And the poet displayed that Nestor possessed the sweetness and the attractive quality of rhetoric: but he demonstrated earnestness and winsomeness through the rhetoric of Menelaus, saying about him:

> "But Menelaus spoke out swiftly, few things, but very sweetly"
>
> [*Iliad* 3.213–14].

And he presents Odysseus, wishing to depict through him the swiftness and sharpness and vehemence and brilliance of rhetoric, saying about him:

> "But when he let loose his great voice from his chest, and words resembling wintry snowflakes, then no other mortal could compete with Odysseus"
>
> [*Iliad* 3.221–23].

And the fact that the name of rhetoric was known to the heroes, he transmits [by means of] Phoenix saying to Achilles:

> "For this reason he sent me to teach these many things: that you should be a speaker of words and a doer of deeds"
>
> [*Iliad* 9.442–43].[43] (*Prolegomena Artis Rhetoricae*, Rabe 22–23)

Like Pseudo-Plutarch, this author treats his subject as a rhetorically structured argument, progressing logically from one point to the next and providing examples from the text of the *Iliad* in support of his claims. "It was necessary" for the heroes to have had access to the crafts (δημιουργήματα) of the gods; he implies that as an intermediate generation between gods and mortals, the heroes were endowed with heightened skills, one of which was the ability to speak rhetorically. This ability, he emphasizes, was systematically depicted by Homer: our anonymous author uses seven different verbs (σημᾶναι, εἰσάγει, ἐξέφηνεν, ἐνδείκνυται, εἰσφέρει, εἰκονίσαι, φέρει) to express the poet's work of rhetorical representation. Like other commentators, this author identifies Nestor, Menelaus, and Odysseus as the *Iliad*'s three stylistic exemplars. In contrast to others, however, he does not make them exemplify the three conventional registers of style (grand, middle, and plain), but characterizes the distinctive speech of each by means of descriptive nouns. His final contention brings the argument to its culmination: not only the concept, but indeed the very term "rhetoric" (or at least its related agent noun) was known to the heroes, as Phoenix' use of the phrase μύθων ῥητῆρ' attests.

_⚬ ⚬_

This survey of ancient views on the existence of rhetoric in Homer is certainly not exhaustive, but it should be sufficient to establish the existence of a robust tradition in these views. Along with these extant references, there is also evidence for discussion of the subject in lost works from antiquity. Two treatises by the second-century CE Stoic grammarian Telephos of Pergamon, for example, are attested in the Suda: Περὶ τῶν παρ' Ὁμήρῳ σχημάτων ῥητορικῶν and Περὶ τῆς καθ' Ὅμηρον ῥητορικῆς, titles which suggest an analytical investigation of rhetoric (including rhetorical "figures") in Homer. While the analysis of Homeric speech among these diverse ancient authors tends not to be extensive or systematic, it does reveal a broad lack of prejudice about the capacity of poetry to display formal rhetoric, and of Homeric speakers to be orators and logographers. For all the attention devoted to this idea in ancient scholarship, it is one that has largely disappeared from modern analysis of both Homer and ancient rhetoric. Even the modern understanding of how the ancients viewed rhetoric in Homer is impoverished, as few historians of rhetoric seem to have tracked the diachronic breadth and critical depth of these claims.[44] Kennedy examines a few of them in his article "The Ancient Dispute over Rhetoric in Homer," but sees this notion as a post-Classical development arising out of the polemic between rhetoric and philosophy (part of the philosophers' argument against the claim, by rhetoricians, that rhetoric was a τέχνη).[45] Not surprisingly, then, Kennedy is dismissive of the ancients' claim that rhetoric can be discovered in Homer's speeches: "One would suspect that grammarians and scholiasts were the first to note the existence of formal rhetoric in Homer, since they would have training in rhetorical systems and quite likely would be lacking the historical sense which might have told them that Homer was innocent of the rules that he seems to illustrate."[46] Similarly, Pernot concludes, "Whatever the liveliness and precision with which the ancients developed the theme of 'Homeric rhetoric,' there is surely no question for us moderns of following their path."[47] Is the ancients' view that rhetoric can be found in the speeches of Homeric characters indeed the product of naïve and misguided zeal? To answer this question, I now turn to the evidence of the *Iliad* itself.

CHAPTER TWO

Investigating Homeric Rhetoric

A central tenet of this investigation is that rhetoric is, in the classical Greek conception, a *technê*. It is a skill—learned, taught, and employed with calculation and intention. The first step in any act of rhetoric is gathering information: information about human nature and its points of susceptibility to persuasion; information about the particular audience and its points of susceptibility to persuasion; and information about the techniques of speech that tend to induce persuasion for any given situation or audience. Equipped with this data, the rhetorician may then proceed "scientifically": he makes a prediction about what words will best achieve the desired effect or incite the desired action in his audience, and then crafts his speech accordingly. The success or failure of the speech— judged by favorable or unfavorable audience response—constitutes the outcome of his experiment. The variables, of course, are myriad: since rhetoric deals with human nature and behavior, its reception is subject to the whims of human emotion, psychology, temporary state of mind, present circumstances, and past associations (among other things), all of which may or may not be known to the speaker. Nevertheless, the most successful rhetoric, according to Aristotle's foundational theory, draws upon three touchstones, or "proofs" (*pisteis*): the speaker's character (*êthos*), the audience's disposition (*diathesis*), and the speech's argumentation (*logos*). It then produces from this triangulation the most convincing set of words possible for a given situation.

Because these three touchstones of Aristotelian rhetoric are integral to my analysis of the rhetoric of Homer, I will say a few more words about my use of them as concepts and terms. The passage that establishes them is *Rhetoric* 1.2.3:

τῶν δὲ διὰ τοῦ λόγου ποριζομένων πίστεων τρία εἴδη ἐστίν· αἱ μὲν γάρ εἰσιν ἐν τῷ
ἤθει τοῦ λέγοντος, αἱ δὲ ἐν τῷ τὸν ἀκροατὴν διαθεῖναί πως, αἱ δὲ ἐν αὐτῷ τῷ λόγῳ,
διὰ τοῦ δεικνύναι ἢ φαίνεσθαι δεικνύναι.

Of the *pisteis* produced through speech there are three species; for some are in the
character [*êthos*] of the speaker, and some in disposing [*diatheinai*] the listener in
some way, and some in the speech [*logos*] itself, by showing or seeming to show
something.

I have chosen to use the term *diathesis* to refer to the second of these approaches
("disposing the listener in some way"), rather than the more conventional term
pathos, for several reasons.[1] The first reason involves faithfulness to Aristotle's
text and choice of vocabulary: in the passage above, he makes no mention of
pathos (literally, "emotion," "condition"), but instead provides the somewhat-
unwieldy phrase τὸν ἀκροατὴν διαθεῖναί πως as the second species of proof. I
substitute the noun *diathesis* (with its lexical definitions of "arrangement," "disposition," "means of disposing") for the infinitive verb form. The second and
related reason is that the use of the term *pathos* to describe this approach is, in
fact, a misrepresentation of the full scope of Aristotle's description of it in this
passage. While he later speaks at length of arousing the emotions (*pathê*) in connection with the idea of disposing the listener in some way (*Rhetoric* 2.1–11),
Aristotle clearly intends *diathesis* to include any strategy that is calculated to
create sympathy in the listener, whether by appealing to emotions or by knowing the particular listener and adapting one's argumentative strategy according
to what will best effect his acquiescence. The term *diathesis* conveys this broader
notion of sensitivity to audience psychology, I believe, more accurately than
does the term *pathos*. Indeed, it is a rhetorical category that can be seen to encompass not only *pathos*, but in some cases *êthos* and *logos* as well: an appeal to
the character of the speaker, like an appeal to the emotions, falls under the notion of disposing the audience favorably to the speaker. This alternative understanding of the three-part division of persuasion is borne out in the next three
paragraphs of the *Rhetoric*, with the narrower concept of *pathos* replacing the
broader concept of *diathesis*:

[There is persuasion] through character [*êthos*] whenever the speech is spoken in
such a way as to make the speaker worthy of credence. . . . [There is persuasion]
through the hearers when they are led to feel emotion [*pathos*] by the speech. . . .
Persuasion occurs through the arguments [*logoi*] when we show the truth or the
apparent truth from whatever is persuasive in each case. (1.2.4–6)

In my use of these terms for analyzing Homeric rhetoric, then, I draw a distinction between the techniques of *diathesis* and *pathos* by limiting the latter term to instances in which a speaker targets particular emotions to evoke in his audience: anger, calm, fear, pity, shame, and the like (all of which Aristotle treats in his discourse on the emotions in *Rhetoric* 2.2–11). When the speaker uses other means to dispose the audience favorably—for example, making an appeal based on what he knows of the audience's susceptibilities or preferences, or employing flattery to engender goodwill—I will identify this as *diathesis*.

My aim in this chapter is to identify and analyze the occurrence of rhetoric, using a rigorous and technical understanding of that term, within the direct speeches of Homer's *Iliad*. The fact that Iliadic speeches occur in a narrative context rather than being free-standing (as are Classical orations) adds another layer of variables to the analysis of these speeches' effectiveness. In addition to examining the dynamics between the speaker and his or her audience, therefore, this analysis must touch upon the way that speeches affect (or are affected by) the characterization of speakers within the *Iliad*'s broader narrative. It must also consider the implications of the relationship between speeches and the narrative trajectory, or plot. Discussion of these issues will be woven into my analysis of individual speeches, with broader trends summarized in chapter 3.

I. METHODOLOGY

My approach to analyzing rhetoric in the *Iliad* involves comparing the direct speech of Homeric characters with a system based largely on Aristotle's techniques for effective persuasion. I have chosen Aristotle's *Rhetoric* as a standard because it is as complete and systematic an explication as any from antiquity (Cicero, Dionysius of Halicarnassus, Hermogenes, and others notwithstanding). As Schiappa and Timmerman observe, "Aristotle obviously did not originate the practice of giving deliberative speeches in classical Greece, but he did create an influential taxonomy of terms that grouped, described, and even circumscribed various types of discourse in a particular manner."[2] The *Rhetoric* has the additional benefit of being the earliest systematic treatise on rhetoric to survive, an artifact from a time when the definition and origins of rhetoric were still in the process of being established. It is also better suited to my analysis of Iliadic speeches than are more modern typologies such as that proposed by Anton Fingerle, who identifies different types of Homeric speech, including laments, rebukes, threats, vaunts, and the like; or the speech-act categories developed by Searle (following Austin), namely representatives, directives, commissives, expressives, and declarations.[3] While such typologies and theoretical approaches have been productively deployed in other scholarly work on Homeric speech, they are insufficient to describe a speech's internal rhetoric—the individual arguments and diverse strategies that appear *within* a speech category such as rebuke or directive. For this task, Aristotle proves more apt.

Given the occasional unevenness of the *Rhetoric* and the areas in which it may not give a complete picture of rhetorical possibilities, I have made certain clarifications of and adjustments to Aristotle's system. My goal has been to create a sensible scheme of rhetorical categories and subcategories distilled from Aristotle that can serve as a rubric for "measuring" the presence of rhetorical techniques and degree of rhetorical sophistication in represented direct speech (a rubric that could equally be applied to "real" oratory). Aristotle asserts at the beginning of *Rhetoric* Book 3 that the most basic division of rhetorical speech is between style (*lexis*), arrangement (*taxis*), and "proofs" (*pisteis*). It is the latter element that is the focus of most of the *Rhetoric* (including the entirety of Books 1 and 2), and it is these "proofs," or argumentative techniques, that are of interest to me in comparing Homeric speech with rhetorical speech according to Aristotle.

The first and most important set of techniques in my rubric is comprised of Aristotle's aforementioned three-part division of rhetorical *pisteis* in *Rhetoric* 1.2.3: *êthos* (argument based on the speaker's character); *diathesis* (argument based on putting the audience into a certain frame of mind, of which appeal to emotion, *pathos*, is a major subcategory); and *logos* (argument based on reasoning in speech). The aspects of *êthos* that a speaker commonly invokes, according to Aristotle (2.1.5), are good sense (*phronêsis*), virtue or courage (*aretê*), and goodwill (*eunoia*). As discussed above, *diathesis* encompasses a wide range of audience-focused appeal, ultimately requiring an awareness of the audience's disposition and an understanding of emotions and how to manipulate them (*Rhetoric* 2.1–11).

The components of *logos* are reckoned differently at two different points in the *Rhetoric*, but both groupings are of interest, as they represent further categories of persuasive technique. At *Rhetoric* 1.3.7, Aristotle claims that the components of syllogistic argumentation (*logos*) are threefold: evidence (*tekmêria*), probability (*ta eikota*), and signs (*sêmeia*). We might characterize these components as being "external" aids to *logos*: things that can be pointed out in support of an argument, but that are external to it (the concept of probability can be viewed in this way if we think of it as occurrences that are fixed or predictable, and thus objective in the same way that evidence is objective: both are deictic).

Aristotle identifies two different components of *logos*, however, at 2.20.1: example (*paradeigma*) and enthymeme (*enthumêma*). Example and enthymeme can be thought of as "internal" aids to *logos*—that is, arising from the speaker's own art of argumentation—and thus they complement the external aids listed above. According to Aristotle, *paradeigma* involves either the citation of actual past events (λέγειν πϱάγματα πϱογεγενημένα) or the making up of fables (ποεῖν) (2.20.2). Enthymeme, the rhetorical device to which Aristotle devotes the most attention over the course of the *Rhetoric*, is a rhetorical syllogism comprised of two parts: a premise (*protasis*, 1.3.7), and a conclusion (*to sunagein*, 2.22.3).[4] The conclusion generally expresses the speaker's stated objective, while the premise— which may be either particular or generalized—provides a reason or argument for that conclusion. The conjunctions γάϱ or ἐπεί often introduce an enthymeme premise and connect it to the conclusion, which may either precede or follow the premise. An enthymeme relies on generally accepted opinions, rather than on demonstrated facts, as the "proof" that leads from premise to conclusion; this, for Aristotle, is the fundamental difference between rhetorical and logical reasoning (1.1.11). Both *paradeigma* and enthymeme thus employ argument (*logos*) for their rhetorical effectiveness.

The most fine-grained category of Aristotelian persuasive technique is a subset of enthymeme: namely, the elements or "topics" (*topoi*) of demonstrative enthymemes that Aristotle lists in *Rhetoric* 2.23.1–30. These 28 topics are, as the Greek term suggests, commonplaces used to formulate the premises of enthymemes. Although the topics vary considerably in type—from the practical (such as division or ruling-out of reasons, the ninth topic in Aristotle's list) to the theoretical (such as the argument from greater and less likelihood, topic #4 in Aristotle's list)—they share a degree of argumentative craft which, when inserted into the enthymeme structure, creates a sophisticated rhetorical construction.

Thus my rubric of persuasive techniques, derived from Aristotle, consists of the three "proofs" (*pisteis*) of *êthos*, *diathesis*, and *logos*; *pathos* (a subcategory of *diathesis*), *paradeigma*, and enthymeme (subcategories of *logos*); and 28 topics (subcategories of enthymeme), which will be individually explained as they appear in speeches from the *Iliad*. My examination of Iliadic speeches reveals striking correspondences between the techniques employed by Homeric characters and those described in Aristotle's *Rhetoric* across all categories and subcategories of rhetoric. The accumulated force of such rhetorical complexity in such quantities in the *Iliad* is difficult to explain away as universally occurring, untaught, and unconscious eloquence.

II. MODEL PASSAGES: "CONTROL" AND "PROOF" TEXTS

I now turn to an examination of the *Iliad*'s persuasive speeches in an attempt to assess whether they can meaningfully be described as rhetoric by Aristotle's standards and by the standards of my working definition of rhetoric: *a learned and deliberately practiced skill, involving the deployment of tropes and techniques according to a rule-based system, and aimed at winning an audience's approval or assent.* In collecting speeches for this investigation, I first examined all the direct speeches in the *Iliad* and identified those whose intent was to cause the listener(s) to perform some action or take some attitude in response.[5] This precluded both vaunting speeches on the battlefield, and speeches that consist exclusively of rebuke or blame (not rebuke or blame in the service of persuasion to action). From the resulting field of speeches intended to elicit some behavior, I then further distinguished between those that employ solely command or instruction, and those that summon argumentation in their attempt to convince the listener(s). The former class of speeches—simple commands or instructions—are generally brief, and are unaccompanied by any persuasive elements (appeals, reasons, arguments, examples, invocations to figures of authority, evocations of the past, etc.). Although they are uttered with the intent of stirring the listener to do something or take some attitude, they cannot be categorized as *rhetorical* since they rely solely on the imperative mood of the verbs, rather than on the speaker's arguments, to affect behavior. They are also generally uncontroversial (i.e., unlikely to be contested by the listener).

It is the latter class of speeches—those that summon argumentation and reasons—that are of interest to me, as they suggest an awareness of rhetorical technique. The level of sophistication in these persuasive speeches is the more significant for being only a subset of all the persuasive attempts among the Iliadic speeches. The fact that some speeches (used in certain situations, spoken by certain characters) do *not* make use of devices that would later be classed as "rhetorical," while others do, provides a basis for comparison—an unmarked and a marked set, so to speak. It also suggests a degree of intentionality in the poet's representation of these rhetorical devices: rhetoric in the *Iliad* is not simply a universal practice, coextensive with locutionary acts. Even within this smaller class of what I will call "rhetorical" speeches, there are varying degrees of elaborateness. There are speeches of short or medium length that employ one or two rhetorical devices, such as *êthos, diathesis, paradeigma,* or enthymeme. But there are also a number of longer speeches that present more sophisticated and substantial rhetorical properties. They contain many different rhetorical devices in

combination, often spun out to considerable length, and tend to be more attuned to the audience and to which arguments are best calibrated to persuade
that particular audience.

I will begin my analysis of rhetorical speeches in the *Iliad* by noting several
"control" texts: that is, speeches that seek to elicit some action from the audience
but that lack persuasive techniques or argumentation, and therefore do not meet
my criteria for consideration as rhetoric. One such control text is Priam's speech
to the Trojans at *Iliad* 7.368–78:

> Trojans and Dardanians and companions in arms: hear me
> while I speak forth what the heart within my breast urges.
> Take now your supper about the city, as you did before this,
> and remember your duty of the watch, and be each man wakeful;
> and at dawn let Idaios go to the hollow ships, and speak with
> the sons of Atreus, Menelaos and Agamemnon, giving
> the word of Alexandros, for whose sake this strife has arisen,
> and to add this solid message, and ask them if they are willing
> to stop the sorrowful fighting until we can burn the bodies
> of our dead. We shall fight again until the divinity
> chooses between us, and gives victory to one or the other.

This sort of speech provides a necessary contrast to the proposed rhetorical nature of other speeches that I will discuss below. Priam's primary tactic for spur-
ring his audience to action is his use of the imperative mood in the phrases "hear
me," "take now your supper," "remember your duty," and "be wakeful." No reasons are adduced to these commands; Priam seems to rely on the practical, uncontroversial nature of his proposal, and perhaps also on his status as king (although there is no explicit appeal to his status or identity, such as would constitute
an argument from *êthos*).[6] Although this speech would qualify as a directive in
Searle's speech-act taxonomy, it does not qualify as rhetorical persuasion. This
sort of straightforward combination of command and instruction, devoid of persuasive elements, is very common in the *Iliad*. To cite just a few other examples,
Odysseus uses this combination when speaking with Diomedes during the
night raid in Book 10 (341–48); the gods engage in commanding and being commanded, as when Sleep plies Poseidon with a brief command to stir up the
Greek troops in Book 14 (357–60) and Zeus commands Apollo to embolden
Hector in Book 15 (221–35); and even the great orator Nestor employs this mini-
malist approach when giving instructions to burn the dead and then build a
rampart for defense in Book 7 (327–43).

In contrast with Priam's speech above, a representative example of the more rhetorically nuanced speeches that will form the basis of my argument is Odysseus' exhortation to the Greek assembly at *Iliad* 2.284–332. Odysseus begins by addressing Agamemnon, but shifts his address part of the way through the speech to include the entire audience of Greek warriors.[7] Odysseus here delivers a formal assembly-speech, accompanied by the "rhetorical" gesture of holding the scepter (2.279).[8] The poet characterizes this speech as βουλή (282), and describes the act of speaking with the verbs ἀγορήσατο and μετέειπεν (283). It is a complex speech, involving persuasion from several different angles: Odysseus embeds an exhortation from the mouth of another speaker (Calchas' prophecy at Aulis) within his own exhortation to his audience to fight. I present the formally persuasive / rhetorical elements of the speech—that is, those that correspond to Aristotle's *pisteis* and *topoi*—as follows, highlighted in bold.

Odysseus' speech begins with a reproach to the Achaeans for not adhering to their former promise "to go home only after you had sacked strong-walled Ilion" (286–88). This is an example of what Aristotle would call the **topic of consideration of timing** (ἐκ τοῦ τὸν χρόνον σκοπεῖν, topic #5 in Aristotle's list), discussed in *Rhetoric* 2.23.6; it derives its rhetorical force from comparing promises or behavior before and after a change in circumstance, and pointing out an inconsistency in order to make an argument. This reproach forms the premise to an **enthymeme** of which the conclusion is only implicit, though it will be stated later in the speech: that the Greeks must stay true to their promise and fight the war to the finish. Odysseus emphasizes his reproach with an unflattering simile: "for as if they were young children or widowed women they cry out and complain to each other" (298–90). Such a comparison is calculated to engender in the Achaeans a sense of shame (**pathos**) and thus to put them in a frame of mind to prove themselves courageous—the technique of **diathesis**. The change of circumstance in question, of course, is the long duration of the war, and it is to this topic that Odysseus turns next. Rather than continuing in a rebuking tone, however, he conveys his sympathy for and understanding of his audience's frustration in the following passage:

> In truth, it is a hard thing, to be grieved with desire for going.
> Any man who stays away one month from his own wife
> with his intricate ship is impatient, one whom the storm winds
> of winter and the sea rising keep back. And for us now
> this is the ninth of the circling years that we wait here. Therefore

> I cannot find fault with the Achaians for their impatience
>
> beside the curved ships. . . . (291–97)

The tone of this passage is aimed at putting the audience in a favorable frame of mind (*diathesis*), from the opening *gnômê* (lines 291–93) to the introduction of first-person diction to forge a sense of camaraderie and shared experience (ἡμῖν, 295; οὐ νεμεσίζομαι, 296). Odysseus emphasizes his understanding of the frustration of the Greek soldiers by means of an argument resembling Aristotle's **topic of greater and less** (ἐκ τοῦ μᾶλλον καὶ ἧττον, topic #4, *Rhetoric* 2.23.4), which argues that if something that is lesser in quality or quantity or likelihood is the case, then something that is greater than it in quality or quantity or likelihood can be inferred also to be the case. This is the force of the *gnômê* "Any man who stays away one month from his own wife with his intricate ship is impatient": it is an example of a lesser, but still valid, cause for impatience, of which the greater cause is the situation-specific statement, "And for us now this is the ninth of the circling years that we wait here." The conclusion of this **enthymeme**, then, is the following concession, which also functions as an instance of *diathesis*: "Therefore (τώ) I cannot find fault with the Achaians for their impatience beside the curved ships."

Odysseus launches into a new **enthymeme** construction in lines 297–99. Its premise consists of another *gnômê*—"Always it is disgraceful to wait long and at the end go home empty-handed"—and is followed by an imperative conclusion: "No, but be patient, friends, and stay yet a little longer until we know whether Kalchas' prophecy is true or is not true." The attachment of a purpose clause (ὄφρα δαῶμεν) to this conclusion effects a transition into the second half of the speech's argumentation: the appeal to Calchas' prophecy in lines 299–330. The language Odysseus uses to invoke the memory of Calchas' prophecy foreshadows forensic oratory, beginning with the statement that "you all were witnesses" (ἐστὲ δὲ πάντες / μάρτυροι, 2.301–2). He then relies on the shared memory of his audience, as well as on the authority bestowed by the supernatural events he recounts, to make rhetorical use of a "sign" (σῆμα, 308), namely the omen sent by Zeus at the outset of the Greeks' campaign of a serpent devouring nine sparrows. Odysseus' explicit invocation of a σῆμα here corresponds to one of the three premises (προτάσεις) of rhetorical *logos* that Aristotle identifies in *Rhetoric* 1.3.7: signs (σημεῖα), evidence (τεκμήρια), and probability (τὰ εἰκότα). To make his argument, Odysseus quotes Calchas' interpretation of the omen:

> "As this snake has eaten the sparrow herself with her children,
>
> eight of them, and the mother was the ninth, who bore them,

so for years as many as this shall we fight in this place
and in the tenth year we shall take the city of the wide ways."
So he spoke to us then; **now all this is being accomplished** (τὰ δὴ νῦν πάντα
τελεῖται). (326–30)

The strategy of quoting another's words is itself a persuasive strategy, as both
Irene de Jong and Deborah Beck have observed, since embedded quotation
invokes an external authority to reinforce the argument of the speaker.[9] Here,
Calchas' interpretation of the bird omen serves as both sign and evidence for
Odysseus' conclusion that the Argives should fight, since the prophecy about
the ten-year duration of the war is being fulfilled before their very eyes. This
also acts as an appeal to another topic that anticipates Aristotle: the **topic
of consequences by analogy** (ἐκ τοῦ ἀνάλογον ταῦτα συμβαίνειν, topic #16,
Rhetoric 2.23.17), which deduces similar consequences for two occurrences
based on a correspondence between those occurrences. Because everything
has gone according to Calchas' prophecy thus far ("so for [nine years] shall
we fight in this place"), Odysseus argues, we can therefore expect the rest
of the prophecy ("in the tenth year we shall take the city of the wide ways")
to be borne out. This is the implication of his observation that "now all this
is being accomplished." His complex speech-within-speech argument is in
turn the premise to a broader **enthymeme**, whose conclusion—an imperative command—brings the speech to a close: "Come then, you strong-greaved
Achaians, let every man stay here, until we have taken the great citadel of
Priam" (2.331–32).

This speech represents the concerted use of multiple techniques for effective
rhetoric as catalogued by Aristotle, spanning all three levels of specificity that I
described above: *logos* and *diathesis* (including *pathos*) on the most basic level;
several different enthymemes on the middle level; and three of Aristotle's detailed "topics of demonstrative enthymemes" on the most specialized level. The
result of this μῦθος (as it is labeled in 2.335) can be judged by the audience response: "So he spoke, and the Argives shouted aloud, and about them the ships
echoed terribly to the roaring Achaians as they cried out applause to the word of
godlike Odysseus" (333–35). The effectiveness of the speech in achieving its goal
is implicit rather than explicit, since it is immediately followed by speeches from
Nestor and before the Argives resume their fighting stations. But Odysseus'
speech is the one that turns the tide of the army's sentiments, and as such can be
deemed effective—which, as we shall see, is more than can be said for many
other "rhetorical" speeches in the *Iliad*. The relationship between rhetorical

sophistication and successful persuasion, in Homer as in later oratory, is not one of simple correlation.

III: RHETORICAL SPEECHES IN THE *ILIAD*

Odysseus' speech at *Iliad* 2.284–332 provides one of the lengthier, more elaborate, and more wide-ranging examples of rhetoric in the *Iliad*, but rhetorical argumentation can be seen across a broad spectrum of speech lengths and complexities within the poem. In all, I have identified a total of 58 rhetorical speeches in the *Iliad*. This section presents my analysis of a representative sample (18) of these 58 speeches, encompassing a variety of speakers and rhetorical situations. (Analysis of the remaining speeches and their rhetorical techniques can be found in the appendix.) Since my analysis of these speeches has turned up no predictable distribution of techniques that would make it possible to create meaningful subcategories based on, for example, speakers or speech length or density of rhetorical techniques, I have concluded that a chronological ordering of the catalogue is best.[10] The rhetoric of these speeches is conditioned on their position within the narrative and their relationship to other speeches around them. Simple chronological organization thus gives the most natural and easy-to-follow path to the big picture that emerges: namely, that many of the *Iliad*'s speakers engage in complex rhetorical argumentation comparable to that expounded in Aristotle's treatise.

Each distinct use of a technique that corresponds to Aristotle's rhetorical framework or terminology is marked in bold.

I. The first speech in the *Iliad* that exhibits rhetorical argumentation in the service of persuasion is Nestor's speech to Agamemnon and Achilles at 1.254–84.[11] He addresses the two heroes in an effort to end their quarrel, and opens by shaming them for the sorrow that their quarrel is bringing upon the Greeks: ὦ πόποι, ἦ μέγα πένθος Ἀχαιΐδα γαῖαν ἱκάνει ("Oh, for shame. Great sorrow comes on the land of Achaia," 254). Nestor elaborates upon this πένθος in the following lines, envisioning the glee of Priam if he were to discover the Greeks' internal quarrel (255–58). This constitutes an argument from the **topic of the consequence** (ἐκ τοῦ ἀκολουθοῦντος προτρέπειν ἢ ἀποτρέπειν, topic #13, *Rhetoric* 2.23.14), which looks to the consequences of an action in order to exhort or dissuade; the topic is in turn an **enthymeme** premise whose conclusion is the simple command ἀλλὰ πίθεσθ' (259)—that is, "be persuaded" to cease from quarreling.

Nestor then makes an appeal based on his own *êthos*, beginning with the authority engendered by his seniority (ἄμφω δὲ νεωτέρω ἐστὸν ἐμεῖο, 259). He also invokes the example of men he has dealt with in the past: "Yes, and in my time I have dealt with better men than you are, and never once did they disregard me" (260–61).[12] This argument employs two topics: the **topic of an earlier judgment about the same or a similar matter** (ἐκ κρίσεως περὶ τοῦ αὐτοῦ ἢ ὁμοίου, topic #11, *Rhetoric* 2.23.12)—in this case, the earlier judgment of others concerning Nestor's competency as a counselor; and the **topic of greater and less** (ἐκ τοῦ μᾶλλον καὶ ἧττον, topic #4, *Rhetoric* 2.23.4). The latter topic reasons as follows: if the men of an earlier generation, who were greater warriors than you, obeyed me (καὶ μέν μευ βουλέων ξύνιεν πείθοντό τε μύθῳ 273), how much more should you, lesser warriors, obey (ἀλλὰ πίθεσθε καὶ ὕμμες, 274). In lines 262–72, Nestor expands upon this description of an earlier generation of superior men in order to provide a *paradeigma* for his current audience: κάρτιστοι δὴ κεῖνοι ἐπιχθονίων τράφεν ἀνδρῶν·/κάρτιστοι μὲν ἔσαν καὶ καρτίστοις ἐμάχοντο ("These were the strongest generation of earth-born mortals, the strongest, and they fought against the strongest," 266–67). He again highlights his own *êthos* by counting himself a part of their company (καὶ μὲν τοῖσιν ἐγὼ μεθομίλεον, 269). At the end of this paradigmatic section, Nestor inserts a short, capping **enthymeme** that is rife with the vocabulary of persuasion; his imperative conclusion, "Do you also obey (ἀλλὰ πίθεσθε καὶ ὕμμες)," is followed by the gnomic premise, "since to be persuaded is better (ἐπεὶ πείθεσθαι ἄμεινον)" (274).

In the final part of his speech (1.275–84), Nestor addresses each of the quarreling rivals in turn, and tailors his appeal to the individual. He turns to Agamemnon first, commanding him (with a flattering nod to his high status, ἀγαθός περ ἐών, 275) not to take Briseis away from Achilles, and adding as an afterthought the reminder that the Achaeans themselves had given her to him (275–76). Turning to Achilles, he argues from an **enthymeme** that again takes the form of a conclusion / command supported by a *gnômê*: "Nor, son of Peleus, think to match your strength with the king, since (ἐπεί) never equal with the rest is the portion of honour of the sceptred king to whom Zeus gives magnificence" (277–79). The next lines attribute to the two feuding heroes different aspects of *aristeia*, an attempt to engender good feeling (*diathesis*) through flattery and recognition of their individual claims to superiority. "Even though you are the stronger man (σὺ καρτερός ἐσσι), and the mother who bore you was immortal," Nestor concedes to Achilles, "yet is this man [Agamemnon] greater (ὅ γε φέρτερός ἐστιν) who is lord over more than you rule" (280–81). Finally, Nestor makes a personal appeal to Agamemnon to end the speech, relying on the pull of his *êthos* with the plaintive words "even I (αὐτὰρ ἔγωγε) entreat you to give over your bitterness against Achilleus" (282–83). This constitutes the conclusion to a final **enthymeme**. The premise is grounded in desperation; Nestor begs Agamemnon to give up his anger because Achilles "stands as a great bulwark of battle over all the Achaians" (282–84), thus employing the **topic of consideration of incentives and disincentives** (σκοπεῖν τὰ προτρέποντα καὶ ἀποτρέποντα, topic #20, *Rhetoric* 2.23.21). This topic involves providing persuasive or dissuasive arguments to spur the listener to action: for example, Aristotle observes, people will be likely to take an action if it is "possible and easy and advantageous" (δυνατὸν καὶ ῥάδιον καὶ ὠφέλιμον, *Rhetoric* 2.23.21). Nestor's speech pleases Agamemnon, who calls it κατὰ μοῖραν (1.286), but it is unsuccessful in its aim to stem the hostilities between the two warriors.

II. In the famous *diapeira* episode, Agamemnon makes a speech (2.110–41) that is unique in its rhetorical aim: he exhorts the Greek army to withdraw from Troy with the expectation that his speech will, in fact, persuade them to do the opposite (he confides to the leaders beforehand that it will be a test, ἔπεσιν πειρήσομαι, 2.73).[13] This attempt at reverse psychology backfires, however. Although Agamemnon can be an ineffective speaker in the *Iliad* when he *wants* to persuade (e.g., in his speech to Teucer, 8.281–91), here, ironically, he is effective when he intends *not* to persuade.[14] His faux-rhetoric is all too persuasive, given his audience's state of mind. Agamemnon begins with an appeal to the supposedly hostile will of Zeus. "Zeus son of Kronos has caught me fast in bitter futility," claims Agamemnon, citing the god's fickle dealings with him (111–15). He reports that Zeus has commanded him to return home to Argos, and, as an argument for resigning to this command, offers the **gnômê** that Zeus "is too strong, who before now has broken the crests of many cities and will break them again, since his power is beyond all others" (116–18).

A subtle attempt at counterpersuasion can be observed in Agamemnon's emphasis on the shame that will arise from giving up: "And this shall be a thing of shame for the men hereafter to be told, that so strong, so great a host of Achaians carried on and fought in vain a war that was useless against men fewer than they, with no accomplishment shown for it" (2.119–22). This constitutes an argument from an assumed knowledge of his men's frame of mind (**diathesis**), as Agamemnon (mis-) calculates that their emotions of shame and honor will arouse them to protest. By dwelling at great length, and with a vivid illustration, on the fact that the Greeks outnumber the Trojans (122–30), Agamemnon is employing *auxesis* or expansion, which Aristotle identifies as a common aspect of persuasion in *Rhetoric* 2.18.4–5.[15] Agamemnon then returns to his earlier defeatist theme, citing the great number of Trojan allies, "who drive me hard back again and will not allow me, despite my will, to sack the well-founded stronghold of Ilion" (132–33). This observation (carrying the weight of experiential truth for the audience) provides the first premise of an extended **enthymeme**. As the second premise, Agamemnon uses an argument from *diathesis* all too effectively, stirring up his audience's emotions of pity and longing for their homes and families, as well as of frustration at the fruitlessness of their efforts:

> And now nine years of mighty Zeus have gone by . . .
> and far away our wives and our young children
> are sitting within our halls and wait for us, while still our work here
> stays unfinished as it is. . . . (134–38)

The enthymematic conclusion follows in the form of the command "come then, do as I say, let us all be won over; let us run away with our ships to the beloved land of our fathers" (139–40). Perhaps imagining that this command will strike the Greek army as cowardly, Agamemnon adds a further premise—highly debatable—in the final line of his speech: ". . . since (γάρ) no longer now shall we capture Troy of the wide ways" (141). But however flawed his assumptions and his claims, Agamemnon's use of *diathesis* is unwittingly in line with his audience's sentiments. The men take his speech at face value and are persuaded: "So he spoke, and stirred up the passion in the breast of all those who were within that multitude and listened to his counsel" (2.142–3).

III. The next two speeches are part of the same interaction: a quarrel between Zeus and Hera at the beginning of Book 4 over the outcome of the war. The narrative has just seen the cataloguing of Greek and Trojan forces in Book 2 and the duel between Menelaus and Paris in Book 3. Zeus makes reference to the latter event as he initiates the quarrel with a speech (4.7–19) that is equal parts blame and deliberation. Its aim is to discourage dissension and maverick action among the gods, and to reach a consensus on the best course for resolving the war. To this end, he addresses the assembled gods, specifically targeting Hera and Athena with "offensive words" (κερτομίοις ἐπέεσσι, 4.6). His first move is to provoke Hera into action by comparing her unfavorably with Aphrodite as a protector of her hero: while Hera and Athena are "sitting apart, looking on at the fighting, and take their pleasure," Aphrodite actively "stands by her man and drives the spirits of death away from him" (9–11). Once again, we see an appeal to shame used as rhetorical strategy, an example of Zeus deploying *diathesis.* He knows what will most rankle his target, for, as we see throughout the *Iliad*, Hera despises everything about Aphrodite: her character, her support of the Trojans, and her methods of achieving her aims.

Having incited Hera in this way, Zeus turns to the assembled gods with the exhortation to let reason and mutual advantage prevail in making peace between Trojans and Greeks, based on Menelaus' victory in the duel (4.13–19). He first issues a call for deliberation (φραζώμεθ', 14). The exhortation "Let us consider then how these things shall be accomplished" is followed by two opposing options: "whether again to stir up grim warfare . . . or cast down love and make them friends with each other" (14–16). This exhortation represents an **enthymeme** conclusion; as a rationale and premise for the exhortation, Zeus plaintively offers a best-case scenario: "If somehow this way could be sweet and pleasing to all of us, the city of lord Priam might still be a place men dwell in, and Menelaos could take away with him Helen of Argos" (17–19). The appeal to a solution that would be "sweet and pleasing to all of us" exemplifies Aristotle's **topic of consideration of incentives and disincentives** (topic #20). Zeus does not argue strongly for this proposed peaceable solution, however; he merely advocates that some sort of solution be considered. This leaves his speech to end on an oddly indecisive note, and it is thus perhaps unsurprising that the speech fails to placate Hera and Athena ("Hera and Athena muttered," 4.20), and that Zeus concedes to Hera's demands in the negotiations that follow (4.37).

IV. With the tide already turned in her favor by Zeus' concession speech at 4.31–49, Hera makes a speech at 4.51–67 that presents her specific demands for the course of the war. The rhetorical nature of her speech indicates that she does not take Zeus' concessions for granted, and is still concerned with persuading him. She opens with a concession of her own: Zeus may destroy any of her three favorite cities in the future without opposition (51–56). Then she moves to flattery of Zeus' strength; knowing that he prides himself on this quality, she employs the technique of *diathesis*: "In malice I will accomplish nothing, since you are far stronger (πολὺ φέρτερός)" (56). Finally, in anticipation of her demands, she makes a strong appeal to her *êthos* as part of an **enthymeme** premise in lines 58–61. Her work and will ought to be carried out because of her identity and status, she argues. She is a god (58), of the same race as Zeus (58), the firstborn daughter of Kronos (59), and the wife of Zeus (60–61). In line 61, she reminds Zeus that he is "lord over all the immortals," simultaneously flattering him (*diathesis*) and claiming authority for herself by association with him. Having thus laid the groundwork for her demands, she begins her enthymematic conclusion with a modest exhortation that she and Zeus "both give way to each other" (62) as an example to the other gods. She moves at last to pure commands: "give orders to Athene to visit horrible war again on Achaians and Trojans, and try to make it so that the Trojans are first offenders" (64–67). In progressing from concession, caution, and respect to bold demands, Hera has assessed her audience correctly and crafted an effective speech. The decisive success of the speech is evident from the narrator's cap: "Nor did the father of gods and men disobey her" (4.68).

V. Sarpedon addresses Hector at 5.472–92 with a rhetorically rich exhortation to fight. This speech is itself spurred by a brief exhortation delivered by Ares (in the guise of Akamas) to the Trojan army in 5.464–69. Sarpedon's opening tactic employs *diathesis* through a taunt designed to arouse the emotion of shame: "Where now, Hektor, has gone that strength that was yours?" (472). Continuing to question Hector's dedication to the fighting, Sarpedon makes an appeal to the **topic of consideration of timing** (ἐκ τοῦ τὸν χρόνον σκοπεῖν, topic #5, *Rhetoric* 2.23.6): Hector made a boast in the past (φῇς που) "that without companions and without people you could hold this city alone, with only your brothers and the lords of your sisters" (473–74). However, he is failing to fulfill this boast in the present; as Sarpedon notes, "I can see not one of these men now (νῦν)" (475). He draws attention to the concrete, visual evidence of not seeing Hector's family, and continues to evoke shame in his addressee by claiming that his brothers and brothers-in-law "slink away like hounds who circle the lion, while we, who are here as your companions, carry the fighting" (476–77). This reminder of Sarpedon's own contribution to the war effort works simultaneously as an appeal to *êthos* and as a *paradeigma*, and he develops these techniques in 478–84 as he details the personal sacrifices he has made to support the Trojans. This passage also initiates an extended **enthymeme**, for which the premise is an argument from the **topic of greater and less** (topic #4):

> I have come, a companion to help you, from a very far place . . .
> Yet even so I drive on my Lykians, and myself have courage
> to fight my man in battle, though there is nothing of mine here
> that the Achaians can carry away as spoil or drive off.
> But you: you stand here, not even giving the word to the rest
> of your people to stand fast and fight in defence of your own wives. (5.478–86)

Hector and the Trojans—with greater responsibility and more to lose than Sarpedon and the Lycians—should be fighting with proportionally greater ferocity; this is not, however, the case.[16] Having stated this as a premise (and as another source of shame), Sarpedon concludes the enthymeme with the command not to "be taken as war-spoil and plunder by the men who hate you" (488). He invokes both fear and shame (*pathos*) in the last lines of his speech, warning that the Greeks' imminent assault on Troy should be a constant concern for Hector (490), as should be the avoidance of reproof (κρατερὴν δ' ἀποθέσθαι ἐνιπήν, 492)—reproof such as Sarpedon himself is now issuing. The speech is effective, and indeed merits the unusually descriptive narrative comment that "his word (μῦθος) bit into the heart of Hektor" (5.493). In response, Hector is depicted leaping from his chariot, shaking two spears, and roaming throughout the army "stirring men up to fight and waking the hateful warfare" (494–96).

VI. Andromache makes a poignant rhetorical appeal to Hector at 6.407–39, begging him to stay within the walls of Troy. Her first argument combines a threat ("Your own great strength will be your death") with an appeal to pity ("and you have no pity [οὐδ' ἐλεαίρεις] on your little son, nor on me, ill-starred, who soon must be your widow") (407–9). Both of these considerations are calculated to evoke an emotional response in her husband (*pathos*), and thus to dispose him favorably to her eventual request (*diathesis*). Andromache continues her speech by expanding upon these two rhetorical approaches (*auxesis*), providing a vivid depiction of the threat to Hector's life and the pitiable consequences that his death will have for his loved ones:

> For presently the Achaians, gathering together,
> will set upon you and kill you; and for me it would be far better
> to sink into the earth when I have lost you, for there is no other
> consolation for me after you have gone to your destiny—
> only grief; since I have no father, no honoured mother. (409–13)

As Aristotle observes in the *Rhetoric*, pity is "pain at an apparently destructive or painful evil happening to one who does not deserve it and which a person might expect himself or one of his own to suffer. . . . The kind of people who think they might suffer are those . . . that have parents or children or wives" (*Rhetoric* 2.8.2–5). Thus Andromache, as Hector's wife, is uniquely able to invoke pity; she depicts his suffering at the hands of the Achaeans, and she herself embodies the suffering of "one of his own." Here and elsewhere in the speech, she draws upon the technique of *êthos* by keeping her personal history and her identity as Hector's wife at the forefront of her appeal. Lines 414–28 contain Andromache's narration of her own pitiable past, in which her father and brothers had been killed by Achilles and her mother by Artemis. This narration ends with a repetition and expansion of her statement of bereavement in line 413: "Hektor, thus you are father to me, and my honoured mother, you are my brother, and you it is who are my young husband" (429–30). The cry for pity expressed in this sentiment (*pathos*), which invests and concentrates all familial relationships in one person, Andromache's addressee, serves as the premise to an **enthymeme**. Its conclusion is the plea, "Please take pity (ἐλέαιρε) upon me then, stay here on the rampart" (431). A second enthymematic premise follows, appealing to the **topic of consideration of incentives and disincentives** (topic #20): "that you may not leave your child an orphan, your wife a widow" (432). Andromache ends her speech on a practical note, urging Hector to muster the Trojan forces to the most vulnerable part of the city walls (433–39). Though Hector is moved by her words ("All these things are in my mind also, lady," 6.441), his own sense of honor and shame keep him from acceding to her request.

VII. Agamemnon addresses an exhortation to Teucer at 8.281–91, notable because the situation hardly seems to call for a persuasive speech, as Teucer is already acquitting himself brilliantly in the battle (273–79). Agamemnon opens with a flattering and respectful address (*diathesis*) in 281, calling Teucer "dear heart" and "lord of your people." This is followed by an **enthymeme** consisting of the simple conclusion / command "strike so" (βάλλ' οὕτως) and the lengthier premise "thus you may be a light given to the Danaans, and to Telamon your father" (282–83). While the invocation of the Danaans in their time of need constitutes a mild appeal to Teucer's sympathies as a leader of soldiers, the invocation of Teucer's father is an even stronger use of *diathesis*. Agamemnon elaborates this appeal in lines 284–85 in order to play on the emotions of filial affection and sense of obligation: "Telamon your father, who cherished you when you were little, and, bastard as you were, looked after you in his own house. Bring him into glory, though he is far away." (This strategy will be used more prominently later in the poem, when Phoenix in Book 9 and Priam in Book 24 invoke the figure of Peleus when attempting to persuade Achilles.) The reminder of Teucer's past and the implied debt he owes to Telamon shade into the premise of a new **enthymeme**, of which the conclusion is the command "bring him into glory" (285).

But Agamemnon strikes a discordant note by reminding Teucer that he is a bastard (σε νόθον, 8.284) in the midst of his appeal, thus undermining his attempt to put Teucer in a favorable frame of mind. Such mishandling of the *diathesis* technique is typical of Agamemnon, and is the foremost reason for the frequent failure of his rhetoric. Agamemnon ends his speech with an appeal to the **topic of consideration of incentives and disincentives** (topic #20), promising rewards to Teucer *if* the gods ever grant the Greeks victory over Troy (286–91). The rhetoric of this promise is weak on several levels, however: he puts a condition (the capture of Troy) on the promise; he takes care to note that Teucer will receive his reward only after Agamemnon does ("First after myself I will put into your hands some great gift of honour," 289); and the incentives themselves are remarkably paltry, a series of single possible rewards rather than an accumulation of several (in stark contrast with Agamemnon's lavish peace-offering to Achilles in Book 9, for example): "a tripod, or two horses and the chariot with them, or else a woman" (290–91). The speech ends on this stingy note, and its ineffectiveness is quickly manifest. Teucer rebuffs the exhortation as unnecessary and patronizing with the words, "Son of Atreus, most lordly: must you then drive me, who am eager myself, as it is?" (8.293–94). Agamemnon's arguments may have partaken of rhetorical devices, but his application of them—and his insensitivity to his audience—dooms the speech's persuasive power. As is the case for many of the *Iliad*'s characters, Agamemnon's speaking ability—or lack thereof—is a significant aspect of his characterization.[17]

VIII. Hector addresses the Trojans and their allies at 8.497–541 in a battlefield speech following a period of Trojan success in the fighting, as they have pressed forward to the Achaean ships. It is a speech aimed at both exhorting his audience to fight and convincing them to adopt his strategy in the present. Hector opens with a command (κέκλυτέ μευ, 497) followed by an explanation of his proposed course of action: namely, that the Trojans should halt their pursuit of the Greeks now that it is nightfall (498–502). He bolsters the Trojans' confidence (*diathesis*) by postulating that the Argives would have been thoroughly defeated if not for an external and temporary circumstance: "the darkness . . . beyond all else rescued the Argives and their vessels" (500–501). Beginning with the hortatory subjunctive command to "be persuaded by black night" (πειθώμεθα νυκτὶ μελαίνῃ, 502), Hector issues a series of simple, practical commands for nighttime preparations in lines 503–9. The final command—to bring piles of firewood—turns into the conclusion of an **enthymeme**, which is followed in turn by two premises. These premises progress from the more practical and mundane concerns to the more strategic and far-reaching: "so that (ὥς) all night long . . . we may burn many fires" (508–9); and "so that not (μή) in the night-time the flowing-haired Achaians may set out to run for home" (510–11). A second **enthymeme** follows, beginning with the conclusion that "not thus in their own good time must they take to their vessels, but in such a way that a man of them at home will still nurse his wound" (512–13), and supported by an explanatory premise: "so that (ἵνα) another may shrink hereafter from bringing down fearful war on the Trojans" (512–16). This last argument draws upon the **topic of consideration of incentives and disincentives** (topic #20), as Hector envisions the Greeks so harassed by Trojan strength that they would be dissuaded from future fighting.

Another multifaceted **enthymeme** construction follows this one, as Hector commands the heralds to instruct the boys, old men, and women in Troy to complete various tasks in order to guard the city in lines 8.517–22. These commands—acting as enthymematic conclusions—culminate in the general admonishment to "let there be a watch kept steadily" (521), followed by the premise "lest (μή) a sudden attack get into the town when the fighters have left it" (522). This premise is a straightforward appeal to the **topic of the consequence** (topic #13). Hector caps his instructions and their attendant premises with another conclusion: "Let it be thus . . . as I tell you" (523), and he repeats the sentiment for emphasis in the following line, characterizing his own speech as a μῦθος (524). He follows this command with a prayer to the gods in 526–28 that the Trojans might be able to drive off the Greeks.

In the final portion of his speech, Hector draws on his own bold character (*êthos*) as motivation. He asserts his willingness to fight Diomedes despite the uncertainty of the outcome, thereby providing an inspiration for his men:

> [Tomorrow] I shall know if the son of Tydeus, strong Diomedes,
> will force me back from the ships against the wall, or whether I
> shall cut him down with the bronze and take home the blooded war-spoils.
> Tomorrow he will learn his own strength, if he can stand up to
> my spear's advance; but sooner than this, I think, in the foremost
> he will go down under the stroke, and many companions about him. (8.532–37)

This note of confidence is extended into the speech's conclusion, a complex wish tied to an appeal to probability (*eikos*):

> Oh, if I only
> could be as this in all my days immortal and ageless
> and be held in honour as Athene and Apollo are honoured
> as surely as this oncoming day brings evil to the Argives. (538–41)

Here, Hector makes the postulation that defeating the Greeks is such a likely outcome that he would entrust his greatest wish to the same likelihood.[18] It is a bold, almost reckless, note on which to end his speech—one that puts a twist on that Classical-era rhetorical standby, the argument from probability. But it drives home the speech's overall strategy of stirring up the emotions of confidence and optimism in the Trojan warriors in preparation for the next day's battle. As a result, the Trojans immediately shout their approval (8.542) and implement Hector's plan.

IX. Nestor steps into the midst of a quarrel in the Achaean assembly at 9.53–78, making a speech addressed primarily to Diomedes (whose speech immediately preceded his own), secondarily to Agamemnon (who has proposed withdrawing from Troy, a plan opposed by Diomedes), and thirdly to the assembled Achaean army (which has expressed approval of Diomedes' upstart sentiments).[19] Nestor's speech is thus a rhetorical balancing act, attempting to do several things at once: to persuade the addressees individually of different things; to reconcile Agamemnon and Diomedes to each other; and to restore damaged morale and establish strategic tasks for the army. In its attempt to mediate between two feuding parties without offending either one of them, this speech is reminiscent of Nestor's speech to Agamemnon and Achilles at 1.254–84. Here, Nestor relies heavily on the technique of *diathesis*, tailoring his words to each specific addressee in turn. He begins by extending compliments to Diomedes, observing that Diomedes is superior to his peers in both battle prowess and assembly-speaking: "Son of Tydeus, beyond others you are strong in battle, and in counsel (βουλῇ) also are noblest (ἄριστος) among all men of your own age" (53–54). He also praises the speech that Diomedes has just delivered (55–56 and 58–59), but criticizes it for falling short of completion, offering the famous assessment, "Yet you have not made complete your argument" (ἀτὰρ οὐ τέλος ἵκεο μύθων, 56). Such an assessment suggests that both speaker and audience share an objective standard for argumentative or persuasive skill, and that Diomedes measures up well with his peers in this skill; but that, in his immaturity, he lacks the ability to fully utilize the capacities of rhetoric for a given situation. In contrast, Nestor says, he himself possesses this ability by virtue of greater age and experience, and he will proceed to model it: "But let me speak, since I can call myself older than you are, and go through the whole matter (πάντα διίξομαι), since there is none who can dishonour the thing I say (μῦθον), not even powerful Agamemnon" (60–62). This represents perhaps the most emphatic argument from *êthos* in the *Iliad*, from the speaker most prone to appealing to his own *êthos*. Nestor gestures toward his age and status as he pronounces himself immune to the possibility of dishonor that seems to plague all other heroes in the poem.[20] What follows is, as Martin has noted, Nestor's instruction-by-example of a "complete" μῦθος for his younger comrade.[21]

Nestor initiates his general exhortation to the Achaean audience with an admonitory **gnômê**: "Out of all brotherhood, outlawed, homeless shall be that man who longs for all the horror of fighting among his own people" (9.63–64). Bryan Hainsworth notes the effect of this proverb on the audience: "Nestor is cunningly forestalling (as Akhilleus did not in Book I) a violent reaction to his reasonable proposals. . . . The gnome suits Nestor's age (cf. Aristotle *Rhetoric* 1395a for the appropriateness of proverbs to the elderly) and is a characteristic part of his rhetorical armament."[22] This strategy is also an instance of *diathesis*, as it primes Nestor's audience to be receptive to his peacemaking efforts. He next delivers a series of practical instructions in 65–68, operating on the assumption that the Greeks will stay and fight but making no mention of Agamemnon's proposal to withdraw. As he transitions from suppressing criticism to expressing praise, Nestor continues to show sensitivity to the Greek commander's dignity, addressing the next lines (68–73) directly to Agamemnon. Although he issues several direct orders to Agamemnon ("take command," 69; "divide a feast among the princes," 70), he interweaves them with flattering reminders of Agamemnon's status and power: "since (γάϱ) you are our kingliest" (69); "all hospitality is for you; you are lord over many" (73). With this well-placed employment of *diathesis*, Nestor preserves the unity of the army and saves face for a leader whom Diomedes had just labeled a coward.

Nestor ends his speech with a return to a more generalized exhortation, applicable to Agamemnon, Diomedes, and the whole assembled army. This exhortation takes the form of an **enthymeme**, beginning with the conclusion "When many assemble together, follow (πείσεαι) him who advises the best counsel" (9.74–75). The premise draws on the **topic of consideration of incentives and disincentives** (topic #20), as Nestor warns that "in truth there is need for all the Achaians of good close counsel, since (ὅτι) now close to our ships the enemy burn their numerous fires" (75–77). Having reminded his audience of the significance of the upcoming night for their fortunes (78), Nestor ends his instructive display of diplomatic rhetoric. The speech is a twofold success: it persuades the Achaeans to take action ("So he spoke, and they listened hard to him, and obeyed [ἐπίθοντο] him, 9.79); and it teaches Diomedes how to accomplish a τέλος μύθων. Martin observes that, subsequent to this "expert teaching" from Nestor, "Diomedes grows in rhetorical ability through the rest of the poem," and by the time he speaks in Book 14, "he has learned how to construct an impregnable speech."[23]

X. Phoenix's embassy speech to Achilles (9.434–605) is marked by its expansion (*auxesis*) of several rhetorical approaches. Its length alone—at 171 lines, it is the longest speech in the *Iliad*—commands the audience's attention and endows it with special significance. Martin has documented the *Iliad*'s equation of size with importance, observing that "length is a positive speech value. The assignment of length in speech by the narrator Homer produces our impressions about the importance of a given episode and also of a speaker."[24] Much scholarly attention has been lavished on this speech; among those that focus on its content are the treatments of Held (1987), Nagy (1999), Rosner (1976), Scodel (1982 and 2002), and Willcock (1964). Many of these scholars note aspects of Phoenix's persuasive strategy that correspond to an Aristotelian rubric for rhetoric, though they do not discuss these aspects in terms of rhetoric or Aristotle. Judith Rosner, in analyzing the parallels between this speech and the themes of the *Iliad* as a whole, discusses what I would identify as Phoenix's use of *diathesis* when she notes that Phoenix "concentrates on Peleus' hospitality," shifting "away from the materialistic outlook of Odysseus / Agamemnon into the humanity and *xenia* of Peleus / Achilles."[25] Gregory Nagy observes Phoenix's assertion that the embassy members are the comrades "most dear" (φίλτατοι) to Achilles (9.522)—employing the same term he will use to describe the companions of Meleager later in the speech (9.586), and, I would note, making an appeal to *êthos*.[26] Ruth Scodel focuses her analysis on the relationship of the character of Phoenix in the *Iliad* to what the audience would have known about him via tradition; commenting on Phoenix's character (*êthos*), she notes that "his 'leadership' was presumably intended to get the embassy through the door and win them a fair hearing."[27] George Held points out the parallels between this speech and the supplications of Chryses in Book 1, Patroclus in Book 16, and Priam in Book 24; he notes particularly the similarity in the roles of Phoenix and Priam with relation to Achilles (they are both substitute father-figures), and their correspondingly similar arguments—yet another appeal to *êthos*.[28] James Boyd White recognizes in Phoenix's speech two major strains of appeal, the logical (as represented by the Meleager myth and its argument that Achilles will receive the gifts of honor if he joins battle now, but will lose them if he refuses) and the ethical. "Phoenix's more effective appeal is ethical," White argues, "based on his special standing in the household and life of Achilles."[29] But while these scholars and others have treated broad rhetorical patterns or individual strategies within the speech, no analysis has catalogued Phoenix's full use of formal rhetorical techniques.

Phoenix opens his appeal by using *pathos*, attempting to stir up Achilles' emotions with the combination of a "stormburst of tears" (9.433) and a plea that he take pity on Phoenix in his old and dependent state (437–38). This plea expands into a call for loyalty to the wishes of Peleus (438–43), and a reminder of Achilles' obligation to Phoenix due to his service as Achilles' childhood mentor and instructor (438–43). Phoenix vows that he will follow Achilles wherever he goes, and uses this vow as an opportunity to expand upon his own youth and exploits, placing particular emphasis on his relationship with Achilles as a surrogate son (447–95)—a strong invocation of *êthos*.[30] Phoenix' identity and proximity to Achilles, as well as his own pitiable history, lend authority and emotional weight to his appeal. The climax of this autobiographical excursion is posed as a multifaceted **enthymeme** in which Phoenix states the persuasive purpose of the speech for the first time (62 lines into the speech). This enthymeme begins with a premise, then moves to a conclusion, and finally offers two further premises. In the first premise, Phoenix continues to remind Achilles of their shared past:

> And, godlike Achilleus, I made you all that you are now,
> and loved you out of my heart . . .
> So I have suffered much through you, and have had much trouble,
> thinking always how the gods would not bring to birth any children
> of my own; so that it was you, godlike Achilleus, I made
> my own child, so that some day you might keep hard affliction from me. (485–95)

Phoenix implies that his past devotion to Achilles has put Achilles under obligation, and he now attempts to redeem that obligation by making a request. This request comprises the *enthymeme* conclusion: "Then, Achilleus, beat down your great anger" (496). In support of this command, Phoenix offers a second premise, a reproach—"It is not yours to have a pitiless heart" (496–97)—that hints at his intimate knowledge of Achilles' character. He builds upon this reproach with a third premise in the form of a *paradeigma* for Achilles to follow: "The very immortals can be moved; their virtue and honour and strength are greater (μείζων) than ours are, and yet with sacrifices and offerings for endearment, with libations and with savour men turn back even the immortals in supplication. . . ." (497–501) This final argument appeals not only to a *paradeigma*, but also to the **topic of greater and less** (topic #4), with its reminder to Achilles that if even the gods (who, as superior beings, have greater prerogative for anger) can relent, surely he (as a mere mortal) is capable of following suit.

Phoenix follows this enthymeme with a parable—a relatively rare strategy for Iliadic speeches.[31] He relates the myth of the Litai, personified goddesses of supplication, and the ominous fate that awaits those who repudiate prayers or pleas. This warning serves as the first premise of another **enthymeme**—even more intricate than the previous one—which is structured as follows: premise 1, conclusion 1, premise 2, premise 3, premise 4, conclusion 2, premise 5. (Since this entire cluster of premises and conclusions contributes to the same point, I consider them all part of the same enthymematic structure.) The first premise includes the parable of the Litai, which culminates in an argument from the **topic of consideration of incentives and disincentives** (topic #20): "If a man shall deny them, and stubbornly with a harsh word refuse, they go to Zeus, son of Kronos, in supplication that Ruin may overtake this man, that he be hurt, and punished" (9.510–12). From this pronouncement Phoenix draws the enthymeme's first conclusion, "So, Achilleus: grant, you also, that Zeus' daughters be given their honour" (513–14). As the second premise, Phoenix notes the change in Agamemnon's attitude, using this as an argument which resembles Aristotle's **topic of the same men not choosing the same thing, but a different thing, before and after [some mitigating circumstance]** (ἐκ τοῦ μὴ ταὐτὸ τοὺς αὐτοὺς ἀεὶ αἱρεῖσθαι ὕστερον ἢ πρότερον, ἀλλ᾿ ἀνάπαλιν, topic #18, *Rhetoric* 2.23.19):

> Were he not bringing gifts and naming still more hereafter,
> Atreus' son; **were he to remain still swollen with rancour,**
> **even I would not bid you throw your anger aside,** nor
> defend the Argives, though they needed you sorely. **But see now,**
> **he offers you much straightway, and has promised you more hereafter.** (515–19)

The construction of this premise goes beyond simply Phoenix's use of an argument suggesting that a change in circumstances demands a change of heart. He also exerts the force of his own *ēthos*—toward which Achilles is predisposed—into the suggestion. In addition, he sympathizes with Achilles' view of Agamemnon by characterizing the king as "swollen with rancour" (ἐπιζαφελῶς χαλεπαίνοι, 516) and by "siding" with Achilles in the potential situation he lays out, a gesture of *diathesis*. Only then does he supply the twist that Agamemnon does *not* in fact remain "swollen with rancour": "But see now, he offers you much straightway, and has promised you more hereafter" (519). Premise 3 of this enthymeme is contained within the broader argument of premise 2: namely, the **topic of con-**

sideration of incentives and disincentives (topic #20) invoked by this mention of Agamemnon's bribe in line 519.

Premise 4 makes its argument from the *êthos* of the embassy members. These men, Phoenix argues, are both the best of the Achaeans and the dearest to Achilles personally: "He has sent the best (ἄριστοι) men to you to supplicate you . . . those who to yourself are the dearest (φίλτατοι) of all the Argives" (9.520–22).[32] Phoenix implies that the quality of the messengers demands a favorable response to their message, and he states his conclusion (conclusion 2 of this complex enthymeme) in the next lines: "Do not you despise their argument (τῶν μὴ σύ γε μῦθον ἐλέγξῃς) nor their footsteps, though before this one could not blame your anger" (522–23). Phoenix sets up his argument such that Achilles' refusal to accede to the embassy's request is construed as an act of disrespect (ἐλέγξῃς) toward the individuals involved, an especially egregious charge considering that they have just been identified as Achilles' φίλτατοι. A final premise (premise 5) supports this conclusion by employing the **paradeigma** of heroes of old: "Thus it was in the old days also, the deeds that we hear of from the great men, when the swelling anger descended upon them. The heroes would take gifts; they would listen, and be persuaded (πέλοντο παράρρητοί τ' ἐπέεσσι)" (524–26). The adjective παράρρητος—a precursor to technical rhetorical terminology, and cognate with ῥήτωρ—appears only twice in Homer (the other instance is *Iliad* 13.726, where Polydamas admonishes Hector to "be persuaded"), and nowhere else in Greek literature. Its sense of "open to (rhetorical) persuasion" is a remarkably explicit example of the Iliadic characters' attentiveness to the persuasive arts.

Phoenix then transitions seamlessly from this multifaceted enthymeme to a new section in 9.529–605 that expands on the theme of heroes of old. The crowning **paradeigma** of his speech is, of course, the tale of Meleager. The significance of this myth, and its parallels with Achilles' situation, have received thorough scholarly treatment (see, for example, Willcock 1964; Rosner 1976; and Nagy 1999, 103–9). In strictly rhetorical terms, the entire story serves as the paradeigmatic premise to a final **enthymeme**, whose conclusion comes at the end of Phoenix's speech. This premise ends with the account of Meleager's capitulation to his wife's pleas to fight: "So he gave way in his own heart, and drove back the day of evil from the Aitolians; yet these no longer would make good their many and gracious gifts" (597–99). The enthymeme conclusion follows: "Listen, then; do not have such a thought in your mind; let not the spirit within you turn you that way, dear friend" (600–601). Three final considerations— additional premises of the same enthymeme—bring the speech to a close. The first draws upon the **topic of consideration of timing** (topic #5), as Phoenix warns

Achilles that "it would be worse to defend the ships after they are burning" (601–2). The second premise employs the **topic of consideration of incentives and disincentives** (topic #20): "The Achaians will honour you as they would an immortal" (603). In the final premise, an argument from the **topic of the consequence** (topic #13), Phoenix warns that "if without gifts you go into the fighting where men perish, your honour will no longer be as great, though you drive back the battle" (604–5).

With this admonition, Phoenix ends his tour-de-force persuasive effort. No matter how skillful and well-argued the rhetoric, however, his speech was destined to be unsuccessful because of Achilles' predetermined (and preordained) stance.[33] Achilles is deferential in his response to Phoenix, but refuses to be persuaded, turning back the old man's final argument ("The Achaians will honour you as they would an immortal") with the reply "such honor is a thing I need not" (9.607–8). It is apparent here that no amount of brilliant argumentation can substitute for either knowing the key to the particular listener's frame of mind (*diathesis*), or possessing the right character (*êthos*) to appeal to that listener—rhetorical positions that, as I will discuss in the coda to chapter 3, only the figures of Patroclus and Priam bring to Achilles.[34]

XI. Nestor's address to Patroclus at 11.656–803 is, to use Martin's description, a "digressive" speech.[35] Its ultimate aim is to convince Patroclus to make an appeal to Achilles that will lure him back into battle; this aim does not come into view explicitly, however, until near the end of the speech (lines 764–802). In the opening lines, Nestor asks rhetorical questions about Achilles' behavior; he presumably hopes that his appeals to shame and pity will affect Patroclus, who is best positioned to persuade Achilles. By cataloguing the misfortunes and injuries of the Achaeans in 655–64, Nestor is using an emotional appeal to arouse his audience's pity (**pathos**) and thereby to produce sympathy for his cause (**diathesis**). He continues this appeal with a reproach: "Meanwhile Achilleus brave as he is cares nothing for the Danaans nor pities them. Is he going to wait then till the running ships by the water are burned with consuming fire for all the Argives can do, till we ourselves are killed one after another?" (664–68) From here, Nestor launches into an extended narrative depicting his own past exploits (670–762), triggered by the wish that he were still young and strong. Through this narrative—recounting the battle between Nestor's Pylians and the hostile Epeians—Nestor asserts his own *êthos* to gain credibility. It also serves as a **paradeigma** of courage even in the face of opposition (i.e., his father's opposition to his participation in battle). Hainsworth observes that "Nestor's reminiscences have, from his standpoint, two purposes. First, to use an incident from his heroic youth in order to insist on his credentials and the value of his words . . . second, indirectly to admonish or exhort. . . . Patroklos should overcome Akhilleus' opposition and insist on leading the eager Myrmidons to war."[36]

Following this *paradeigma*, which comprises the bulk of his speech, Nestor makes a transitional statement with ominous overtones, directed obliquely at Achilles: "But Achilleus will enjoy his own valour in loneliness, though I think he will weep much, too late, when his people are perished from him" (11.762–64). Only at this point does he turn at last to address Patroclus. Lines 765–90 evoke a shared past between speaker and addressee, as Nestor recalls his long-ago visit to Achilles and Patroclus to invite them to join the Trojan war. Nestor relies heavily on *diathesis* in this section, as evidenced by his affectionate opening vocative ὦ πέπον and his immediate mention of Patroclus' father: "Dear child, surely this was what Menoitios told you that day when he sent you out from Phthia to Agamemnon" (765–66). In recounting this scene of the meeting between himself and the two father-and-son pairs at the home of Peleus, Nestor chooses to emphasize certain memories and to suppress others based on the particular audience (Patroclus) and what is likely to affect his emotions. This is evident in the way that Nestor quickly passes over Peleus' words to Achilles with the description "And Peleus the aged was telling his own son, Achilleus, to be always best in battle and pre-eminent beyond all others" (783–84). (The conversation between Peleus and Achilles is invoked by Odysseus in his embassy speech to Achilles at 9.225–306; see appendix, speech VI.) In contrast, he quotes the entire speech from Menoitius to Patroclus, a speech whose words are uncannily pertinent to the present moment and Nestor's particular ends: " 'My child, by right of blood Achilleus is higher than you are, but you are the elder. . . . You must speak solid words (πυκινὸν ἔπος) to him, and give him good counsel, and point his way. If he listens to you (πείσεται) it will be for his own good' " (786–89). Various commentators have questioned the veracity of Nestor's convenient quotation, with Martin observing that Nestor is "not necessarily recounting 'what happened' . . . Nestor selects the one detail from the alleged 'instructions' of Peleus that will contrast most with his own recapitulation of another speech of advice, that made by Patroklos' father, suggesting that the companion of Achilles should instruct and guide him."[37] But whether or not this quotation reflects the reality of a long-ago conversation between fathers and sons, it has a powerful rhetorical function within Nestor's argument. Along with serving to dispose Patroclus favorably toward Nestor, this fabricated quotation contains an appeal to *êthos*. Beck has shown that Greek characters in the *Iliad* "tend to use direct quotations in their speeches to reinforce directives by invoking the authority of particular figures whose stature is widely recognized," and who are "comparatively uncontroversial sources of authority that lie beyond the political struggles of the camp."[38] This is exactly the role that Patroclus' distant father plays: an unimpeachable authority figure whom Nestor can leverage for persuasive effect.

The entire recollected scene, ending with Nestor's reproach to Patroclus that "this is what the old man told you, you have forgotten" (11.790), serves as the premise of an **enthymeme**. It provides a motivating reason for the conclusion that follows: "Yet even now you might speak to wise Achilleus, he might be persuaded (πίθηται)" (790–91). Nestor then offers two further premises, the first a projection of a hopeful outcome ("Who knows if, with God helping, you might trouble his spirit by entreaty [παρειπών]," 792–93), the second a *gnômê* ("The persuasion [παραίφασις] of a friend is a strong thing," 793). The vocabulary of persuasion—πίθηται, παρειπών, παραίφασις—is explicit here, and Nestor's phrasing is carefully calculated: he employs optative verbs rather than imperatives, and two different conditional clauses, thus couching the proposal as a humble suggestion to Patroclus.

The final portion of Nestor's speech (11.794–803) contains a proposal for a new tactic. In the event that Achilles might persist in his refusal to be persuaded, Nestor suggests to Patroclus a backup plan that will preempt any counterargument such as those that Achilles had made to the embassy in Book 9. He expresses his plan to Patroclus simply, using imperative verbs: "Let him send you out . . . let him give you his splendid armour to wear to the fighting" (796–98). For my treatment of the rhetorical argumentation contained these lines, see speech XIII below (Patroclus' speech to Achilles at 16.21–45, which quotes these lines of Nestor almost exactly). Nestor's speech is ultimately effective, both in the short term, as it stirs Patroclus' feelings and prompts him to obey the old man (11.804–5); and in the long term, as it achieves the desired goal: Patroclus will implement Nestor's suggestions in his speech to Achilles in Book 16, and will draw Achilles into battle through his death.

XII. An example of brief but effective battlefield rhetoric is Ajax's speech to the Greek army at 15.502–13. It immediately follows a similar exhortation from Hector to the Trojan troops, almost as though the two rival warriors are speaking in remote antiphony, unbeknownst to each other. In fact, the narrative of Book 15 leaps back and forth from Hector to Ajax in a series of such speeches, interspersed with fighting scenes, over the course of lines 425–741. In this speech, Ajax begins by addressing his audience with a rebuke (αἰδώς, Ἀργεῖοι, 502) that appeals to the emotion of shame (a use of *pathos* technique). He then makes a sarcastic argument from absurdity: "Do you expect, if our ships fall to helm-shining Hektor, you will walk each of you back dryshod to the land of your fathers?" (504–5). This question admits of only one answer, effectively forcing the audience to conclude that they have no choice but to fight and save the ships. In addition, the threat that it expresses invokes the **topic of consideration of incentives and disincentives** (topic #20); with their proverbial bridges burned, the Greeks have the ultimate incentive to fight. Ajax's second rhetorical question calls on the evidence of his audience's own ears for persuasive force, as he asks whether they can hear Hector urging his men to burn the Greek ships (ἦ οὐκ . . . ἀκούετε, 506–7). In keeping with the sarcastic tone of the speech, Ajax invests his warning about Hector with a sinister absurdity: "He is not inviting you to come to a dance. He invites you to battle" (508). The speech ends with an **enthymeme**, which begins with the exhortation to "close in and fight with the strength of our hands at close quarters" (510). As premise for this conclusion, Ajax offers a statement of generalized truth (*gnômê*)—namely, that it is better to take a risk on a bold action than to wait passively for inevitable defeat (as the Greek soldiers are currently doing):

> Better to take in a single time our chances of dying
> or living, than go on being squeezed in the stark encounter
> right up against our ships, as now, by men worse than we are. (511–13)

Such an argument appeals to another of the enthymeme topics that Aristotle identifies, the **topic of examining whether a better course of action could be taken than that which is being advised or carried out** (εἰ ἐνδέχετο βέλτιον ἄλλως . . . σκοπεῖν, topic #25, *Rhetoric* 2.23.26). By posing a choice between the bravery and honor of a momentary struggle, and the shame of being slowly "squeezed" (στρεύγεσθαι) by inferior men, Ajax is also employing *diathesis*: his audience will be inclined favorably toward what they see as the honorable course of action. This combination of argumentation and awareness of his audience's psychology renders Ajax successful, and the Greeks' response is conveyed by the same formula that had followed Hector's corresponding speech in line 15.500: "So he spoke, and stirred the spirit and strength in each man" (514).

XIII. Patroclus makes an emotional appeal to Achilles at 16.21–45 for which most of the persuasive strategies had been suggested by Nestor at 11.656–803 (see above, speech XI). Patroclus' primary aim is to convince Achilles to rejoin the war; his secondary aim (knowing that he is unlikely to succeed in the first) is to convince Achilles to allow him to fight in his stead. He opens the speech with a brief use of *diathesis*, flattering Achilles by calling him φέρτατ' Ἀχαιῶν ("greatest of the Achaians," 21). Whether a calculated allusion on Patroclus' part or not, φέρτατος is the same adjective that Nestor had earlier used for Agamemnon when contrasting him with the καρτερός Achilles (1.280–81). In making the claim that none of the Achaeans (not even Agamemnon) stands ahead of Achilles in greatness, Patroclus is surely mindful of the struggle for superiority and τιμή that has dominated the poem's action and Achilles' consciousness thus far—a consideration that will be confirmed by Achilles' response at 16.49–100. Patroclus then moves on to a different kind of *diathesis*—an appeal to the emotion of pity (*pathos*) for comrades in distress, instead of to the emotion of pride. He gives an amplified account of the Greek warriors' dire situation in lines 22–29, detailing the wounds of the major chieftains. This account functions like the premise of an enthymeme in that it gives a reason for Achilles to take action, but Patroclus never actually states an enthymematic conclusion or makes an explicit request. Instead, he anticipates a negative response to his attempt to persuade Achilles, and launches into a series of reproaches in 29–35: Achilles is impossible (ἀμήχανος), nurses his anger (χόλος, ὃν σὺ φυλάσσεις), is accursedly brave (αἰναρέτη), and above all is unnaturally pitiless (νηλεές). Another premise that does not attain full realization as an enthymeme can be found in the reproachful rhetorical question of lines 31–32, "What other man born hereafter shall be advantaged unless you beat aside from the Argives this shameful destruction?"

Patroclus then moves on to the second part of the speech (16.36–45), quoting almost word-for-word the speech that Nestor had suggested he use at 11.793–803 (the only difference being his use of second-person rather than third-person verbs in reference to Achilles).[39] Patroclus proposes an alternative solution to the Greeks' woes in the event that Achilles persists in his refusal to enter battle. This proposal takes the form of an extended **enthymeme** whose conclusions are the simple commands "Send me out" (38) and "Give me your armour" (40). Each of these commands is followed by a premise that argues from the **topic of the consequence** (topic #13): "Send me out . . . and I may be a light given to the Danaans" (38–39) is the first construction; "Give me your armour . . . so perhaps the Trojans might think I am you, and give way from their attack, and the fighting sons of the Achaians get wind again after hard work" (40–43) is the second. The *gnômê* that "there is little breathing space in the fighting" (43) extends the argument of the second premise. Patroclus' final statement offers yet another premise to this multifaceted enthymeme, as he cites the observable fact that fresh fighters are more effective than tired ones: "We unwearied might with a mere cry pile men wearied back upon their city, and away from the ships and the shelters" (44–45).

Patroclus' rhetoric is as successful as he could have hoped, given the stubbornness of Achilles and the will of Zeus. After a long speech of deliberation (16.49–100), Achilles reluctantly assents to letting Patroclus join the battle. It is a curious note that in this speech Patroclus does *not* use the technique—so common among Iliadic speakers—of appealing to his own *êthos*, based on his identity as Achilles' closest companion. This is especially striking given that Patroclus seems to be the only person (thus far) who can persuade Achilles to do anything in the *Iliad*, and, as Nagy has noted, it is his status as Achilles' πολὺ φίλτατος . . . ἑταῖρος (17.411, 655) that ultimately will enable him to do what all the other Greeks have tried and failed to do: persuade Achilles to fight.[40] But Patroclus' failure to use *êthos* in this speech is not the whole story. Instead of invoking *êthos* verbally, Patroclus *performs* what is in effect the same appeal through gesture and attitude—as though he himself stands as a sign, or σῆμα, indicating the correct course of action to Achilles. The "semantic" nature of this performance accompanying Patroclus' speech is noted both by the narrator ("Meanwhile Patroklos came to the shepherd of the people, Achilleus, and stood by him and wept warm tears," 16.2–3) and by Achilles himself ("Why then are you crying like some poor little girl, Patroklos, who runs after her mother and begs to be picked up and carried, and clings to her dress, and holds her back when she tries to hurry, and gazes tearfully into her face?," 16.7–10). Another indication of the performative quality of Patroclus' rhetoric is the narrator's description of his delivery: his speech is framed by the phrases "groaning heavily" (βαρὺ στενάχων, 20) and "supplicating in his great innocence" (λισσόμενος μέγα νήπιος, 46). His offer to serve as "a light given to the Danaans" and to wear Achilles' armor so that he can impersonate Achilles further situates Patroclus in the role of a σῆμα, a visual marker—to Achilles above all.

XIV. Hera delivers a speech to Zeus at 16.440–57 in order to dissuade him from saving his son, Sarpedon, from his fated death at Patroclus' hands. The speech can be seen as comprised of two enthymematic arguments, the first dissuasive and the second hortatory. Hera's first **enthymeme** begins with a conclusion that she clearly does not favor: the command "Do it, then" (443). The premises to this enthymeme point out why such an action would be a bad idea, beginning with the warning that the other gods will disapprove if Zeus favors his son: "but not all the rest of us gods shall approve you" (443). This is an appeal to the **topic of consideration of incentives and disincentives** (topic #20) on Hera's part, as she knows that the approval of and unity among the Olympian gods is essential to Zeus' ability to maintain power. She issues a further warning in lines 445–49 resembling Aristotle's **topic of an earlier judgment about the same or a similar matter** (topic #11), which derives its force from an appeal to precedent. In this case, Hera argues that if Zeus goes against precedent in this matter by saving Sarpedon, he will *set* a dangerous precedent; the other gods would clamor for their own children to be saved contrary to their destinies, "since (γάρ) around the great city of Priam are fighting many sons of the immortals. You will waken grim resentment among them" (448–49). This line of reasoning also partakes of the argument from the **topic of the consequence** (topic #13); the consequence if Zeus were to defy Sarpedon's destiny would be chaos and potentially rebellion among the gods. Hera follows these dire warnings with another **enthymeme**, one that takes a gentler tone. Though acknowledging the pain it will cause Zeus, Hera exhorts him to submit to fate, concluding, "No, but if he is dear to you, and your heart mourns for him, then let him be, and let him go down in the strong encounter underneath the hands of Patroklos" (450–52). Her premise offers a measure of consolation to Zeus by reminding him that death and "painless" (νήδυμον) sleep will escort Sarpedon back to his homeland, "where his brothers and countrymen shall give him due burial" (454–57). As is consistently the case, Hera's rhetoric is effective in persuading Zeus; he does not disobey her (οὐδ' ἀπίθησε, 16.458).

XV. Glaucus issues an elaborate rebuke and challenge to Hector at 17.142–68 in the midst of the battle over Patroclus' body.[41] This speech is characterized by the narrator as a χαλεπὸς μῦθος (17.141), and at times it resembles a forensic prosecution speech, as Glaucus attempts to motivate Hector through accusations and appeals to shame. Glaucus begins by commenting on the disparity between Hector's appearance and reputation, and his actual weak performance in battle: "Hektor, splendid to look at, you come far short in your fighting" (142–43). In arousing the emotion of shame (*pathos*), Glaucus is seeking to put his listener in the right frame of mind to be persuaded (*diathesis*). He follows this opening gambit with an **enthymeme**, beginning with the conclusion: "Take thought now how to hold fast your town. . . ." (144–45). Its premise argues from the **topic of the consequence** (topic #13): "since (γάρ) no Lykian will go forth now to fight with the Danaans for the sake of your city, since (ἐπεί) after all we got no gratitude for our everlasting hard struggle against your enemies" (146–48). The accusation that Hector has neglected the allies becomes more pointed in Glaucus' following rhetorical question, an argument from the **topic of greater and less** (topic #4):

> How then, o hard-hearted, shall you save a worse man in all your
> company, when you have abandoned Sarpedon, your guest-friend
> and own companion, to be the spoil and prey of the Argives,
> who was of so much use to you, yourself, and your city
> while he lived? (149–53)

Glaucus then threatens to lead his Lycians homeward and abandon the war effort, so that "the headlong destruction of Troy shall be manifest" (154–55). It is a threat designed to arouse Hector's fear.

Glaucus' next tactic—also drawing upon *pathos* in that it is calculated to incite an emotional response—is to issue a challenge calling for evidence of the Trojans' μένος: "For if the Trojans had any fighting strength (μένος) that were daring and unshaken, such as comes on men who, for the sake of their country, have made the hard hateful work come between them and their enemies, we could quickly get the body of Patroklos inside Ilion" (17.156–59). This contrafactual condition employs a mixture of logic and shaming to bring home its rhetorical point, much as the forensic oratory of Classical Athens (Demosthenes comes to mind) would later do. The logical strain of argumentation continues in Glaucus' next lines, which appeal to the **topic of consideration of incentives and disincentives** (topic #20): "If, dead man though he be, he could be brought into the great city of lord Priam . . . the Argives must at once give up the beautiful armour of Sarpedon, and we could carry his body inside Ilion" (160–63). Glaucus ends his speech with a return to his original tactic, namely an appeal to Hector's sense of shame. His contemptuous attack on Hector's character—insulting him with an unfavorable comparison to Ajax—is calculated to spur him to action: "No, but you could not bring yourself to stand up against Aias of the great heart, nor to look at his eyes in the clamour of fighting men, nor attack him direct, since he is far better (φέρτερος) than you are" (166–68). Glaucus' approach to *diathesis* here and throughout this speech—namely, invoking the emotion of shame—reverses its more typical usage as a technique for putting the listener in a sympathetic, favorable frame of mind toward the speaker. Nevertheless, it serves the same rhetorical purpose as do all uses of *diathesis*: it disposes the listener to do what the speaker wants him to do. In this case, Glaucus calculates his words to put Hector on the defensive—to stir up in him an angry frame of mind that will make him eager to prove Glaucus' taunts wrong and to fight

more fiercely for Patroclus' body. The success of this rhetorical and psychological strategy can be seen from Hector's response to the speech. He expresses
annoyance but ultimately compliance with Glaucus' desires: "Glaukos, why did
a man like you speak this word of annoyance (ὑπέροπλον ἔειπες)? . . . Come
here, friend, and watch me at work" (17.170, 179). Glaucus' use of *diathesis* has
produced the desired effect.

XVI. As Hector prepares to leave the walls of Troy to face Achilles in single
combat, Priam begs him not to go. Priam's speech (22.38–76) opens with an **enthymeme** whose conclusion is the imperative plea "do not wait the attack of this
man alone, away from the others" (38–39). The enthymeme premise is an appeal
to the **topic of consideration of incentives and disincentives** (topic #20), in which
Priam dispenses with flattery and instead offers naked realism: "You might encounter your destiny beaten down by Peleion, since he is far stronger (πολὺ
φέρτερος) than you are" (39–40). Priam then expresses his own sentiments toward Achilles (41–43), from which he transitions to the strategy of arousing pity
(*pathos*) in Hector by cataloguing the loss of his many sons at Achilles' hands
(44–53). This catalogue ends with a use of the **topic of greater and less** (topic #4)
that serves as the premise to another **enthymeme**. The death of his sons Lykaon
and Polydoros, Priam asserts, may be a source of sorrow to the Trojan people;
but it is "a sorrow that will be fleeting beside their sorrow for you, if you go
down before Achilleus" (54–55). From this premise, Priam draws an enthymematic conclusion in the form of a command: "Come then inside the wall, my
child" (56). A further premise is added, arguing from the **topic of consideration
of incentives and disincentives** (topic #20): "so that (ὄφρα) you can rescue the
Trojans and the women of Troy, neither win the high glory for Peleus' son, and
yourself be robbed of your very life" (56–58).

Lines 22.59–71 comprise Priam's vivid, impassioned, and extended appeal to
Hector to have pity on him. This appeal takes the form of a projection about the
future if Hector does not heed his request:

> Oh, take pity on me, the unfortunate still alive, still sentient
> but ill-starred, whom the father, Kronos' son, on the threshold of old age
> will blast with hard fate, after I have looked upon evils
> and seen my sons destroyed and my daughters dragged away captive. . . .
> And myself last of all, my dogs in front of my doorway
> will rip me raw, after some man with stroke of the sharp bronze
> spear, or with spearcast, has torn the life out of my body. (59–68)

In this section, Priam invokes both *êthos* and *pathos* to put Hector in the desired frame of mind. His explicit call for pity (πρὸς δ' ἐμὲ τὸν δύστηνον ἔτι φρονέοντ' ἐλέησον, 59), and the vision of future disaster that follows, constitute an emotional appeal similar to the one Priam will express in his speech to Achilles at 24.486–506 (see below, speech XVII). Like that speech, this one manipulates the psychology of the addressee—his son, in this case—by emphasizing the proximity of the sufferer to himself, a technique discussed by Aristotle in the *Rhetoric*:

> Let pity be [defined as] a certain pain at an apparently destructive or painful evil happening to one who does not deserve it and *which a person might expect himself or one of his own to suffer*, and this when it seems close at hand. . . . The kind of people who think they might suffer are those . . . that have parents or children or wives; for these are their "own" and subject to the sufferings that have been mentioned. (*Rhetoric* 2.8.2–5; italics added)

Note that Aristotle identifies the sympathetic character of pity: pity does not have to be linked only to what might befall oneself, but may be felt for the sake of loved ones. This is the rhetorical use of pity that Priam is using to sway Hector, and that he will deploy later in his appeal to Achilles.

An extended *gnômê* closes Priam's speech. It functions as the premise of a final **enthymeme**, though the accompanying conclusion is only implicit: "For a young man all is decorous when he is cut down in battle and torn with the sharp bronze, and lies there dead . . . but when an old man is dead and down, and the dogs mutilate the grey head and the grey beard and the parts that are secret, this for all mortality, is the sight most pitiful" (22.71–76). In its invocation of pity, this truism also partakes in *pathos* (as has so much of Priam's appeal to his son) in order to dispose him favorably (*diathesis*). Priam leaves the enthymematic conclusion—a renewal of his demand that Hector refrain from facing Achilles—unstated, and indeed never returns to the urgent plea of the speech's opening. This could be interpreted as a lack of rigor in logical argumentation, or alternatively as indicative of the old man's desperation; he focuses on his own fears and pitiable state instead of emphasizing those considerations that might better persuade his addressee. Perhaps partly for this reason, and no doubt also because of the will of Zeus, Hector is unmoved by the speech: "[Priam] could not move (ἔπειθε) the spirit in Hektor," we are told at 22.78.

XVII. Priam delivers his famous appeal to Achilles to return Hector's body at 24.486–506. His opening tactic is an indirect appeal to pity, based on the association between himself and Achilles' father: "Achilleus like the gods, remember your father, one who is of years like mine, and on the door-sill of sorrowful old age. And they who dwell nearby encompass him and afflict him" (486–92).[42] By visualizing Peleus' sad and lonely experience and comparing it to his own, Priam avails himself of the rhetorical strategy of *pathos*. He also deploys the strategy of *êthos* by invoking his own past as a powerful king in order to emphasize the pitiable depths to which he has fallen, and by employing gesture and words to perform his current state: that of an old man, vulnerable and inoffensive. In all of this, Priam intends Achilles to recognize the traits of his own father; he uses this association, in turn, to put Achilles in a sympathetic frame of mind (*diathesis*). The way that Priam manipulates the emotion of pity is a practical embodiment of Aristotle's theoretical discussion of pity in *Rhetoric* 2.8.2–5 (see discussion of speech XVI above); Aristotle identifies this avenue of appeal as especially effective on those with parents and children.

Priam continues to focus on arousing pity within Achilles by recounting the loss of his own sons and the sorrow it has brought on him (αὐτὰρ ἐγὼ πανάποτμος 24.493), an ominous precedent for the parallel with Peleus. In this section, he uses amplification (*auxesis*) of the numerical magnitude of his loss to emphasize the piteousness of his situation:

> I have had the noblest
> of sons in Troy, but I say **not one of them** is left to me.
> **Fifty** were my sons, when the sons of the Achaians came here.
> **Nineteen** were born to me from the womb of a single mother,
> and other women bore the rest in my palace; and of these
> violent Ares broke the strength in the knees of **most of them**,
> but **one was left me** who guarded my city and people, **that one**
> **you killed** a few days since as he fought in defence of his country,
> Hektor. (493–501)

Colin Macleod identifies in this passage yet another Aristotelian technique: "By numbering and classifying his sons Priam gives more weight to his loss: cf. Arist. *Rhet.* 1365a10 'a single subject when divided into parts seems more impressive.'"[43] Although this technique of dividing something into constituent parts is not one of Aristotle's "topics for demonstrative enthymemes," it is included in his analysis of deliberative rhetoric under the rubric of how to argue effectively that a thing is good or advantageous (*Rhetoric* 1.7.31). Macleod further observes that the fact "that Priam goes on . . . to treat Hector as his 'only' son has argumentative and emotive value. It stresses the analogy between himself and Peleus; it also represents the strength of his grief at losing Hector."[44] Here, at last, Priam introduces the reason for his visit. His request takes a deferential form: no imperative demand, only the statement that "I come now to the ships of the Achaians to win him back from you" (501–2). As a premise, he offers a simple argument from the **topic of consideration of incentives and disincentives** (topic #20): "I bring you gifts beyond number" (502). Whether he is attuned to the fact that Achilles is historically unmoved by gifts, or is simply a canny judge of effective rhetoric for a given audience, Priam touches on the incentive only briefly. Instead, he offers a final **enthymeme** that returns to his original tactics of *êthos* and *pathos*. The conclusion—"Honour then the gods, Achilleus, and take pity (ἐλέησον) upon me"—is followed by a premise that brings the speech full circle: "remembering your father, yet I am still more pitiful (ἐλεεινότερός περ)" (503–4).

In the final lines of the speech, Priam points to his own gesture of self-abasement in order to stir up the pity of Achilles (*pathos*): "I have gone through what no other mortal on earth has gone through; I put my lips to the hands of the man who has killed my children" (24.505–6). This deictic technique, with the speaker using himself as a σῆμα ("sign"), is one that we have seen exercised on Achilles in the past (see speech XIII above, Patroclus' speech to Achilles at 16.21–45). It also strikingly embodies Aristotle's teaching on how to arouse pity rhetorically:

> And since sufferings are pitiable when they appear near at hand . . . necessarily those are more pitiable who contribute to the effect by gestures and cries and display of feelings and generally **in their acting** (ὑποκρίσει); for they make the evil seem near by making it appear before [our] eyes. . . . For this reason **signs** (σημεῖα) and **actions** (πράξεις) [contribute to pity]. (*Rhetoric* 2.8.14–16)

Priam is clearly effective in stirring up Achilles' emotions; the narrator takes care to note that Ὣς φάτο, τῷ δ' ἄρα πατρὸς ὑφ' ἵμερον ὦρσε γόοιο ("So he spoke, and stirred in the other a passion of grieving for his own father," 24.507). A bond is thus forged between the two enemies as they weep together. It will take more discussion, however, before Achilles is persuaded to agree fully to Priam's request.

XVIII. The final speech in this catalogue of selected rhetorical speeches occurs after the tempest between Achilles and Priam has passed and Achilles has relinquished Hector's body, prompted more by the gods' orders than by Priam's rhetoric (24.560–62). One final act of persuasion is needed, however: at 24.599–620, Achilles attempts to convince Priam to cease from grieving and take sustenance, just as others had urged Achilles to do when he was in mourning for Patroclus (19.216–37, 303–4). After opening his speech with a reminder of his concession to Priam (599–601), Achilles launches into an **enthymeme** to make his case. The conclusion is stated in the form of the simple command "now you and I must remember our supper" (μνησώμεθα δόρπου, 601); but as Macleod points out, Achilles' use of a first-person verb indicates "sympathetic participation," a subtle touch of *diathesis* exerted to encourage Priam.[45] The enthymeme premise is spun out at greater length, for it involves the *paradeigma* of the Niobe story (602–17). Achilles begins this *paradeigma* with a clear statement of the behavior to be followed: "For (γάρ) even Niobe, she of the lovely tresses, remembered to eat (ἐμνήσατο σίτου), whose twelve children were destroyed in her palace" (602–3).[46] Having repeated the phrase "she remembered to eat" one more time in 613, Achilles caps the *paradeigma* with a restatement of his conclusion in 618–19: "Come then, we also, aged magnificent sir, must remember to eat (μεδώμεθα . . . σίτου)." He ends his speech on a consoling note, reminding Priam that when he returns to Troy he will be able to mourn Hector at length, and assuring him that Hector "will be much lamented" (620). By showing consideration for Priam's greatest concern—giving his son a proper burial—Achilles employs the crucial persuasive element of *diathesis*. His speech is effective: Priam does not respond verbally, but he assents to eating (24.627–28).

CHAPTER THREE

Patterns of Aristotelian Rhetoric in the *Iliad*

From the preceding survey and analysis of the *Iliad*'s rhetorical speeches, it is possible to observe several patterns, both among rhetorical techniques used and among speakers who employ these rhetorical techniques. Certain speakers emerge from this analysis as the most "successful" rhetoricians in the *Iliad*—that is, those whose rhetorical speeches most often achieve the desired response from the audience—and while some of the results are predictable (Nestor scores highly), others are more surprising (Hera's rhetorical success stands out not just among the gods, but among all speaking characters). It should be noted that rhetorical techniques in the direct speeches of the *Iliad* do not usually correspond to poetic formulas; rather, they are deployed as part of persuasive arguments tailored to a particular audience and situation. This chapter ends with a discussion of the influence of plot considerations on the success of persuasive attempts.

I. TECHNIQUES

Figure 1 (see below) is a summary of the total number of various Aristotelian rhetorical techniques that appear in the 58 speeches analyzed in chapter 2 and the appendix. I have included enthymeme, *diathesis*, *êthos*, *paradeigma*, *gnômê*, and topics in this graphic summary of Aristotelian techniques. Though I noted instances of emotional appeal, or *pathos*, when analyzing Iliadic speeches, I do not include *pathos* in this summary because it is not a technique labeled by Aristotle as such; emotional appeal in Aristotle's account seems to be a subset of

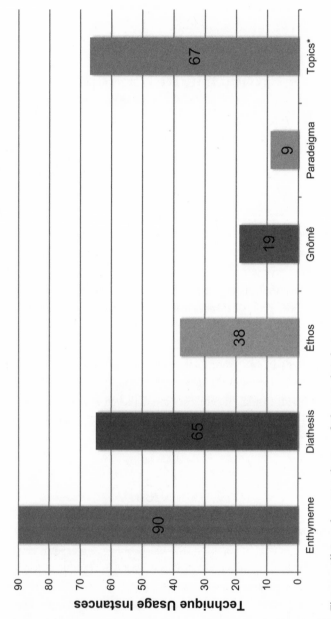

Figure 1. All Speeches: Distribution of Rhetorical Techniques
*See text discussion on p. 79.

"disposing the audience favorably," that is, *diathesis*. I have also chosen not to include the instances of *eikos* argument and *auxesis* technique in this graphic summary, since they appear relatively infrequently (3 and 6 times, respectively) in the 58 speeches. None of the speeches contains fewer than two rhetorical techniques, and the number of distinct techniques in a single speech reaches as high as 18 (in Phoenix's Book 9 appeal to Achilles). Enthymemes are almost universally employed, appearing in all but 2 speeches. *Diathesis* appears in all but 15 speeches; at least one topic in all but 18 speeches; *êthos* in 27 out of the 58 speeches; *gnômê* in 19 of the 58; and *paradeigma* in 8 of the 58. The prevalence of enthymemes (usually supported by topics, *gnômai*, or *paradeigmata*) speaks to the importance of argumentation, or *logos*, within the speeches. The accumulation of these diverse techniques, often combined into complex lines of argumentation, forms the basis of my case for the existence of a learned and systematized practice of rhetoric in Homer.

Although not differentiated in the figure, the different Aristotelian topics that make up the 67 uses of topics in the speeches are, in descending order of frequency: Topic #20 (consideration of incentives and disincentives), with 37 instances; Topic #4 (greater and less), 10 instances; Topic #13 (consequence), 8 instances; Topic #5 (consideration of timing), 5 instances; Topic #11 (an earlier judgment about the same or a similar matter), 2 instances; and 1 instance each of Topic #6 (turning against the adversary the things said by the adversary against the speaker), Topic #10 (induction), Topic #16 (consequences by analogy), Topic #18 (the same men not choosing the same thing, but a different thing, before and after [some mitigating circumstance]), and Topic #25 (examining whether a better course of action could be taken than that which is being advised or carried out).

II. SPEAKERS

The distribution of the *Iliad*'s rhetorical speeches according to speaker is presented in figure 2 (see below). Nestor delivers the greatest total number of rhetorical speeches, a reflection of his dominance in both quantity and quality of persuasive speech in the *Iliad*. "If the attribution of advanced age and command of speech is not an especially unique one," Keith Dickson observes, "it still remains true that Nestor is the most conspicuous embodiment of these traits in the poems."[1] Hector's high number of rhetorical speeches is on the one hand surprising, given the narrator's evaluation of him as better at fighting than at speaking (*Iliad* 18.252). But since Hector is relatively isolated in his leadership

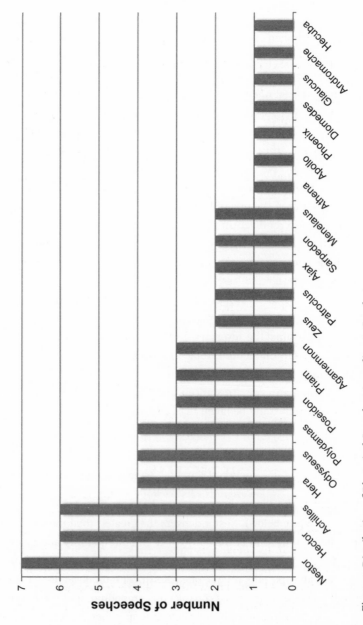

Figure 2. Distribution of Rhetorical Speeches According to Speaker

role among the Trojans—in contrast with the Greeks' assortment of heroes offering deliberation in the assembly and exhortation on the battlefield—the bulk of the persuasive speaking on the Trojan side falls to Hector.[2] Perhaps the most surprising result of this part of the survey is that Hera, with four speeches in the catalogue, exceeds all other gods in rhetorical productivity and is near the top among all speaking characters. The reason for this may be that she stands to benefit more than most characters in the epic from deploying persuasive speech: her opposition to Zeus through much of the *Iliad* provides motivation for using persuasion (since force would be impossible), while her position as Zeus' wife provides the opportunity.

Figure 3 (see below) presents a summary of the individual Aristotelian rhetorical techniques employed by each speaker. Nestor is an outlier in terms of his overall copiousness, and Phoenix in the number of techniques per speech (due to his extended Book 9 persuasion speech), but otherwise, the speakers who employ persuasion in the *Iliad* use a fairly regular distribution of these techniques. No strong patterns emerge linking particular speakers with particular techniques: all the major rhetorical categories that Aristotle identifies seem to be at the disposal of all of these speakers, though of course the sample size of rhetorical output varies greatly. The nine instances of *paradeigma*—the most infrequently used technique—come from just four speakers: Nestor, Achilles, Phoenix, and Sarpedon. This group includes the *Iliad*'s oldest speakers (Nestor and Phoenix) as well as an outstanding warrior of divine parentage on each side of the battlefield (Achilles and Sarpedon), suggesting a correlation between *paradeigma* usage and venerable characters that tend to address the weightiest diplomatic matters.

Differences in the use of rhetorical techniques by gods and mortals are difficult to detect. The five divinities represented in the catalogue partake of the same variety of techniques as do the human speakers, with one exception: aside from a single instance in a speech of Poseidon (which is addressed to a human character, Idomeneus, rather than to a fellow god), divine speakers do not employ the technique of *gnômê*. Put statistically, just one of 19 instances of *gnômê* (5 percent) comes from a god, even though gods deliver 11 of the 58 rhetorical speeches (19 percent) in the *Iliad*. This pattern makes sense given that *gnômai* generally involve statements from a human perspective about the gods' behavior or the nature of the world, and thus would be of little relevance to argumentation between gods. There is no clear distinction apparent between the slate of rhetorical techniques used by male and female speakers, or by Greek and Trojan speakers. This does not of course mean that there are no differences between

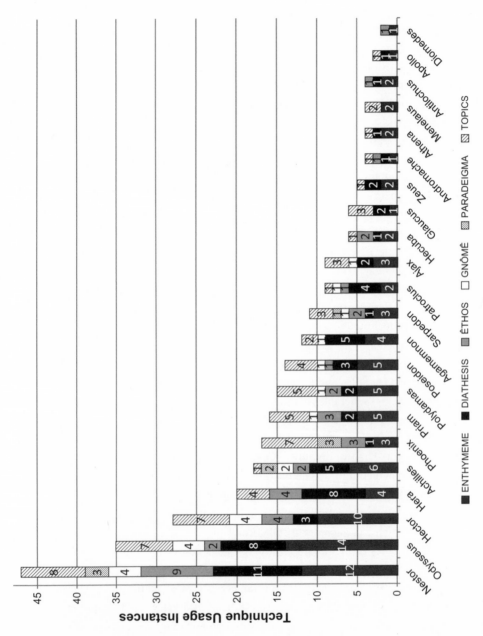

Figure 3. Distribution of Rhetorical Techniques According to Speaker

divine and human speech, or the speech of individual characters; Martin (1989), Mackie (1996), and Worman (2002), among others, have noted the significant distinctions in speaking styles among Iliadic characters. It simply indicates that many rhetorical techniques that Aristotle would later catalogue are used by Iliadic speakers of all types as they attempt to persuade others. Rhetorical speech is not limited to the usual suspects (Nestor, Odysseus, Achilles, etc.), but is quite widespread among the characters and situations of the *Iliad*.

Although Nestor enjoys the distinction of delivering the most rhetorical speeches and using the most rhetorical techniques of any speaker in the *Iliad*, quantity is by no means the only criterion for speaking prowess. It may reasonably be asked, what of the relative rhetorical *success* of all these speakers? Since nearly all the rhetorical speeches I have analyzed are accompanied by a narrative indication of whether or not the addressees approve and / or heed the speakers' words, it is possible to trace speakers' effectiveness at persuasion. Of course, such an evaluation of effectiveness must take into account that larger forces within the narrative can at times overrule the effects of a given speech, making it impossible to deem the speech a rhetorical success or failure purely on its own merits. (The relationship between rhetorical speeches and the plot of the *Iliad* is discussed in section III below.) For this reason, instances in which there is some ambiguity about the rhetorical effectiveness of a speech on its internal audience—either because the audience response is unstated, or because the plot or characters involved clearly necessitate a speech's failure to persuade (Phoenix to Achilles at 9.434–605, Patroclus to Achilles at 16.21–45, Polydamas to the Trojans at 18.254–83, and Andromache, Priam, and Hecuba to Hector at 6.407–39, 22.38–76, and 22.82–89, respectively)—are discounted.

Of the remaining speeches, who is the most "successful" rhetorician (based upon the speaker's ability to achieve the desired effect on his or her audiences)? By this calculation, the answer is Hector: all six speeches that he delivers convince his audience to take the action that he wants (however misguided that action might be from the narrative perspective). Six out of Nestor's seven speeches are successful; the exception is his speech at 1.254–84, which fails in its object of reconciling Achilles and Agamemnon (for more on the reasons for this "failure," see section III below). Thus the persuasive prowess of both Hector and Nestor is borne out in the result, as well as in the number, of their speeches. Among the other characters with more than one rhetorical speech, most have mixed results. Even the two great Homeric heroes, Achilles and Odysseus, fail in some cases to persuade—Achilles in his first speech to Priam (24.518–51), Odysseus in his speeches to Achilles (9.225–306, 19.155–83, and 19.216–37). A notable exception to these mixed results is Hera, whose four rhetorical speeches are all successful. No speaker among this group is characterized as especially ineffective except for Zeus, whose first of two rhetorical efforts in the poem (4.7–19) fails to convince Hera of the need for a compromise in the outcome of the war, and whose second (14.313–28) is the product of Hera's manipulation, and is thus superfluous. Although it may seem surprising that the father of the gods rarely persuades others to do his bidding, the key concept here is *persuasion*. Zeus is masterful at giving *commands*; Martin has spoken of him as "the source of all authority in the poem" based on his forceful and effective *muthoi*.[3] Consequently, the king of the gods has little need for (and thus, perhaps, little practice in) the art of persuasive argumentation. When a need for persuasion does arise, Zeus is no match for his consort, who must rely on wheedling and tricky speech rather than on pure authority to achieve her ends.

III. RHETORIC AND PLOT IN THE *ILIAD*

My overarching contention is that the *Iliad*, through the direct speeches of its characters, demonstrates a systematic employment of persuasive techniques corresponding to the practice that would come to be categorized as "rhetoric" in the fourth century; in particular, these techniques closely match the system explicated in Aristotle's *Rhetoric*. Homeric speeches lend themselves so readily to rhetorical analysis in part because they tend to be delivered in patently rhetorical contexts (e.g., the assembly, the battlefield), and in part because they are embedded into a narrative, with the result that audience responses are reported. Aristotle identifies deliberative rhetoric as either hortatory or dissuasive (συμβουλῆς δὲ τὸ μὲν προτροπὴ τὸ δὲ ἀποτροπή, *Rhetoric* 1.3.3); such deliberative rhetoric, he observes, is concerned with the future (1.3.4) and with exhorting what is expedient (1.3.5). This deliberative model is the category under which most or all of the *Iliad*'s rhetorical speeches fall.[4] That these speeches take place in a fictional narrative context, however, complicates the process of determining their rhetorical success. Taking rhetorical success to mean the effectiveness of a speaker at persuading or motivating his audience to a desired action or state of mind, one might ask how the demands of the *Iliad*'s plot, and the narrative conception of fate, interact with the characters' rhetoric. Do these "speech-external" factors affect the speakers' persuasive success or failure? And to what extent do the constraints of characterization affect the rhetoric of different speakers, and the receptivity of different audiences?

There is no question that all of the speeches in the *Iliad* affect the plot, to a greater or lesser degree. But plot considerations, as well as the character of speaker and audience, can in turn affect the speeches: that is, there are times when even rhetorically skillful speeches must fail. Such incongruity can usually be explained by the mismatch between the values of speaker and audience. Nestor's plea for Agamemnon and Achilles to cease their quarrel at 1.254–84 is a rhetorically nuanced and complex speech, but it nevertheless fails to placate the rivals (Achilles in particular). This is a necessary outcome for reasons of plot, since the entire plot of the *Iliad* would have been short-circuited if Nestor had been successful in soothing the *mênis* of Achilles. But Nestor's failure to persuade also makes sense given the character of Achilles: like so many speakers after him, Nestor does not comprehend the depth of outrage Achilles feels, nor that words alone are not enough to repair the breach between him and Agamemnon. To cite another example, Polydamas' prudent argument that the Trojans should withdraw from the battlefield in anticipation of Achilles' arrival at 18.254–83 is rhetorically sound, but doomed by both plot necessity (Achilles' upcoming *aristeia* and Hector's tragic insistence on facing him), and the character of Hector (proud and courageous to the point of foolhardiness). The eloquent speeches of Priam and Hecuba to Hector in Book 22—last, desperate efforts to dissuade their son from confronting Achilles—are unsuccessful for the same reason. Most prominent of all is the failure of Phoenix's tour-de-force embassy speech to Achilles, despite its wide range of rhetorical techniques and sensitivity to its addressee. Phoenix's attempt is doomed before it even begins for the same reason that nearly all speakers who attempt to persuade Achilles fail. The thread of the epic narrative, glossed as the will of Zeus (Διὸς δ' ἐτελείετο βουλή) in *Iliad* 1.5, is directly linked to the actions of Achilles. Achilles' actions are governed, in turn, by the idiosyncrasies of his character, namely his heroic values and knowledge of his own fate.[5] This renders him nearly impervious to persuasive arguments (a point of note that I explore briefly in the coda below).

Such instances in which persuasion attempts fail in accordance with the combined factors of plot and characterization are not the norm, however. More often than not in the *Iliad*, it is possible to trace a correspondence between "good" rhetoric and a positive audience response, or between "bad" rhetoric and a failure to persuade; there are even speeches that contain a mixture of both and are received accordingly (such as Diomedes' passionate outburst at 9.32–49, acclaimed by the Achaeans but critiqued by Nestor). Examples of good rhetoric leading to the speaker's desired outcome abound: Hera's clever employment of *diathesis* when wheedling Zeus, Hector's appeals to the Trojan troops, Nestor's strategic advice to younger warriors, and Sarpedon's exhortations to Hector and Glaucus, among others. Examples of bad rhetoric are fewer, but include Zeus' ill-conceived effort to placate Athena and Hera at 4.7–19, Agamemnon's awkward attempt to exhort Teucer at 8.281–91, and Polydamas' antagonistic proposal of a battle strategy to Hector at 12.211–29—all of which fail to persuade. The common denominator in these rhetorical failures is the speakers' insensitivity to the character and attitude of their addressees—or, to put it in Aristotelian terms, a lack of disposing the listener (*diathesis*).

To be sure, no literary representation of speech can be treated as an artifact of rhetoric in the same way that a freestanding fifth- or fourth-century oration can be. The suspense of the plot and the character of the audience only add to the complexity of variables present in the *Iliad*'s persuasion situations—and sometimes, as we have seen, those factors render the internal rhetoric ineffective. But rhetoric can be identified even when it does not achieve its persuasive aim. Indeed, the presence in the *Iliad* of rhetoric that fails to persuade because of its poor quality is vital to my contention, for it provides a basis for comparison with rhetoric of good quality. If both skillful and unskillful rhetoric are represented in Homeric direct speeches, with the former succeeding and the latter failing, this implies an awareness of standards for practicing and judging rhetoric. It also implies the possibility of a system by which rhetorical persuasion can be mastered (presumably through oral *didaxis* and *praxis*) to a greater or lesser degree. As the meta-rhetorical Iliadic passages listed in the introduction indicate, the conceptualization of persuasive speech as a technical skill—practiced with varying degrees of success by different speakers in different situations—comes from both the Iliadic narrator's voice, and the words of the characters themselves.

CODA: PERSUASION AND ACHILLES

Among the patterns that have emerged through this analysis of the *Iliad*'s rhetorical speeches, there is one outlying point of interest which stands at the intersection of rhetoric, plot, and character: namely, that Achilles is the object of a disproportionate number of the persuasion attempts in the *Iliad*.[6] This is not entirely surprising, given that the plot of the epic revolves around Achilles and his involvement in the war; it is, however, notable that certain distinct patterns surround the attempts to persuade Achilles. Although many characters try (among them Agamemnon, Odysseus, Phoenix, Ajax, Lycaon, Hector, and the kings of the Achaeans as a collective), only two speakers in the entirety of the *Iliad* are actually successful at persuading Achilles to do something that he had been previously opposed to doing. These two are Patroclus, who persuades Achilles to allow him to enter battle in Book 16; and Priam, who persuades Achilles to relinquish Hector's body in Book 24. The explanation for Patroclus' success is fairly simple: he is Achilles' "nearest and dearest," and thus the persuasion is based purely on Patroclus' *êthos*, his identity. The reason for Priam's success is more complex and difficult. His *êthos* would appear to be the farthest thing from persuasive to Achilles—he is the father of Achilles' bitterest enemy, and Achilles is the murderer of his son. But through his rhetoric, Priam is able to forge an *êthos* that appeals to Achilles by analogy with Achilles' own father. Achilles responds favorably to the invitation to transfer his pity for Peleus onto Priam. In addition, both Patroclus and Priam take the approach of embodying signs (σημέια) for Achilles, pointing to themselves as argumentative "evidence" through both gesture and deictic self-reference. Examples of the former are Patroclus' tears and clinging to Achilles at 16.2–20 and Priam's tears and suppliant gestures at 24.477–512; examples of the latter are Patroclus' command to "send me out . . . and I may be a light given to the Danaans" (16.38–39) and Priam's command to "take pity on me . . . I put my lips to the hands of the man who has killed my children" (24.503–6).

PART TWO

The Genealogy of Rhetoric from Homer to Aristotle

CHAPTER FOUR

Explaining the Correspondence between Homeric Speech and Aristotelian Theory

The remarkable points of correspondence between the techniques of persuasion used in Homeric speech and those appearing in Aristotle's *Rhetoric* raise the question of how this correspondence might have arisen—a question made more intriguing because it seems to have gone largely unacknowledged by Aristotle himself (Aristotle's treatment of Homer will be discussed in chapter 6, section III). There are three possible explanations for the rhetorical similarities between Homer and Aristotle: (1) common sources for both authors; (2) the universality of rhetoric, implying that Aristotle arrived at his theories apart from and independent of any Homeric contribution to the discipline; and (3) the impact of Homeric represented speech on the development of formal rhetoric, culminating in Aristotle's work. Investigating this last possibility (option 3) will involve examining the historical and literary processes in Greece that might have led from Homer's poetic representation of rhetoric to Aristotle's canonical treatise. Chapters 5 and 6 will thus treat texts in the intervening centuries between Homer and Aristotle, both poetic (Hesiod, Homeric Hymns, Pindar, tragedy) and theoretical (the sophists and Plato), looking specifically at instances of rhetoric in these texts that might be comparable to the rhetoric of speeches from the *Iliad*. My discussion of option 2, the possibility that rhetoric is a universally occurring, unlearned phenomenon, will be informed in part by a comparative examination of rhetoric in non-Greek ancient narratives. While it is impossible to answer definitively questions such as "Did Homer invent rhetoric?" and "Was Aristotle borrowing from Homer in developing his rhetorical theory?" due to their speculative nature, my intention is to identify the most plausible account of the transmission of rhetoric in Homeric poetry into the formal, Classical manifestation of rhetoric in oratory and theory.

I. COMMON SOURCES

It is theoretically possible that both Homer and Aristotle drew on the same pre-Homeric material in creating their respective representations of a rule-governed system for persuasive speech. The lack of attestation for pre-Homeric sources beyond a few references to the shadowy figures of Orpheus and Musaeus, however, makes it impossible to argue for this possibility in any meaningful way. Although various works of poetry are attributed to the mythical figure of Orpheus, known for his gifts at singing and lyre-playing, the earliest such attributions date to the late-sixth or early-fifth century BCE.[1] And even if a tradition of Orphic poetry did predate the Homeric epics, its subject matter—centered on religious ritual, theogonies, cosmogonies, metempsychosis, and the like (which we know from the appropriation of Orphic material by the Pythagoreans, Bacchic mysteries, and other mystery cults)—makes it unlikely that such poetry would have contained the type of rhetorical paradigms that Homeric poetry exhibits. The figure of Musaeus occupied a place similar to and allied with Orpheus in Greek tradition, but with even less claim to being an actual historical figure. His name is often invoked in the Classical era and later as an early (pre-Homeric) poet, but he served primarily as the mouthpiece for a variety of oracles and poetry on religious and eschatological themes.[2] Ultimately, even if the Homeric epics were derived from earlier sources, the fact that subsequent Greek literature does not acknowledge such sources suggests that the epics must have effectively assimilated and superseded any source material. What is relevant to this study is that the Homeric epics represent the earliest surviving Greek literature, and that no earlier literary source can be invoked. Given the unique "debate culture" that prevailed in ancient Greece, however, actual speaking practices could well have functioned as a common source of rhetorical material for Homer and Aristotle (for further discussion of Greece as a debate culture, see section II below). Although this project focuses on the influence of Homeric poetry on rhetorical theory and practice, there is little doubt that speaking practices in Greece influenced Homeric poetry as well.

II. UNIVERSALITY OF RHETORIC

In seeking to explain the correspondences between Homer's and Aristotle's depictions of effective rhetoric, it is necessary to consider the possibility that Homeric speakers are simply using a mode of speech that is universally available, an innate human capacity. Henrich Plett distinguishes between what he calls "primary grammar," or ordinary speech, and "secondary grammar," or rhetorical language.[3] Do the Homeric poems portray characters who employ "primary grammar," merely mimicking a mode of unlearned, everyday communication that occurs naturally in society? Or do they, in fact, represent a consciously deployed, rule-governed system for persuasion through their characters' speech—the marked phenomenon of "secondary grammar"?

As I seek to answer this question, it is worth revisiting my definition of the term "rhetoric." This term has been conceived of and deployed in numerous ways throughout history, and perhaps no modern scholar has devoted more study to the subject than George Kennedy. Kennedy's *Comparative Rhetoric* provides a useful articulation of three different historical conceptualizations of the term "rhetoric," from most to least specific. The first of these reads:

> Some might argue that "rhetoric" is a peculiarly Western phenomenon, a structured system of teaching public speaking and written composition, developed in classical Greece, taught in Roman, medieval, renaissance, and early modern schools, and, with some revisions, still in use today.[4]

As is appropriate for the narrowest definition of the term, this definition makes mention of a didactic system encompassing both speaking and writing. This definition, observes Kennedy, is only "a subset of a more general meaning that also goes back to the beginnings of Western rhetorical consciousness." He explains the second and more general meaning thus:

> A common brief definition of "rhetoric" in classical antiquity was "the art of persuasion," or in Aristotle's fuller form (*Rhetoric* 1.2.1) "an ability, in each case, to see the available means of persuasion."[5]

The invocation of Aristotle's *Rhetoric* marks this definition as the one generally understood in Classical Greece (and which gradually evolved into the school-curriculum rhetoric described in the first passage). Although the translated phrase "art of persuasion" may sound like a casual and nontechnical activity to the modern English-speaking ear, the original context of the phrase, and the word τέχνη in connection with persuasion, denoted just the opposite: that persuasion was a technique, a skill. But there is a yet broader understanding of rhetoric, according to Kennedy. This understanding

> existed in Greece before "rhetoric," that is, before it had the name that came to designate it as a specific area of study. "Rhetoric" in this broader sense is a universal

phenomenon, one found even among animals, for individuals everywhere seek to persuade others to take or refrain from some action, or to hold or discard some belief. . . . Rhetoric, in the most general sense, may thus be identified with the energy inherent in an utterance (or an artistic representation): the mental or emotional energy that impels the speaker to expression, the energy level coded in the message, and the energy received by the recipient who then uses mental energy in decoding and perhaps acting on the message. Rhetorical labor takes place.[6]

Surely this final and most wide-ranging definition of rhetoric as "energy [mental or emotional] inherent in an utterance"—which can be expressed by a monkey's call of warning or a stag's roar of competition over a mate (to cite two of Kennedy's examples)—qualifies as a universal and innate capacity of living creatures. But it is a modern construal of a term that has traditionally had a much more precise definition, as attested in the first two Kennedy passages above. This more precise definition of rhetoric is what I am concerned with in this study. To revisit my working definition, first put forward in the introduction: *Rhetoric is a learned and deliberately practiced skill, involving the deployment of tropes and techniques according to a rule-based system, and aimed at winning an audience's approval or assent.*

Which of these definitions of rhetoric most aptly describes the practice of characters in the Homeric epics? Clearly, the Homeric poet represents his characters employing Kennedy's most general definition of rhetoric, namely "mental or emotional energy that impels the speaker to expression, the energy level coded in the message, and the energy received by the recipient." Homer *is*, in this sense, depicting a common and universal practice of rhetoric. But does the poet also depict rhetoric in the sense of that term which has prevailed from Aristotle's up to our own time—the "structured system," the "ability, in each case, to see the available means of persuasion"? Based upon my examination of Iliadic speeches in chapter 2, I would argue that indeed Homer exhibits both an awareness of rhetoric (not a theoretical awareness, but a recognition of technique-governed persuasion as a skill to be cultivated); and an internalized systematicity in its practice. Across a wide spectrum of Homeric speakers, the degree of sophistication in arguments, variety in tropes, and sensitivity shown to the particular audience is too marked to be an accidental or unconscious phenomenon. The presence of such rhetorical qualities in *some* Homeric speeches, but not in others, further indicates the marked, nonuniversal nature of the phenomenon. It is possible see traces of a (nonliterate) cultivation of speaking techniques in the persuasion represented in the *Iliad*. Such cultivation would consist of oral instruction passed on from an older warrior to a younger one, as with Phoenix instructing Achilles or Nestor instructing Diomedes in the art of speaking.[7]

In order to contextualize synchronically my claim that Homeric "rhetoric" is not simply a universal phenomenon, I have looked at several works of non-Greek literature that predate or are roughly contemporaneous with the Homeric epics, and that are roughly similar in form (i.e., narrative with embedded direct speech). What follows is a very brief overview of the appearance of rhetoric in three major ancient non-Greek texts (for a helpful and more in-depth overview of rhetoric in ancient literate societies, Kennedy's *Comparative Rhetoric* is an excellent resource). I have found that in the represented speeches of these works, it is possible to identify occasional instances of a few of the rhetorical tropes that exist in Homer, such as rebukes that appeal to shame and simple, isolated enthymemes. But on the whole, these speeches are of the type that I did *not* include in my reckoning of rhetorical speeches in the *Iliad* based on criteria of complexity and technical sophistication.

In ancient Near Eastern literature, the most obvious parallel to the Homeric epics is the *Epic of Gilgamesh*, which in its fullest surviving version (the Standard Babylonian version) dates to around the seventh century BCE, although there are numerous earlier versions of the epic; individual tales dealing with the character of Gilgamesh originate as far back as the third millennium BCE.[8] Most of the direct speeches in the standard version of *Gilgamesh* involve information exchange or simple instructions, with no rhetorical techniques adduced—or, at least, with few of the rhetorical techniques found in Greek literature (such as logical argumentation, *diathesis*, etc.).[9] Sara Denning-Bolle has noted "stylistic devices used in Mesopotamian narrative literature that are also present in dialogic contexts. These include repetition, parallelism, metaphor, simile, and stories-within-stories."[10] As examples of these stylistic devices, she points to the fact that the flood narrative in *Gilgamesh* is contained within a speech addressed by Utnapishtim to Gilgamesh; that Gilgamesh rejects the advances of Ishtar in a speech that "repeats an earlier dialogue of hers with another prospective lover"; and that Enkidu "recounts his dream of the gods' dialogic counsel in his dialogue with Gilgamesh."[11] But although each of these instances of embedded direct speech "jolts the reader or listener for a moment," in the words of Denning-Bolle, none of them is actually used for *persuasive* purposes. That is, none of these stories or dialogues within character speech in *Gilgamesh* is part of an effort to convince the internal audience of something, in the way that Homeric rhetorical speeches do.

There are a few exceptions, however. Tablet II of *Gilgamesh* contains a speech in which Gilgamesh attempts to enlist Enkidu's help in attacking the monster Humbaba, a seemingly impossible heroic task. Gilgamesh employs several rhetorical techniques in his attempt to persuade his comrade; they are more simple and brief in expression than are similar techniques among Homeric speakers, but they are rhetorically recognizable nonetheless. First, Gilgamesh stirs up the emotion of shame in Enkidu (*pathos*) with the words "Why, my friend, do you speak like a weakling? With your spineless words you [make me] despondent" (*Gilgamesh* II.232–33).[12] He then employs logical argument in the form of an enthymeme with an unstated (or perhaps lost—the text is fragmentary here) conclusion. The premise takes the form of a *gnômê*: "As for man, [his days] are numbered, whatever he may do, it is but wind. . . ." (II.234–35). By reminding Enkidu of human mortality, Gilgamesh is suggesting that it is irrational to fear death—the implied enthymematic conclusion being that Enkidu should join him in this risky endeavor. A second, parallel enthymeme follows, in which Gilgamesh points to Enkidu's own past experience with wilderness survival as evidence that he is well prepared for this task:

> You were born and grew up [in the wild:]
> even lions were afraid of you, [you experienced] all.
> Grown men fled away [from your presence,]
> Your heart is tried and [tested in] combat.
> Come, my friend, [let us hie] to the forge! (*Gilgamesh* II.237–41)

Gilgamesh relies on an assertion of Enkidu's identity and experience as a persuasive element in the face of his fears. Though this tactic might be seen as flattery and thus an example of *diathesis*, Enkidu's previous fears and his subsequent continued resistance to Gilgamesh's proposal (II.274–86, III.230–31) indicate that this is not an effective use of that tactic. The speech serves more to establish Enkidu's heroic qualities for the reading audience, and to set up dramatic tension for the upcoming Humbaba episode, than it does to illustrate rhetorical persuasion.

A few more rhetorical instances dot the surviving *Gilgamesh* material. Tablet III depicts the Elders of Uruk using *gnômai* to support their command to Gilgamesh as he ventures out to fight Humbaba: "'Who goes in front saves his companion, who knows the road protects his friend.' Let Enkidu go before you" (III.4–6). This construction is an enthymeme, though of the simplest kind. Tablet V contains fragments of Enkidu's hortatory speech to Gilgamesh, which includes words intended to shame the hero into action. Finally, Kennedy observes that "the debate of the gods [in Tablet VII over whether Gilgamesh or Enkidu must die because of their offenses], which is really a trial of the two warriors, shows some awareness of what in Western rhetorical theory is called 'stasis theory,' the determination of the question at issue."[13] This "debate," however, consists mainly of three gods making progressive declarations: first Anu asserts that "between these two [let one of them die!]"; then Enlil proposes that they "let Enkidu die"; and finally Shamash unsuccessfully protests punishment of the "innocent Enkidu," pointing out that Enlil was responsible for motivating the warriors' actions: "Was it not at your word that they slew him?" (III?.col. I, from a supplement to missing lines in Tablet VII). Other than this final point, which incorporates a rhetorical question but does not lead to any change in the decision to punish Enkidu, the gods' "debate" does not present any persuasive techniques. The remainder of the *Epic of Gilgamesh* contains commands, instructions, and storytelling, but nothing else resembling rhetorical persuasion.

Few other works of Near Eastern literature offer an exact comparison with Homer by containing represented persuasive speech.[14] Elements of a rhetorical voice do appear in the Egyptian epistolary tradition, however. In surviving letters from fourteenth-century BCE Egypt, for example—a collection known as the "Amarna Letters," addressed to the king of Egypt from various correspondents in Mesopotamia, Syria, and Palestine and treating official, business, and personal topics—Kennedy notes that "ethos, pathos, and logical argument are all used as means of persuasion."[15] *Êthos* is demonstrated in the letters, for example, by means of letter-writers "citing honorable actions of the past" to demonstrate their good character; *pathos* by writers describing their terrible circumstances in pleas for assistance from the king; logical argument by enthymeme, as when writers accompany their requests to the king with a rehearsal of their prior deeds of service.[16] Such an array of Aristotelian categories within Egyptian rhetoric is the exception rather than the rule, however. Michael Fox argues that *êthos* alone is "the major mode of persuasion in Egyptian rhetoric," and that "didactic wisdom literature gives no thought to argumentation as such and shows no awareness of the possibility that argumentation could operate independently of ethos."[17] Kennedy discusses the fact that Near Eastern rhetorical instruction tends to emphasize the virtues of restraining one's tongue— either to silence or to necessary speech—and waiting for the right moment to speak.[18] This is apparent in surviving writings such as the Egyptian *Instructions of Ptahhotep* (on which see Fox 1983) and the Biblical book of Proverbs. These instructional works have more in common with Greek wisdom literature than with the represented persuasion found in Homer. (For discussion of the relationship between Greek wisdom literature and rhetoric, see chapter 5, section III.)

Although it is beyond my capacity to discuss them in any depth here, the literary traditions of China and India have produced literary works traceable as far or farther back than the epics of Homer. Both of these cultures possess ancient literature in which direct speech is embedded into a narrative: the Chinese *Shūjīng* (translated into English as *Classic of History, Book of History,* or *Book of Documents*) is a compilation of documents that record the deeds and sayings of early Chinese dynasties, and the Sanskrit epics *Mahābhārata* and *Ramayana* recount tales of wars, heroes, and gods early in the Indian literary tradition. What follows is a brief look at the rhetorical content of several direct speeches in these works.

The *Shūjīng* held a revered place in Chinese literature as "the oldest and most sacred of historical texts, and attributed to the greatest sages of antiquity."[19] It is one of the "Five Classics" of ancient Chinese literature, and consists of documents dating from roughly the twenty-fourth to the eighth century BCE.[20] According to tradition, Confucius was responsible for the assembly and arrangement of the *Shūjīng*'s collection of documents. Direct speech forms the bulk of its material; connected and framing narrative is rare. On rhetoric in the *Shūjīng*, Kennedy observes that instances of persuasion make little use of arguments from *pathos*, more of arguments from *êthos*, and tend to employ inductive rather than deductive argumentation (i.e., favoring appeals to example, precedent, and authority, but rarely employing enthymemes or the argument from probability).[21] Mary Garrett has examined the differences between "Western" and Chinese rhetorical theories concerning the emotions (the notion of *pathos*), although she is concerned not with representations of rhetoric in literature so much as with broad cultural comparisons. The differences are stark, Garrett argues: in Classical China, "what those in power desired was not assent to one proposal, but a deep imprinting of particular attitudes, loyalties, and predilections in the entire population so that pleading or coercion on specific occasions would not be necessary, only the issuance of directives and occasional exhortations."[22] This agrees with Burton Watson's characterization of the arguments that were used, according to the *Shūjīng*, by leaders in the Chou dynasty to establish their authority after overthrowing the previous emperor. These new leaders

> sought for some philosophical principle or concept to justify their action and assist them in persuading the Yin people to cooperate with the new regime. They found such a justification in the concept of the mandate of Heaven, which teaches

that the would-be founders of a new dynasty, by their just and virtuous actions, receive from Heaven—a vague, half-personalized spiritual power which rules the universe—a command to set up a new rule.[23]

This describes closely the rhetorical strategy of appeal to and reliance on external sources of authority, invoked by the speaker in a heavy-handed method of persuasion. Such a method generally indicates that the speaker holds most of the power in the relationship and the audience holds little or none; thus the need for a more winsome, audience-sensitive approach to persuasion (through *diathesis* and argumentation, for example) is unnecessary.

It is this power dynamic that governs most of the communications depicted in the *Shūjīng*. Much of what might qualify as persuasion in this text comes in the form of commands, admonition, or wisdom speech, usually exchanged between a ruler and one of his ministers. A typical example appears in a section called "The Documents of Yü," in which the minister Yü advises the sovereign Kao Yao as follows:

> Find your repose in your (proper) resting-point. Attend to the springs of things; study stability; and let your assistants be the upright:—then shall your movements be grandly responded to, (as if the people only) waited for your will. Thus you will brightly receive (the favour of) God;—will not Heaven renew its appointment of you, and give you blessing?[24]

The rhetoric in this speech takes a gnomic or proverbial form common to wisdom texts from a wide range of cultural traditions. The only truly rhetorical component of the speech—the point at which Yü progresses from issuing *gnômai* to making an enthymematic argument—comes at the end, when he suggests that there will be a positive result if Kao Yao takes his advice. A minister may (deferentially) offer the favor of Heaven as an incentive in order to persuade a sovereign *Shūjīng*; this is the slightly less rhetorically rigid counterpart to a sovereign invoking the mandate of Heaven in order to command obedience from his subjects. Neither method, however, bespeaks rhetorical complexity or sophistication.

A closer analogue for Homeric rhetoric may be found in ancient Indian epic. The subject matter of the *Mahābhārata*—a familial war between the Kauravas and the Pandavas over rights to the kingdom of the Kurus—bears some resemblance to that of the *Iliad*. The *Mahābhārata's* origins in popular oral tradition likely date to the eighth or ninth century BCE, though the earliest preserved textual portions are not older than 400 BCE.[25] The epic remains a tangle of differing chronological layers (with the last accretions to the text coming as late as 400 CE) and genres (genealogy, religious philosophy, lament, etc.). Despite the narrative focus on genealogical succession and war, however, the role of effective speech is not insignificant. According to Kennedy, the *Mahābhārata* "describes a society in which debate among nobles on political issues was frequent, important, sophisticated, and popular."[26] The nature of heroism in the *Mahābhārata*, as in the Homeric epics, is tied to skill in speaking as well as in fighting: Kevin McGrath observes that the warrior Karna in particular is renowned for "his boasting and capacity for skilful verbal assault," and is described as the "best of speakers," *vadatām vara*.[27]

One such instance occurs in Book 1 of the epic, when Karna enters an arena of warriors dueling for show, and engages in a battle of words and weapons with his rival and half-brother, Arjuna. Near the beginning of their encounter, Karna delivers the following challenge:

> This stage is open to all, so what of you, Phalguna? Barons are those who are the strongest. Law obeys might. Why abuse, which is the whimpering of the weak? Talk with arrows, Bhārata, until before your teacher's own eyes I carry off your head with mine![28] (1.8.126)

The primary rhetorical device used in this speech is that of shaming the addressee, which Karna effects through a combination of provocative questions, the accusation of weakness, and the confident assertion that he will kill Arjuna before his own teacher's eyes. Karna expresses the desired object of this speech—that is, getting Arjuna to agree to a duel with him—in the briefest of phrases, the command "Talk with arrows." This phrase gives the speech a conventional enthymematic structure, with the command acting as the enthymeme conclusion while the aforementioned elements of shaming provide the motivating premise. Indeed, Karna is a hero who revels in the act of boasting, even though he is certainly not alone in this practice, as McGrath notes: "For it is usually the case that heroes, the Indo-European hero in general and the *Mahābhārata* hero in particular, boast before combat and verbally assail their opponent."[29] McGrath analyzes a lengthy dialogue between Karna and Karpa in Book 7 in which Karpa criticizes, and Karna defends, Karna's well-established habit of elaborate boasting before combat.[30]

Despite the value placed on speech in the *Mahābhārata*, however, direct speeches in the epic do not often involve sustained rhetorical argumentation aimed at persuasion. Instead, the speech genres of boasting / vaunting, invective, pure commands, and conversational dialogues conducted in private predominate. McGrath's study of six major dialogues in the *Mahābhārata* involving Karna, the hero most renowned for his speech, demonstrates the recurring qualities of admonition, prediction, criticism, and debate.[31] Only one of these dialogues centers on a persuasion attempt: Kunti's failed attempt to convince her son, Karna, to switch loyalties in the impending war (5.55.143). She makes use of two rhetorical devices in this speech: her own *êthos* as Karna's mother (a strategy that backfires, since she had abandoned him as a baby and this is their first interaction since that time); and an offer of incentives, namely the fortune of the Pandava king Yudhisthira and the status of "a heroic *Pārtha*." Kunti's speech thus draws upon only the most basic categories of rhetorical technique.

This brief look at comparative data offers some context for judging whether the kind of persuasive speech found in Homer is a universally practiced phenomenon (one that would later come to be labeled "rhetoric"); whether that phenomenon is an unlearned or a learned mode of human communication; and whether, if learned, it differs or innovates in any significant way from roughly contemporary non-Greek representations of persuasion. To varying degrees, the *Epic of Gilgamesh*, the *Shūjīng*, and the *Mahābhārata* do exhibit a set of basic strategies common to persuasion attempts across multiple ancient cultures: appeals to *êthos* or authority; *gnômai*; and the offer of incentives. But these strategies are deployed less frequently, and with less elaboration, than they are in the *Iliad*. In addition, the Homeric stable of rhetorical strategies goes well beyond this basic set, which suggests that a developed system of rhetoric exists in Homer that cannot be explained simply as universal human persuasive practice. That the rhetorical qualities of Homeric speech stand out within ancient literature can be explained partly in reference to a broader cultural distinction that has been much noted by scholars of the ancient world: the propensity of ancient Greek society for public debate, argument, and competition. From the very earliest Greek poetry to the legal and political oratory of the late Classical era (and, much later, the stylized and elaborate argumentation of the Second Sophistic), ancient Greece functioned as a "debate culture," one in which power was won and negotiated through competitive and persuasive speech.[32] Buxton, who presents a survey of the role of persuasive argumentation in the ancient Near East as compared with that in ancient Greece, comes to the following conclusion: "On the whole, evidence from other Near Eastern cultures supports the picture . . . according to which classical Greece was remarkable both for its range of contexts for public debate and for the radical nature of the issues open to argumentation."[33] My own contention pushes these observations even further to argue that Homeric poetry not only represents a debate culture, but shows that this culture practiced rhetoric in a more technical and advanced sense (comparable with Classical-era oratory and the systems laid out in rhetorical theory) than has been heretofore recognized, or than we find in any comparable ancient literature.

A final comment on the distinction between a universally available, "accidental" rhetoric and a learned, rule-governed rhetoric comes from Aristotle himself. At the very beginning of his *Rhetoric*, he observes that

> all [people], up to a point, try both to test and uphold an argument and to defend themselves and attack. Now among the general public, some do these things **at random** (εἰκῇ) and others **through an ability acquired by habit** (διὰ συνήθειαν ἀπὸ ἕξεως). . . . (1.1.1–2)

Aristotle here presents the two different forms that an untheoretical practice of persuasive speech can take: (1) something that occurs universally, or randomly, without calculation; and (2) something that must be learned and consciously cultivated by habit, an ability, implying the existence of greater and lesser degrees of sophistication and success. It is this latter, more specialized conception of rhetoric that I believe is in evidence in the speeches of the *Iliad*. Aristotle then goes on to tout his own project of observing and theorizing such an ability:

> But since both ways are possible, it is clear that it would also be possible to do the same by [following] a path; for it is possible **to observe** (θεωρεῖν) the cause why some succeed **by habit** (διὰ συνήθειαν) and others **accidentally** (ἀπὸ τοῦ αὐτομάτου), and all would at once agree that such observation is the activity of an **art** (τέχνη). (1.1.2)

While this statement clearly lays out Aristotle's view of theoretical activity, it also reiterates the distinction between habitual / cultivated and accidental rhetoric. In Aristotle's very first dichotomy regarding rhetoric, then, consciously rhetorical practice (such as that of many Homeric speakers) and meta-rhetorical theory (such as Aristotle's) both stand in opposition to "random"—perhaps we could say "instinctive"—attempts to argue a point.

III. THE RHETORICAL LEGACY OF HOMER

A final possible explanation for the close correspondence between rhetorical elements in Homeric speech and Aristotle's rhetorical theory is that Homer informed and influenced Aristotle through a sort of cultural osmosis. Unlike the ancient commentators on rhetoric whose views were examined in chapter 1, Aristotle does not acknowledge Homer as an inventor of or precursor to rhetoric; he cites Homer in the *Rhetoric* only to illustrate relatively superficial figures of style, such as metaphor and asyndeton. Perhaps Aristotle recognized Homer's use of *êthos*, *diathesis*, enthymeme, topics, and the like and chose to ignore this fact in his treatise (which offers little credit to rhetorical predecessors of any kind). Perhaps he was genuinely blind to the possibility that the earliest Greek poetry provided clear illustrations of the *technê* he was describing. Aristotle's treatment of Homer in the *Rhetoric* will be explored further in chapter 6. What cannot be disputed is that he was deeply familiar with the Homeric epics; this much is clear from his own analysis of Homer elsewhere (most notably in the *Poetics*). Whether Aristotle was conscious of it or not, then, it seems unlikely that the rhetorical sophistication and the consistent patterns of argumentation found in Homer's direct speeches failed to inform his rhetorical system, or that of the sophists and handbook-writers that preceded him.

CHAPTER FIVE

Rhetoric in Archaic Poetry

If indeed Homeric speech is a significant (and largely unacknowledged) source for later rhetorical theory, how was a system of rhetorical persuasion transmitted from Homer to Aristotle—crossing lines of time, genre, and medium (oral to written)? Did it find its way into other forms of Archaic literature along the way? In an attempt to answer these questions, I have surveyed the role of rhetorical speech at representative moments in the chronologically intervening literature: the Homeric Hymns, Hesiod's poetry, varieties of Archaic lyric, tragedy, and sophistic oratory. This survey, necessarily brief though it must be, brings to light noteworthy points of comparison between Homeric poetry and the literature that follows it with regard to the understanding and portrayal of rhetoric. Insofar as it is possible to trace a "literary lineage" for rhetoric in the Archaic age, pointing to the use of persuasive techniques in Archaic poetry, and evaluating the techniques' similarity and possible indebtedness to those found in Homer, I have attempted to do so. Two basic observations emerge from this survey. First, no representation of rhetoric within Archaic literature approaches Homer's in terms of its detailed and wide-ranging employment of rhetorical techniques. Second, when complex rhetoric is depicted during this period, it tends to be in literature that bears an affinity to the Homeric epics in genre and / or subject matter. Thus, as we will see, certain Homeric Hymns and the military exhortation elegies of Callinus and Tyrtaeus are the only Archaic works that contain rhetorical speech bearing a strong resemblance to Homeric rhetoric. It is these works that might be seen as propagating the "literary lineage" for rhetoric from Homer, a lineage that continues through tragedy and certain sophistic works in the fifth century, and thence to the rhetorical theories of Plato and Aristotle in the fourth. In general, however, examples of complex rhetoric—that is, speech that involves the range of logical argumentation, *diathesis*, and *êthos* appeals— are few and far between in the Archaic period, a fact that only highlights the innovation displayed by the Homeric poems in this regard.

I. HOMERIC HYMNS

The dating and origins of the Homeric Hymns are murky, and even when only the longer poems are considered, their composition likely spans more than a hundred years.[1] We know from a variety of ancient sources (the opening lines of Pindar's *Nemean* 2, for example) that hymns were often performed by rhap- sodes as preludes (*prooimia*) to a performance of epic material.[2] There is thus a natural relationship between hymns and epic; in addition, the two genres have certain shared characteristics: both portray the gods as characters, possess a narrative arc, and take the form of hexameter poetry. Indeed, the Hymns share a number of formulae, and occasionally even full verses, with Homer—a fact that, according to Martin West, "is not surprising in view of the Hymns' cre- ation and transmission among a professional rhapsode class."[3] The Homeric Hymns (and the other Archaic literature examined in this chapter) are of inter- est to this project insofar as they contain rhetorical speech that can be compared with that in Homeric poetry. In drawing such a comparison, it is, of course, important to consider the differences in genre and subject matter between the Hymns and the Homeric epics. The Hymns' inherently religious nature and purpose distinguish them from the epic genre. The long Hymns, however, pos- sess a significant formal similarity to Homeric epic in that they are narrative hexametric poems containing direct speech and dialogues between characters. This means that there are opportunities within the Hymns for representing persuasive discourse of the sort that we have seen in Homer. The degree to which these opportunities produce instances of rhetorical speech varies among the individual long Hymns.

Only the four longest Hymns—the *Hymn to Demeter,* the *Hymn to Apollo* (counting the Delian and Pythian portions of the *Hymn to Apollo* as a unity[4]), the *Hymn to Hermes,* and the *Hymn to Aphrodite*—are relevant for this investigation, as the shorter Hymns do not contain instances of persuasive direct speech.[5] I treat these four Hymns in the order of their traditional numbering, beginning with the *Hymn to Dememter* (*Hymn* 2). The examples of rhetoric in this Hymn are sparse, as nearly all of its "rhetorical" speeches consist of only a command attended by an enthymematic premise. Two such speeches occur during an early exchange in which Demeter begs Helios for information on the whereabouts of her daughter. Demeter speaks first:

> Helios, have regard for me, **if ever I have gladdened your heart either by word or deed** (εἴ ποτε δή σεο / ἢ ἔπει ἢ ἔργωι κραδίην καὶ θυμὸν ἴηνα). . . . Look down from the sky with your rays over the whole earth and sea: so tell me truly if perchance you have seen who it is, of gods or mortals, that has taken her away from me by force against her will and gone off with her.[6] (*H. Dem.* 64–73)

Demeter's plea is comprised of a straightforward **enthymeme**. The conclusion—the action that she is attempting to engender in Helios—is her command to "have regard for me," "look down from the sky," and "tell me" if you can identify my daughter's kidnapper. The motivating premise attached to this command is an appeal to her own *êthos* as a provider and friend to Helios: she has, in the past, "gladdened your heart either by word or deed." This quid pro quo argument is a rhetorical standby, already familiar to Greek audiences from Thetis' appeal to Zeus at *Iliad* 1.503–4 ("Father Zeus, if ever before in word or action I did you favour among the immortals, now grant what I ask for").

Helios readily assents to Demeter's request, offering her the desired information and expressing his sympathy for her situation. But once he has revealed her daughter's kidnapper, Helios attempts to persuade Demeter of something in turn:

> So, goddess, end your loud lamenting; there is no call for you to rage for ever like this to no purpose. Aïdoneus, the Major General, is not an unsuitable son-in-law to have among the gods, your own brother, of the same seed. As for privileges, he has the portion he was allotted originally in the threefold division. . . .
> (*H. Dem.* 82–86)

Here again the persuasive element of the speech is a single **enthymeme**. Helios states the object of his persuasion as a command ("end your loud lamenting"), and provides a purely mercenary calculation as the motivating premise—an appeal to Aristotle's **topic of consideration of incentives and disincentives**. Based on Hades' status, Helios argues, his rape of Korê is transformed into an advantageous marriage, which Demeter should accept—perhaps even gladly. This brusque reasoning in an attempt to make his listener cease her lament is a far cry from Achilles' emotionally evocative and sympathetic argument for the same cause, addressed to Priam at *Iliad* 24.599–620 (see chapter 2, speech XVIII). Demeter, of course, remains unappeased.

The next instance of rhetorical persuasion in the *Hymn to Demeter* occurs after the disguised Demeter has made her way to Eleusis, and comes before the Eleusinian queen Metaneira. Demeter has already suggested to Metaneira's daughters that she could serve as a nursemaid for their young brother, but Metaneira realizes that she is dealing with an important personage in disguise, and thus takes pains to use persuasive language in extending the formal job offer:

> Greetings, lady, for I do not expect you come from low parents, but ones of standing. . . . Now that you have come here, you shall have as much as I have myself. Just rear this boy for me. . . . If you were to raise him and see him to young manhood's measure, **then any woman who saw you might well envy you, so richly would I repay you for his nurturing** (ἢ ῥά κέ τίς σε ἰδοῦσα γυναικῶν θηλυτεράων / ζηλώσαι· τόσα κέν τοι ἀπὸ θρεπτήρια δοίην). (*H. Dem.* 213–23)

Metaneira's proposal displays a more nuanced level of argumentation than do the two previous speeches, in that it includes other rhetorical elements in addition to the simple **enthymeme** based upon an incentive of reward. The opening greeting is both deferential and flattering, a clear attempt on Metaneira's part to dispose Demeter favorably (*diathesis*). She then makes a gesture that establishes equality between Demeter and herself with respect to status and possessions. The assertion that "you shall have as much as I have myself" shows that Metaneira knows the importance of gaining her audience's trust by showing good will (*êthos*). She subsequently uses the **topic of consideration of incentives and disincentives** in order to convince Demeter to raise her child, offering both material ("I will reward you richly") and psychological ("other women will envy you") enticements. The speech is a success, as Demeter "gladly" agrees to take on the responsibility (225–30).

It might be argued that a final instance of represented rhetoric in the *Hymn to Demeter* occurs in Hermes' speech to Hades at 347–56, which conveys Zeus' demand that Hades relinquish Persephone to her mother. This is not so much a case of attempted persuasion, however, as it is a command attended by rationale for that command. Earlier, Zeus had instructed Hermes to "persuade Hades with soft words," using a common Homeric formula for characterizing persuasive speech (μαλακοῖσι παραιφάμενος ἐπέεσσιν, 336)—but the inarguable nature of the message is apparent in its rhetorical form as well as in Hades' response (he "did not demur from the command (ἐφετμή) of Zeus the king," 358). Indeed, the aspect of persuasion in this speech is rendered moot by Hermes' opening lines: "Zeus the father has instructed me to bring illustrious Persephone out from the Darkness to them." Hades cannot argue with the speaker or fail to comply, because Hermes is simply following instructions from Zeus—as Hades, too, must do. Hermes offers a premise that gives the command an enthymematic form:

> so that her mother may set eyes on her and cease from her wrath and her dreadful
> resentment against the immortals. For she is purposing a grave thing, to destroy
> the feeble stock of earthborn humankind by keeping the seed hidden in the soil,
> and so diminishing the immortals' tribute (*H. Dem.* 349–54).

Still, this premise is more of an obligatory formal element than an actual attempt to persuade; the effectual part of the speech, as far as Hades is concerned, is that the command comes from Zeus.

These speeches constitute the full spectrum of represented persuasion within the *Hymn to Demeter*. Several characters issue pure commands in the Hymn (e.g., Demeter commanding Metaneira to have her people build the goddess a temple (270–74), and Rhea giving Demeter the command from Zeus to make the earth produce grain once again, 467–69), but these commands do not achieve the status of rhetoric in that no persuasive arguments are attached.

The *Hymn to Apollo* (*Hymn* 3) contains the smallest proportion of direct speech to narrative out of all the long hymns; perhaps this is because the narrative voice in this Hymn is particularly assertive, often speaking in the first or second person (e.g., 1–29, 140–50, 165–81, 207–46, 545–46) as though engaging in direct speech himself. Despite this statistic, the two speeches in the *Hymn to Apollo* that do contain rhetorical persuasion are more complex in their argumentation than the persuasive speeches in the *Hymn to Demeter*. The first of these occurs during the Delian portion of the Hymn: Leto's attempt to convince the personified island of Delos to host Apollo's birth and future temple:

> Delos, if only you would be willing to be the seat of my son, Phoibos Apollo, and
> establish his rich temple on your soil! No one else is ever going to engage with you
> or honor you, for I do not see you ever being rich in cattle or sheep, nor will you
> bring forth a harvest or grow abundant fruit trees. But if you have the temple of
> Apollo the far-shooter, all men will bring you hecatombs as they congregate here,
> and you will have the savor of the fat ever going up beyond measure, and you will
> feed your inhabitants from the hand of others, for you do not have richness under
> your soil. (*H. Ap.* 51–60)

Leto's approach to persuading Delos puts a subtle psychological twist on the straightforward enthymeme argument from incentives. She builds her case gradually: she begins with a plaintive "if only" exclamation that conveys her own vulnerability as well as her wishes, the **enthymeme** conclusion; next she points out Delos' natural disadvantages and needs, thus laying the groundwork for her audience to be receptive to her request; and finally she proposes a mutually beneficial solution (the **topic of consideration of incentives and disincentives**). Along with these incentives—Delos will gain honor and popularity as well as wealth if she assents—Leto incorporates a measure of *diathesis* into her rhetoric. She knows and uses her audience's points of weakness in order to offer a flattering, attractive future to the island. Leto's proposal meets with some resistance: Delos responds by expressing apprehension about Apollo's unpredictable character and requesting the guarantee of an oath from Leto (62–82). Although Delos' request is not itself accompanied by any arguments such as would qualify it as rhetorical, she does successfully negotiate a favorable "deal," as Leto agrees to swear the oath. Thus both goddesses bolster their own interests through this rhetorical exchange.

The Pythian portion of the *Hymn to Apollo* contains a persuasive speech uttered by the personified fountain Telphousa, a response to Apollo's assertion that he will establish a temple within her locality. That Apollo baldly asserts his intention to appropriate Telphousa for his purposes—rather than requesting permission to do so—stands in contrast to the earlier interaction between Leto and Delos in a parallel situation. Whereas Leto had seen it necessary to persuade her audience, Apollo, in the words of Andrew Miller, "displays an abruptness and apparent insensitivity quite alien to his mother's character. Where Leto first broaches her request hypothetically, next suggests reasons why Delos should be willing to listen, and finally makes an attractive proposal of quid pro quo, Apollo issues a flat statement of intent that totally ignores Telphusa's interest in the matter."[7] Such disregard for his audience's feelings and for the efficacy of rhetoric does not serve Apollo well. Telphousa responds by growing angry (κραδίην ἐχολώσατο, 256) and channeling this anger into a deceptive counterproposal, couched in respectful and winsome terms. After addressing Apollo as ἄναξ ἑκάεργε to open the speech, she attempts to dissuade him from his plan with several arguments, followed by a counterproposal:

> I will speak out, and you must take it to heart. You will always be bothered by the clatter of racehorses, and of mules being watered from my divine springs; here people will want to gaze at well-built chariots and the clatter of racing horses, rather than at a big temple with a mass of wealth inside it. **No, if you would take my advice (of course you are nobler and more powerful than I, lord, and your strength is supreme)** (ἀλλ᾽ εἰ δή τι πίθοιο [σὺ δὲ κρέσσων καὶ ἀρείων / ἐσσὶ ἄναξ

ἐμέθεν, σέο δὲ σθένος ἐστὶ μέγιστον]), make it at Crisa, in the hollow of Parnassus: there there will be no noise of chariots or clatter of racing horses round your well-built altar, but just the same the thronging peoples would bring their gifts for Ie-Paieon, and your heart would be glad as you received the fine offerings from the surrounding peoples. (*H. Ap.* 261–74)

Telphousa first offers reasons (enthymematic premises) for why Apollo's plan is faulty. These premises appeal to his desires for comfort and for honor and attention; she points out how her locality lacks those things in a negative argument from the **topic of consideration of incentives and disincentives**. She then turns this argument around in her proposed alternative: if Apollo does what she suggests in the deferentially couched **enthymeme** conclusion ("if you would take my advice, make it at Crisa"), honor and reward are sure to follow. Employing the **topic of consideration of incentives and disincentives** positively now, Telphousa promises that the proposed locale would lack the problems of her territory, and that Apollo's "heart would be glad" at the offerings he would receive. In addition, she exerts the technique of *diathesis* by means of the flattering aside, "of course you are nobler and more powerful than I, lord." Miller calls Telphousa's speech "a small masterpiece of rhetoric, for like Leto—and conspicuously unlike Apollo—she speaks unerringly to the interests and desires (as she conceives them) of her auditor."[8] It is accordingly a successful piece of persuasion, for we find out in the line after her speech that "so saying she persuaded the Far-shooter, intending that renown (κλέος) in the land should be her own" (275–76).

This completes the account of speeches in the *Hymn to Apollo* that could be considered rhetorical. Although other speeches in the Hymn include Hera's diatribe against Zeus to the other Olympians (311–30) and her prayer to Earth, Heaven, and the Titans to grant her a son not fathered by Zeus, namely the serpent Typhaon (334–39), they contain no arguments or persuasive techniques. Apollo gives two speeches of command to the Cretan sailors late in the poem (475–501 and 532–44), but they are simply instructions for establishing and tending his temple. The second of these speeches, as Clay observes, constitutes a different sort of authoritative speech: Apollo's first oracle.[9] Apollo utters these commands with the assumption that he will be obeyed and that persuasion is unnecessary, much as he had done in his speech to Telphousa.

The *Hymn to Hermes* (Hymn 4) is, of all the Homeric Hymns, the richest in both rhetorically constructed direct speech and meta-reference to the persuasive power of speech.[10] It has the greatest number of direct speeches within the narrative (20) of any of the Hymns, and a higher proportion of direct speech to

narrative than all the other longer Hymns save the *Hymn to Aphrodite* (in which
a single speech from Aphrodite to Anchises constitutes one-third of the hymn's
total lines): 48 percent of the *Hymn to Hermes* is direct speech.[11] Such emphasis
on speech is, of course, appropriate to the god whose power lies in tricks and
clever reasoning, and this power is on abundant display in the Hymn.[12] Hermes
indeed classifies his own divine powers as a τέχνη; he boasts to his mother
Maia that ἐγὼ **τέχνης** ἐπιβήσομαι ἥ τις ἀρίστη ("I am going to embark on the
finest of **arts**," 167) as he moves to assert his position among the Olympian gods.
This τέχνη proves to be skill in both deeds (invention and thievery), and words
(glib and beguiling rhetoric). The first portion of the Hymn (1–153) primarily
chronicles Hermes' deeds, while the remainder (154–580) focuses on his verbal
interactions with other characters. Although I am concerned primarily with this
latter portion, there are a few earlier instances of Hermes' speech that do establish aspects of his speaking prowess. Jenny Strauss Clay observes that enigmatic
rhetoric is characteristic of two of Hermes' early speeches, namely his addresses
to the tortoise whose shell he appropriates for constructing a lyre, and to the old
farmer from Onchestus who sees him stealing Apollo's cattle:

> Speech, insofar as it involves communication or mediation between individuals,
> belongs to Hermes' domain. But the rhetoric of Hermes is of a peculiar sort;
> persuasive, seductive, and deceptive, it is characteristically ambiguous and rid-
> dling, concealing as much as revealing, and abounding in double and ulterior
> meanings. . . . Hermes' domain, then, is not the sphere of language that lays
> claim to truth, but rather that use of language whose goal extends outside itself
> and which is a means to an end: persuasion, seductive rhetoric, lies, oaths, perju-
> ries, and even magical incantations.[13]

Hermes' first use of persuasive speech comes when he addresses the farmer from
Onchestus (90–93). It is a modest persuasive attempt, perhaps befitting the sim-
plicity of its humble audience; Onchestus is the only mortal character in the
poem. Hermes employs an **enthymeme** predicated on the **topic of consideration
of incentives and disincentives**, promising to grant fruitfulness to the farmer's
grapevines if he stays quiet about what he has seen: "You will indeed be well in
wine when these all bear fruit . . . [if you] don't see what you've seen, and don't
hear what you've heard" (91–92). The encounter ends with no indication of the
old man's response, and only later will it become clear that Hermes' request was
ineffective, as the farmer betrays him to Apollo (187–211).

Hermes' speech to the farmer is only a precursor, however, to the rhetorical
outpouring that occurs once Apollo confronts Hermes about the theft of his

cattle. The ensuing quarrel between the two gods lasts nearly through the end of the poem. Apollo's initial volley is a short **enthymeme** argument comprised of a command plus a threat designed to evoke the emotion of fear (*pathos* in service of *diathesis*): "Tell me where my cows are, double quick, otherwise we two shall quarrel in no seemly fashion: I shall take you and hurl you into misty Tartarus, into the dismal Darkness past help" (254–57). Hermes' response to this threat and to Apollo's implied accusation of theft is a poetic version of Classical-era forensic oratory, a boldly argued defense speech. Even the narrative introduction to the speech (τὸν δ' Ἑρμῆς μύθοισιν ἀμείβετο κερδαλέοισιν, 260) heralds its verbal craftiness. Hermes' contention centers on the probability (or lack thereof) of Apollo's claim:

> I couldn't tell you where they are, or earn a reward for it. **I don't look like a cattle rustler, a strong man** (οὔ τι βοῶν ἐλατῆρι κραταιῷι φωτὶ ἔοικα). That isn't my business, I'm more interested in other things: what I'm interested in is sleeping, and my mother's milk, and having wrappings round my shoulders, and warm baths. I hope no one comes to hear what this dispute was about; it would astonish the immortals, the idea of a newborn child coming through the porch with cattle that dwell in the fields. That's nonsense you're talking. I was born yesterday, my feet are tender, and it's rough ground beneath. If you like, I'll swear a big oath, by my father's head: I promise I'm not to blame personally. . . .
> (*H. Herm.* 264–75)

This neat piece of persuasion incorporates an appeal to *êthos* simultaneously with an argument from *eikos*, with Hermes citing his own youthful age and innocent character as reasons why Apollo's accusation is preposterous. His assertion that "it would astonish the immortals" to hear such a patently absurd accusation is also a *diathesis* strategy, designed to make Apollo fear the other gods' mockery (*pathos*) and thus be disposed to yield his anger. This *eikos* argument serves as the premise for an **enthymeme** whose implied conclusion is that Apollo should drop his accusation. Hermes ends the speech by volunteering to swear an oath—a rhetorical gesture that caps his overall protestation of innocence (albeit with a thinly veiled undertone of mockery, which is not lost on Apollo, as his response, lines 282–92, reveals).[14]

In this speech, Hermes has exemplified the argument from *eikos* that would become central to later forensic oratory, as we know from several references in Aristotle's *Rhetoric*. Among these references is his claim at *Rhetoric* 2.25.8 that *eikos* is one of the four sources of enthymemes, along with paradigm, necessary signs (*tekmêria*), and fallible signs (*sêmeia*). Aristotle also cites the "Art" (*technê*) of Corax and its well-known example (which Plato attributes to Tisias in *Phaedrus* 273a–b) of the varying uses of the argument from probability:

> If a weak man were charged with assault, he should be acquitted as not being a likely suspect for the charge; for it is not probable [that a weak man would attack another]. And if he *is* a likely suspect, for example, if he is strong, [he should be acquitted]; for it is not likely [that he would start a fight] for the very reason that it was going to seem probable. (*Rhetoric* 2.24.11)

Despite Apollo's exasperation with Hermes' actions, and although he sees right through his protestations of innocence, he does show appreciation for his baby brother's clever speech: "My dear sly swindler (ὦ πέπον ἠπεροπευτὰ δολοφραδές), by the way you talk (οἷ' ἀγορεύεις), I reckon you will often be burgling prosperous houses by night" (282–85). The narrator reinforces this characterization of Hermes as unscrupulous rhetorician (sophist) with the comment that "the Cyllenian was hoping to deceive Silverbow with his arts and his wily words" (ὃ τέχνῃσίν τε καὶ αἱμυλίοισι λόγοισιν / ἤθελεν ἐξαπατᾶν Κυλλήνιος Ἀργυρότοξον, 317–18).

The clash between Hermes and Apollo reaches its rhetorical climax in the courtroom drama on Olympus, in which both appeal to Zeus to arbitrate their dispute. Both combatants offer speeches that resemble later forensic oratory: first Apollo for the prosecution, then Hermes for the defense. Apollo's speech (334–64) is a straightforward and correct account of Hermes' fraudulent actions, with no argument adduced—a pure narrative of grievances. Hermes' speech, however, is a variation on his earlier protestation to Apollo, along with several new rhetorical elements:

> Father Zeus, I shall tell you it as it was, for I am truthful and do not know how to tell a lie. He came into our place in search of his shambling cattle today as the sun was just rising. He didn't bring witnesses or observers from the blessed gods, but insisted on disclosure with much duress . . . because he has the delicate bloom of his glorious prime, while I was born yesterday, as he well knows, and I don't look like a cattle rustler, a strong man. Believe me (since you call yourself my dear father) that I didn't drive his cows home. . . . I am in awe of Helios and the other gods, and I love you, and I respect him. You yourself know I'm not to blame. I'll give you a great oath too. (*H. Herm.* 368–83)

Hermes' first line of defense is a blatant claim to having a truthful and trustworthy character (*êthos*). Next, he attempts to discredit his accuser by portraying him as a bully. The contrasting picture that Hermes paints between Apollo, in the strength of his prime, and himself, a newborn, serves both to put Zeus in a sympathetic frame of mind (*diathesis*) and to revisit the argument from *eikos*. To drive home this argument, Hermes repeats a line from his earlier speech, claiming that "I don't look like a cattle rustler, a strong man" (οὔ τι βοῶν ἐλατῆρι κραταιῶι φωτὶ ἐοικώς, 377). He thus invites his audience to view the evidence that his appearance presents. After this, Hermes employs *diathesis* again, first by reminding Zeus that he is his father in order to dispose him favorably, then by flattery, as he professes awe, love, and respect for the gods. This tone of reverence, along with Hermes' promise (once again) to swear an oath, serves to reinforce his character and credibility (*êthos*). Although Zeus is not convinced of Hermes' innocence as a result of the speech, he is nevertheless entertained: "Zeus laughed out loud when he saw the wicked boy making his fine, expert denials (εὖ καὶ ἐπισταμένως ἀρνεόμενον) about the cows" (389–90). Zeus then commands Hermes to lead Apollo "and without deceit to show the place where he had hidden the sturdy cattle." Hermes makes no further attempt to argue his innocence. As Clay points out, he has already achieved his aim: "After all, he had never expected to refute Apollo's charges but, instead, had manipulated the situation to gain access to Olympus and thereby to win official recognition of his divine status and the paternity of Zeus."[15]

A final example of Hermes' rhetorical prowess occurs in his exchange with Apollo regarding the lyre that Hermes has fashioned. Apollo requests the lyre in return for a guarantee: "I shall introduce you to the immortals, to enjoy prestige and fortune. I shall give you fine gifts, and never deceive you" (460–62). This simple offer of incentives is met by "crafty words" (again the phrase μύθοισιν κερδαλέοισιν, 463) from Hermes, who flatters his brother by citing his status and skill at learning any art:

> And they say you have the privilege of prophetic knowledge from Zeus' utterance, Far-shooter, the complete revelation of Zeus' will; in which I myself have now learned that you are richly endowed. You can help yourself to the knowledge you want. But as your heart is set on playing the lyre, play it, make music, and be festive, accept it from me; and you, dear friend, give me **prestige** (κῦδος) in turn.
> (H. Herm. 471–77)

Only after he has thus put Apollo in a favorable state of mind through flattery (*diathesis*) and offered the lyre in an **enthymeme** premise arguing from the **topic of incentives and disincentives** does Hermes casually insert his own demand for prestige (the enthymeme conclusion). "In passing, the wily Hermes hints broadly at the nature of the gift he would like to receive from

Apollo," observes Clay—namely, the sort of reputation, κῦδος, enjoyed by the gods.[16]

Of all the Homeric Hymns, the *Hymn to Hermes* is richest in the technical features of rhetoric that would later be identified in Aristotle's theory. Hermes' defense speeches are a match for some of the Iliadic speeches analyzed in chapter 2 in terms of their range, accumulation, and canny deployment of techniques such as *êthos*, *diathesis*, and *eikos*.

The final long Hymn in the traditional ordering, the *Hymn to Aphrodite* (Hymn 5), contains several speeches intended to persuade. In none of these, however, does the speaker move beyond simple prayer or command attached to a single reason or threat. Thus the level of rhetoric in the *Hymn to Aphrodite* is much the same as that in the *Hymn to Demeter*. The first rhetorical speech in the poem is Anchises' address to Aphrodite at 92–106, in which he promises to build her an altar in return for her blessing:

> I will build you an altar on a hilltop, in a conspicuous place, and make goodly
> sacrifices to you at every due season. Only have a kindly heart, and grant that I
> may be a man outstanding among the Trojans, and make my future offspring
> healthy, and myself to live long and well, seeing the light of the sun and enjoying
> good fortune among the peoples, and to reach the doorstep of old age. (*H. Aph.*
> 100–106)

This **enthymeme** is comprised of a simple premise from the **topic of consideration of incentives and disincentives** followed by a series of requests—in essence, a prayer formula. As Clay observes of this speech, Anchises makes a promise and "upon this promise, in accordance with the normal sequence of prayer, follows a request. . . . It is the prayer of a moderate and sensible man who recognizes the superiority of the gods and the limitations of the human condition."[17] Aphrodite's response contains the Hymn's next instance of rhetorical speech. First, she claims that Anchises was mistaken in taking her for a goddess; then she responds to his offer to build her an altar with a counterproposal, based on her claim to be a Phrygian princess with gifts to offer him:

> Now I beseech you by Zeus and your noble parents (**no humble people would have
> produced such a child as you**) (οὐ μὲν γάρ κε κακοὶ τοιόνδε τέκοιεν): take me, a virgin
> with no experience of love, and show me to your father and your dutiful mother . . .
> [My father and mother] will send you gold in plenty and woven cloth, and you must
> accept the many fine dowry gifts. When you have done that, hold a delightful wedding-
> feast that will impress men and immortal gods. (*H. Aph.* 131–42)

Here, again, is an **enthymeme** based on a premise using the **topic of incentives and disincentives**. While this topic is relatively simple in itself, Aphrodite elaborates upon it through an emphasis on her own biography and situation, an appeal to *êthos*. "In the course of her speech, Aphrodite manages to allude to her virginity, which makes her more desirable as a wife, her elevated social status, and the wealth that marriage to her will bring to Anchises—all in all, a masterful selling job on someone who hardly needs to be sold," Clay notes.[18] In addition to this enthymematic argument, Aphrodite's flattering parenthetical remark—that Anchises appears to be the child of noble parents—shows an attempt to dispose him favorably to her request (*diathesis*).

A final instance of rhetorical persuasion in this Hymn comes at the end of Aphrodite's long speech to Anchises (192–290) in which she reveals her true identity, gives him mythical background on the consequences of a goddess loving a mortal man, and informs him that she will bear him a son. In the final ten lines of the speech, Aphrodite shifts from giving information to making demands:

> You will take him straight away to windy Ilios. If anyone asks you who was the mother that got your dear son under her girdle, be sure to answer him as I tell you: say he is the child of a nymph. . . . But if you speak out and foolishly boast of having united in love with fair-garlanded Cytherea, Zeus will be angry and will strike you with a smoking bolt. There, I have told you everything. Take note of it, restrain yourself from mentioning me, and have regard for the gods' wrath. (*H. Aph.* 280–90)

As a whole, this speech from Aphrodite treats a wide range of subject matter, and compared to other speeches in the Hymns is "of a remarkable length," observes Peter Walcot. "Its contents are more than sufficiently varied to maintain interest—encouragement to Anchises, the stories of Ganymedes and Tithonos, an admission of her own sense of shame, instructions for the child's concealment from the world, and a final order, reinforced with a threat, to keep their mutual secret."[19] But while impressive in its variety, the speech is not particularly rhetorical, in the sense of employing persuasion; Aphrodite's only persuasive argument is the simple **enthymeme** formed by her request combined with the threat of Zeus' wrath (using fear, *pathos*, as a means of disposing Anchises to respond favorably to her request, *diathesis*). By invoking the lightning bolt of Zeus as a deterrent, Aphrodite effectively bullies her way to a promise of compliance from Anchises, and it is here that the Hymn ends.

Clearly, some understanding of rhetorical persuasion is present in the Homeric Hymns. Manifestations of persuasive techniques range from the relatively simple in the *Hymn to Demeter* and *Hymn to Aphrodite* to the more complex in the *Hymn to Apollo* and *Hymn to Hermes*. The narrative situations depicted in each Hymn are, of course, one reason for the differing amounts of persuasive speech that they contain. The *Hymn to Demeter* focuses on the often-solitary grief and endeavors of Demeter, as well as on cultic and ritual aspects of the goddess that are integral to her worship; there is little occasion for persuasion in these contexts. The *Hymn to Hermes*, by contrast, focuses on a string of confrontations between characters that involve accusation, defense, and supplication. In addition, crafty speech is the hallmark of Hermes himself. The persuasive speeches in the *Hymn to Apollo* and particularly the *Hymn to Hermes* nearly match those found in the *Iliad* in terms of their argumentative quality and diversity of techniques (enthymeme, *diathesis*, *êthos*, *pathos*, *eikos*, and the topic of incentives are all used in the *Hymn to Hermes*; only *paradeigma*, *gnômê*, and a greater diversity of Aristotelian topics are lacking from the Hymns in comparison with the stock of techniques used in Iliadic rhetoric). Perhaps more than any other Archaic poetry after Homer, then, the Hymns propagate the literary "lineage" of rhetoric in Archaic Greece—a lineage beginning with Homer and ending with the crystallization of represented rhetorical speech into theory in the writings of the sophists, Plato, and Aristotle.

The widely varying amounts and sophistication of rhetorical speech within the longer Hymns may also suggest something about the Hymns' relative chronology. Although the lack of any external evidence and the fluid nature of the Hymns' early development via oral tradition make it impossible to know their composition dates with any certainty, internal evidence (diction, vocabulary, and certain references) has led scholars to make some postulations. The *Hymn to Hermes* is generally believed to be the latest of the long Hymns, with proposed dates ranging from the mid/late sixth century to as late as the fifth.[20] Scholarly opinion has coalesced around the idea that the *Hymn to Aphrodite* is earliest of the four, dating to the early seventh or possibly even the late eighth century, according to Nicholas Richardson.[21] It is suggestive that these two Hymns, anchoring the beginning and ending points in a tentative relative chronology of the four long Hymns, are the two that contain, respectively, the least and greatest amount of "rhetorical" speech in my analysis. Such a correspondence lends itself to the theory that the understanding and use of rhetorical techniques generally increased over time. Tracing a progression toward increasing rhetorical complexity over time in the Archaic era is difficult when the surviving texts are so few and so disparate in genre, performance context, and structure. The Homeric Hymns are better suited for such an observation than

most Archaic texts because they form a surviving set of generically related poems composed over several hundred years, and because they contain so much
embedded direct speech. A relative chronology based upon increasing rhetorical sophistication in the long Hymns, then, would render the order as *Hymn to
Aphrodite, Hymn to Demeter, Hymn to Apollo,* and finally *Hymn to Hermes* (again
eliding the possibility that the Delian and Pythian portions of the *Hymn to Apollo*
are separate poems). This is the same order that other scholars have proposed
on different grounds.[22] I am by no means arguing that rhetorical sophistication
alone can tell us the relative dates of these Hymns, but rather that, in the case of
the Hymns, a trajectory toward increasing rhetorical complexity over time is cor-
roborated by other relative dating criteria that has been applied to these poems. If
this trajectory is generalized to Archaic literature more broadly (with the caveat
that it is complicated by considerations of genre), then the highly rhetorical
speeches of tragedy and the rise of rhetorical theory in the fifth century can be
seen, in a sense, as the culmination of this trajectory—not as a new invention
altogether. This notion of a trajectory makes the high levels of complex rhetoric
within the Homeric epics look all the more remarkable.

II. HORTATORY ELEGY

What is the place of Archaic lyric poetry in the transmission of rhetoric from its
systematic literary representation in Homer to its systematic theoretical representation in the fifth and fourth centuries? This question is a difficult one to
answer because of the variety of forms and performance occasions, and the
diverse generic terrain, encompassed by the designation "lyric."[23] It is possible
to make a few broad generalizations pertinent to this study: among the formal
characteristics of lyric poetry is a tendency to eschew linear narrative, with its
alternation of authorial voice and character speech. Thus relatively few lyric poems contain instances of the embedded direct speech that occurs in epic poetry.
Any analysis of lyric direct speech aimed at persuasion is complicated by the
difficulty of determining what exactly constitutes "direct speech" in lyric poetry.
For instance, how ought we to account for the self-identified, first-person voice
that characterizes much of Archaic lyric? In these cases, the poet could be seen
as speaking "in character," that is, in direct speech (whether that character is a
prima facie representation of the poet him / herself, or an assumed persona). The
phenomenon of rhetoric in the lyric voice has been treated in considerable depth
by Walker, who argues that lyric poetry contains "epideictic argumentation" and
provides a paradigm for later rhetoric: "The paradigm these poems embody is

that of enthymematic, epideictic argument in sung or spoken verse that is understood to function as civic discourse, or what the sophists would come to call *politikos logos*, and that is therefore also understood to engage its audience in a suasory transaction calling for an act of judgment in response to the enthymemes presented in or through the poem."[24] Walker's analysis of rhetorical poetics in Archaic lyric thus provides a higher-order parallel to my own analysis, as he explores the rhetoric of a poem taken as a whole—a "suasory transaction" between poet and audience—rather than the rhetoric of represented speech. In tracing the literary lineage of rhetoric through the diverse terrain of Archaic lyric, I have attempted to limit my analysis to examples of represented or embedded persuasion, so as to maintain a parallel with the direct speech I have analyzed in Homer and the Homeric Hymns. Lyric poetry in which rhetorical persuasion issues from the first-person poetic voice primarily takes two forms: exhortation poetry and advice poetry. The former includes the hortatory elegies of Callinus and Tyrtaeus, who attempt to motivate their countrymen to military action; the latter falls into the category of wisdom literature, and will be treated in section III. Lyric poetry containing rhetorical direct speech will be examined in section IV.

The seventh-century elegiac poems of Callinus and Tyrtaeus closely echo Iliadic battlefield speeches, an affinity that Joachim Latacz has treated at length.[25] This is perhaps not surprising, given the subject matter of the poems: Callinus' sole surviving elegy is a rousing call to action against an invading enemy (either the Cimmerians or the Magnesians) addressed to his Ephesian countrymen; Tyrtaeus' elegies are primarily concerned with exhorting his fellow Spartans to fight during the Second Messenian War.[26] I examine the rhetorical features of the Callinus elegy (fr. 1 West) as representative of this lyric subgenre. Callinus begins with a fierce indictment of his audience's complacency and cowardice:

> How long are you going to lie idle? Young men, when will you have a courageous spirit? Don't those who live round about make you feel ashamed of being so utterly passive? You think that you are sitting in a state of peace, but all the land is in the grip of war. . . .[27] (1–4)

The overall rhetorical scheme of this poem can be outlined as moving from *pathos* to *logos* (dominated by enthymematic argument). These opening two couplets, with their insistent and scornful questions, plunge immediately into the technique of shaming the audience (a play on their emotions, **pathos**). This technique becomes explicit with the question "Don't those who live round about make you feel ashamed of being so utterly passive?" (οὐδ' αἰδεῖσθ' ἀμφιπερικτίονας /

ὧδε λίην μεθιέντες, 2–3), which invokes external sources of indictment to add fuel to Callinus' shame campaign. In addition, Callinus emphasizes the contrast between the comfortable situation of his intended audience—young men reclining at a symposium, as suggested by the opening line κατάκεισθε—and the desperate straits of their country gripped by war (3–4). This constitutes an appeal to pity to go along with the appeal to shame; both serve the broader function of **diathesis**, as they dispose the audience to heed Callinus' exhortation.

After a lacuna in the text, we find the apparent conclusion to an enthymeme: "even as one is dying let him make a final cast (ἀκοντισάτω) of his javelin" (5). This imperative command sets in motion a series of **enthymemes** in which command-conclusions alternate with reason-premises:

> For (γάρ) it is a splendid honour for a man to fight on behalf of his land, children, and wedded wife against the foe. Death will occur only when the Fates have spun it out. Come, let a man charge straight ahead, brandishing his spear and mustering a stout heart behind his shield, as soon as war is engaged. For (γάρ) it is in no way fated that a man escape death, not even if he has immortal ancestors in his lineage. (6–13)

The enthymematic premises appear here in the form of two **gnômai**, offering reasons for heeding the commands between which they are sandwiched. Of the argument contained in the first *gnômê*—that "it is a splendid honour for a man to fight on behalf of his land, children, and wedded wife" (6–7)—Douglas Gerber, among others, notes that Callinus' emphasis on family as a motivation for fighting is a departure from Homer's emphasis on personal glory.[28] But the second *gnômê*—"Death will occur only when the Fates have spun it out" (8–9)—contains a sentiment familiar from Iliadic speakers. Compare these lines to Sarpedon's battlefield exhortation to Glaucus: "seeing that the spirits of death stand close about us in their thousands, no man can turn aside nor escape them, let us go on" (*Iliad* 12.326–28). Callinus then delivers another imperative ("Come, let a man charge straight ahead," 9), supported by a restatement of the *gnômê* about fate governing mortal life: "For it is in no way fated that a man escape death" (12–13).

To conclude the elegy, Callinus offers a final premise for the enthymematic argument that has been at the center of the entire poem, namely that the Ephesians should fight. This premise takes the form of a fictional *paradeigma*, a tale of two soldiers:

> Often one who has escaped from the strife of battle and the thud of javelins and has returned home meets with his allotted death in his house. But he is not in any

case loved or missed by the people, whereas the other, if he suffer some mishap, is mourned by the humble and the mighty. All the people miss a stout-hearted man when he dies and while he lives he is the equal of demigods. For in the eyes of the people he is like a tower, since single-handed he does the deeds of many. (14–21)

Callinus plays to his audience's self-conceptions, as well as their civic values, in drawing a sharp contrast between the fates of the deserter and the heroic warrior. The former is not "loved or missed by the people" (οὐκ . . . δήμῳ φίλος οὐδὲ ποθεινός), while the latter is revered in life and mourned in death. This implied offer of status within the community for anyone who fights courageously is an appeal to the **topic of consideration of incentives and disincentives**, and resembles the Homeric incentive of κλέος ἄφθιτον; but here again the emphasis is on civic protection rather than on individual glory. Rather than restate his command that the audience rise and fight, Callinus ends the poem with a strong image of the model that they should emulate: a "tower" of strength, who alone does the work of many men. Within a short space, Callinus' rhetoric has incorporated shaming, logical reasoning, and an appeal to his audience's disposition and (presumably) desires—many of the same persuasive tactics that Homer's characters had employed.

Tyrtaeus' fragments 10–12 take a similar rhetorical approach, evoking the emotions of shame and pity and arguing for fortitude in battle with enthymemes predicated on the incentive of glory and admiration from the community, and the disincentive of a life of poverty and shame. In general, Callinus and Tyrtaeus tend to place greater emphasis than do Iliadic speakers on the cause of defending homeland and family, and on the rewards or punishments that a warrior will receive from the civic community for his actions in battle. These elegiac poets nevertheless stand alongside the *Hymn to Apollo* and the *Hymn to Hermes* as containing the closest match, within Archaic poetry, to the rhetoric of Iliadic speakers in terms of variety of techniques and complexity of argumentative structure. This similarity is no doubt attributable to the wartime context and the exhortation function shared by the elegies and many of the *Iliad*'s persuasive speeches.

III. GREEK WISDOM LITERATURE

Nothing in Archaic Greek wisdom literature approaches the degree of complexity and diversity in persuasive argumentation that exists in Homer. For comparative purposes, however, it is worth noting the types of persuasion found in this genre, and I take Hesiod's *Works and Days* and the elegies of Theognis as representatives.[29] Within these works, rhetoric takes a form different from anything we have examined thus far: namely, a didactic first-person authorial voice. The *Works and Days* is the earliest Greek contribution to a long tradition of wisdom literature that originated in the Near East and is marked by exhortation and instruction addressed to a specific person or group—in Hesiod's case, to both his brother Perses and unjust kings.[30] Since Hesiod presents the *Works and Days* in the form of instructive / persuasive discourse, he inhabits a middle ground between the elaborate, technique-heavy rhetoric displayed in persuasive speeches in (for example) the *Iliad*, and the broader sense of rhetoric as it is commonly used in modern literary criticism—that is, an author's attempt to convince his audience of the reality of the literary world he has created.

West, in his commentary on the *Works and Days*, identifies the following features of the authorial voice: "Hesiod uses a variety of means to diversify and strengthen his sermon: myth, parable, allegory, proverbial maxims, threats of divine anger."[31] In terms of Aristotelian rhetorical technique, these features are all varieties of enthymematic premises. The didactic portion of the *Works and Days* is essentially a series of enthymemes whose conclusions—commands to work hard, to follow Justice (*Dikê*), and to cultivate the earth in various ways—are followed by sententious maxims or threats, often similar to each other and usually invoking the gods. The instructive / persuasive mode shows up briefly near the beginning of the poem (27–36), where Hesiod offers a preview of the chiding tone that he will take in earnest with Perses later; it is only in lines 213ff. that Hesiod turns from his mythological focus to the rebuke and exhortation which characterize the poem's second half. Lines 213–47 are representative of Hesiod's authorial rhetoric, as they involve an exhortation followed by a series of *gnômai* (signaled at several points by the word γάϱ). Altogether this forms an extended **enthymeme**:

As for you, Perses, give heed to Justice and do not foster Outrageousness. For (γάϱ) Outrageousness is evil in a worthless mortal; and even a fine man cannot bear her easily, but encounters calamities and then is weighed down under her. The better road is the one towards what is just, passing her by on the other side. Justice wins out over Outrageousness when she arrives at the end; but the fool only knows this after he has suffered. . . . Those who give straight judgments to foreigners and fellow-citizens and do not turn aside from justice at all, their city blooms and the people in it flower. . . . But to those who care only for evil outrageousness and cruel deeds, far-seeing Zeus, Cronus' son, marks out justice. . . .

Upon them, Cronus' son brings forth woe from the sky, famine together with pestilence, and the people die away.[32] (*Works and Days* 213–43)

Although Hesiod gives several different reasons for why Perses should "give heed to Justice" and "not foster Outrageousness," they all make the same essential point: that it is in Perses' best interests to do these things. The enthymematic premise, restated multiple times, alternates between stock incentives and pious threats. Both the incentives and the threats rest on the understanding that the gods—both Zeus and personified Right—are active in dispensing reward and punishment to humans. There is a lack of diversified rhetorical approaches to persuasion here (as in the *Works and Days* more broadly). Hesiod makes no attempt to tailor his argument to Perses specifically—that is, to employ *diathesis*—nor does he appeal to his own *êthos* or try to incite Perses' emotions (unless one deems the vague threats of divine punishment enough to instill emotional fear). The *gnômai* he employs are generalized enough to apply to a much broader audience, as is typical of wisdom literature.

Hesiod then turns his attention and rebuke to the unspecified kings, whom he accuses of treating him unjustly:

As for you kings, too, ponder this justice yourselves. For (γάρ) among human beings there are immortals nearby, who take notice of all those who grind one another down with crooked judgments and have no care for the gods' retribution. . . . Bear this in mind, kings, and straighten your discourses, you gift-eaters, and put crooked judgments quite out of your minds. A man contrives evil for himself when he contrives evil for someone else, and the evil plan is most evil for the planner. (*Works and Days* 248–66)

Not only is the enthymeme pattern the same here as it was in Hesiod's exhortation to Perses, the argument is the same as well: commands followed by threats of divine retribution. This is, indeed, the extent of persuasive technique in the *Works and Days*. There is more of the same type of argumentation in subsequent passages addressed to Perses (274ff.), but there is nothing any more rhetorically complex or varied, judging by Aristotelian criteria of *êthos*, *diathesis*, *logos*, and the numerous subcategories thereof. As West puts it, "Hesiod's arguments for Dike and for work are essentially of a very simple form. Dike is good because the gods reward it. Hybris is bad because the gods punish it. Work is good because it brings prosperity, independence, and hence social status."[33] While Martin has argued convincingly that a highly complex authorial strategy lies behind this "simple form," this complexity is rather on

the "macro" level of narrative than on the "micro" level of rhetorical arguments and techniques.[34]

Greek wisdom literature continues to have a life in Archaic lyric (primarily
elegiac) poetry. The so-called "paraenetic" elegies of Theognis and Solon contain instruction occasionally attended by maxims about the state of society or
the way the world operates, forming strings of perfunctory enthymemes.[35] As
in the *Works and Days*, these enthymemes depend on incentives or threats; likewise, the elegiac authors lack audience-sensitive *diathesis* appeals, and do not
make reference to their own character (*êthos*) as part of their argument. Contributing to these features, perhaps, is the generalized nature of the audience
to which these poets speak. Cyrnus, the frequent addressee in the Theognidean
corpus, has no discernible personality; he is simply the receptacle for Theognis'
instruction, in much the same role as Perses serves for Hesiod. Typical of the
rhetoric of paraenetic elegy is this generalized advice from Theognis:

> Do not seek the company of base men, but always cling to the noble. Drink and
> dine with them, sit with them, and be pleasing to those whose power is great. For
> (γάǫ) from the noble you will learn noble things, but if you mingle with the base,
> you will lose even the sense you have.[36] (1.31–36)

This passage is a prosaic **enthymeme** based on the ***gnômê*** that one becomes like
one's friends, and the implied incentive that good-quality friends will be beneficial. The proverb-admonition formula is the simplest form of rhetorical argument; Theognis makes no attempt to personalize his speech to his addressee,
nor does he give any indication that he knows Cyrnus' points of susceptibility to
persuasion.

While there is some overlap in the methods of persuasion used by Homer
and the authorial voice in wisdom literature, then, there is even more difference. Hesiod and Theognis, like Homer's characters, use basic enthymematic
argumentation (featuring threats, *paradeigmata*, and gnômai) in their attempts
to persuade. All of these methods can be identified in the wisdom literature of
contemporary, as well as earlier, Near Eastern societies.[37] The difference between Homeric speech and Near Eastern wisdom literature appears most prominently in the scope and complexity of the rhetorical techniques used by the two
literatures. Homeric persuasion *includes* basic enthymematic argumentation,
but it also contains much more: the use of a wide variety of Aristotelian topics
as enthymeme premises; arguments and appeals tailored to the particular audience (*diathesis*) and explicit appeals to the speaker's credibility and character
(*êthos*); and the combination of multiple techniques within a persuasive argu-

ment. These features distinguish Homeric speech from the litany of commands and proverbs that characterize Hesiod and Theognis as well as Sumerian, Akkadian, Babylonian, Egyptian, and Hebrew wisdom literature. The constraints of genre go a long way toward explaining the paucity of rhetorical speech within wisdom literature, in that authors of wisdom literature by definition speak from positions of authority. Hesiod's authority to instruct his brother Perses is assumed throughout the *Works and Days*, as is Theognis' authority to instruct Cyrnus in his elegies. Their authorial status—implicit in the wisdom genre—removes the necessity for carefully crafted or sophisticated persuasive argumentation, and in particular the strategy of appealing to *êthos*.

No examination of rhetoric within Greek wisdom literature would be complete without taking account of the Muses as a locus for persuasion in Hesiod. Friedrich Solmsen has pointed out Hesiod's conception of a "twofold gift of the Muses": poetry and effective speech. These gifts are not learned but are simply bestowed by the Muses—on poets such as Hesiod through an "awakening" or "calling," and on kings from birth.[38] This idea is expressed at the end of Hesiod's catalogue of Muses in the *Theogony*, where a description of Calliope's role contains a description of persuasive speech practiced by kings:

> [Calliope] is the greatest of them all, for she attends upon venerated kings too. Whomever among Zeus-nourished kings the daughters of great Zeus honor and behold when he is born, they pour sweet dew upon his tongue, **and his words flow soothingly from his mouth** (τοῦ δ' ἔπε' ἐκ στόματος ῥεῖ μείλιχα). All the populace look to him as he decides disputes with straight judgments; and speaking publicly without erring, he quickly ends even a great quarrel by his skill. For this is why kings are wise, because when the populace is being harmed in the assembly they easily manage to turn the deeds around, **effecting persuasion with mild words** (μαλακοῖσι παραιφάμενοι ἐπέεσσιν). . . . That man is blessed, whomever the Muses love, **for the speech flows sweet from his mouth** (γλυκερή οἱ ἀπὸ στόματος ῥέει αὐδή).[39] (*Theogony* 79–97)

Hesiod's attention to the gift of speech leaves no doubt that he prized persuasive and eloquent words. In contrast to Homer, however, he does not depict the cultivation of this eloquence, or mention the necessity of practice or even skill in speaking; nor do his represented speeches contain any but the most basic argumentative techniques. For Hesiod, honeyed and persuasive words are simply *granted* to kings by the Muses, and thus bear some resemblance to what Marcel Detienne would call "magico-religious" speech—that is, speech that derives its efficacy from religious power rather than from human cultivation.[40]

Despite the relative chronological proximity of the Homeric poems and Archaic wisdom literature, then, there are vast differences between the two in terms of their rhetorical development. Too often, the designation "Archaic" is applied in a way that glosses over distinctions between authors of the time period that it encompasses, and the treatment of speech is one of those distinctions. Discourse in Archaic literature has been described as "arhetorical" (Cole), as possessing "native vigor" (Kennedy), or as "magico-religious," Detienne's term for the characteristic mode of speech in this era, in contrast with the "secular" discourse of the Classical era.[41] These ways of characterizing speech in Archaic literature are themselves problematic, relying as they do on the narrative of Greek society shifting "from *mythos* to *logos*"—a view that I will address in chapter 6, section IV. Suffice it to say here that Detienne and others are, in a very general sense, promoting an idea of the ancient Greek world that has Aristotelian origins: namely, that there is a stark dichotomy between the poetic, magico-religious authoritative discourse of the Archaic age and the prosaic, techno-philosophical authoritative discourse of the Classical era. This line of thinking has produced an unfortunate conceptual barrier to the recognition that a technique-based mode of discourse, namely rhetoric, *does* occur within the earliest Archaic literature. But such thinking also stumbles in its portrayal of Archaic literature as monolithic. While Hesiod and other Archaic wisdom poets might better fit the description of what Detienne calls a "system of thought in which speech . . . was itself regarded as a natural power or dynamic reality acting spontaneously,"[42] this description does not fairly represent the Homeric view of speech. Speech in Homer is not divinely bestowed upon speakers in the form of uncontrolled inspiration. Iliadic speakers cultivate speaking as a skill; they learn and teach it; they employ logical argumentation in the service of persuasion; and they practice persuasive speech with varying degrees of talent and effectiveness (sometimes even disputing each others' prowess, as Polydamas and Hector do at *Iliad* 12.211–50).

IV. LYRIC

Lyric poetry containing embedded direct speech is the final category of Archaic poetry whose rhetorical qualities may be compared with Homer's. The instances of represented character speech in Archaic lyric (much less represented rhetoric) are few, given that the poems tend to be short in length and nonnarrative in form. What instances there are can be found in lyrics whose subject matter is similar to that of the Homeric epics—namely, heroic themes and characters.

The narrative lyric poetry of Stesichorus falls into this category: according to Emmet Robbins, it was "classified in antiquity as ἔπη, for it was suited to epic themes."[43] The 33-line papyrus fragment known as the "Lille Stesichorus" treats a story drawn from the epic cycle and features a speech exhibiting rhetorical elements.[44] In the speech, the unnamed mother of Eteocles and Polyneices (I follow convention in calling her Jocasta) addresses a joint audience of her sons and the prophet Teiresias in an attempt to mediate her sons' dispute before it leads to bloodshed.[45]

The fragment begins with Jocasta addressing Teiresias, who has apparently just delivered a dire prophecy concerning her sons' war and fratricide:

Do not add to my woes the burden of worry,
or raise grim prospects for my future life.
For (γάρ) the immortal gods
have not ordained for men on this holy earth
unchanging enmity for all their days. . . .
they set men's outlook for the day.[46] (PMG 222(b).201–8)

The first element of Jocasta's rhetoric is a simple **enthymeme**, its conclusion (that Teiresias "not add to my woes the burden of worry") supported by the wishful *gnômê* that the gods ordain human relations to be variable. Then, after expressing the hope that Apollo will not fulfill Teiresias' prophecy, Jocasta makes a play for her audience's pity in the form of a death-wish.

But if I am destined to see
my sons slain by each other, if the Fates
have so dispensed, then may
death's ghastly close be mine straightway . . . (PMG 222(b).211–13)

Her expressions of self-pity and threats of self-harm surely are intended more for her sons than for Teiresias. This is a particularly manipulative incarnation of the *pathos* technique, aided by a reference to her own role as mother of Eteocles and Polyneices (*êthos*). Jan Bremer notes that her conditional argument—a wish to die in the event of some disaster occurring—constitutes "a specific variation on a Homeric theme," of which he cites as Homeric examples Priam's address to the Trojans in *Iliad* 24.244–46, Andromache's to Hector in 6.464–65, and Odysseus' to Telemachus in *Od.* 16.106–11, among others.[47] More than simply a "theme," I would argue that it is a rhetorical trope shared by these speakers, calculated both to express their abhorrence of a situation and to engender pity leading to action in their audience (e.g., Andromache to convince Hector to stay out of battle; Odysseus to incite Telemachus to fight the suitors).

In the second half of the speech, Jocasta turns to address her sons explicitly with a conciliatory proposal in the form of an **enthymeme**. As the enthymeme conclusion, Jocasta commands that they employ the impartial method of drawing lots to determine the distribution of their inheritance, with one son receiving the royal palace and the other receiving the remainder of their father's property (219–24). As the enthymeme premise, she offers an appeal to the **topic of consideration of incentives and disincentives**: the chance to avoid, or at least postpone, their prophesied doom:

> This, I think, should prove
> the way to free you from an evil fate
> as this godly seer foretells,
> if truly Kronos' son [is to preserve]
> King Cadmus' people and city,
> and put off to later times whatever ill
> is fated for our clan. (PMG 222(b).225–31)

In addition to the rhetorical strategies that Jocasta employs, her speech bristles with declarations and confident assurances—"Here's how I declare the outcome for you" (219); "This, I think, should prove the way to free you from an evil fate" (225–26)—in the hope that her words will be enough to stave off the events foretold by Teiresias. As Anne Burnett notes, "The speech shows a woman who marshals extraordinary inner forces so as to defeat her own fear, dominate those about her, and evade the expressed will of the gods."[48]

Jocasta's speech is declared effective by the narrator, who comments, "So spoke the lady **with appeasing words** (μύθοις ἀγ[α]νοῖς), seeking to check her sons from combat in the house, and the seer Teiresias supported her. **They agreed** (οἱ δ᾽ [ἐ]πίθο[ντο] . . .)" (232–34). A similar formula for describing appeasing or persuasive speech, ἀγανοῖς ἐπέεσιν, occurs several times in the Iliad (2.164, 180, 189; 24.772). In the single speech of the Lille fragment, the persuasive strategies of a parent addressing her children resemble those of certain Iliadic speeches (particularly the emotionally charged appeals of Andromache, Priam, and Hecuba to Hector). It also serves as a bridge of sorts in the transmission of rhetorical speech to a later genre of poetry; as Robbins observes, the Lille Stesichorus "anticipates tragedy."[49]

The epinician odes of Baccylides and Pindar also contain mythical narratives with embedded direct speech.[50] The speeches in Bacchylides' odes generally serve to inform or praise another character, rather than to attempt to persuade—perhaps not surprising, given the genre's encomiastic function. The only direct speech among Bacchylides' surviving works that depicts a persuasion attempt with significant use of rhetorical techniques occurs not among the epinicians, but in dithyramb 3 (ode 17), which depicts an episode within Thesean myth.[51] As this poem opens, the Athenian ship is sailing towards Crete bearing its human tribute when Minos (having traveled to Athens to hand-pick the 14 Athenian youths) assaults one of the maidens under Theseus' charge. Theseus issues an impassioned rebuke of the king that serves as the catalyst for this poem's central conflict and heroic feat—a superhuman journey in which he reaches the underwater halls of Poseidon and finds favor with queen Amphitrite, only to resurface to the acclaim of the Athenian youths.

Theseus' speech is a persuasion attempt ostensibly aimed at making Minos desist from his rape of Eriboea, but also serving to establish his own role as challenger to Minos' authority and status. His form of address is respectful, underscoring the rebuke that follows:

> Son of peerless Zeus, in your breast you no longer steer thoughts that are righteous: **restrain your arrogant might, hero** (ἴσχε μεγαλοῦχον ἥρως βίαν). Whatever all-powerful Fate has ordained for us from the gods and the scales of Justice confirm, we shall fulfil it as our destined portion when it comes. But **check your disastrous intention** (βαρεῖαν κάτεχε μῆτιν). What if the noble daughter of Phoenix, maiden with love in her name, bore you, peerless among mortals, after union with Zeus under the brow of mount Ida? Why, the daughter of wealthy Pittheus bore me after drawing close to the sea-god Poseidon. . . . Therefore, warlord of the Cnossians, I tell you to **curb an insolence which will bring much sorrow** (πολύστονον ἐρύκεν ὕβριν); for (γὰρ) I should not wish to see the lovely light of immortal Dawn if once you had forcibly assaulted any of this youthful band; sooner than that **we shall display the might of our hands** (χειρῶν βίαν δε[ί]ξομεν), and God will decide the outcome.[52] (17.20–46)

Over the course of the speech, Theseus issues three syntactically parallel commands to Minos that form a sort of rhetorical *tricolon*: "restrain your arrogant might" (23), "check your disastrous intention" (28–29), and "curb your grief-causing insolence" (40–41). These commands are **enthymeme** conclusions for which the premise is the threat that ends the speech. Theseus threatens Minos with βία (the same word that he used to characterize Minos' transgression in line 23), a show of force that will match and overpower Minos' βία. But this stark enthymeme based on evoking the emotion of fear (**pathos**) is not Theseus' only rhetorical strategy. In addressing Minos as "hero" (23) near the beginning of the speech, Theseus shows that he is aware of Minos' birth and status. His applica-tion of the label in the context of rebuke is a sort of aggressive *diathesis*-strategy: it flatteringly suggests that Minos is capable of a hero's behavior, while at the same time indicting him for falling short. As such, Theseus' strategy recalls the antagonistic call to a higher standard appearing in several Iliadic speeches (e.g., Polydamas to Hector at 12.211–29, Hector to Polydamas at 12.231–50, Sarpedon to Glaucus at 12.310–28, and Polydamas to Hector at 13.726–47). In addition, he highlights his own trustworthy character (*êthos*) by contrasting his pious obedience to fate—"whatever all-powerful Fate has or-dained for us from the gods . . . we shall fulfil it as our destined portion"—with Minos' "disastrous intention."

Theseus takes a bolder tone in his next argument, which is a claim to equal footing with Minos in the area of paternity. He refers flatteringly to Minos as βροτῶν φέρτατον (32–33); both the choice of the adjective φέρτατος and the con-text of comparing two heroes in terms of virtue and breeding are, as Herwig Maehler notes, reminiscent of Nestor's conciliatory speech to Agamemnon and Achilles at *Iliad* 1.280–81: εἰ δὲ σὺ καρτερός ἐσσι, θεὰ δέ σε γείνατο μήτηρ, / ἀλλ' ὅ γε φέρτερός ἐστιν.[53] Theseus uses the adjective not so much to placate Minos as to show him respect (*diathesis*), which he in turn demands Minos show to him since he is likewise the son of a god (*êthos*). This flattery constitutes an ad-ditional enthymematic premise for the command to "curb your grief-causing insolence"; Minos should behave in a manner befitting his kingly and heroic status. Having made this appeal to Minos' better nature, Theseus ends the speech on the threatening note discussed above, and with his final words ap-peals to the gods as arbiters ("God will decide the outcome"), once again dis-playing his pious *êthos*. The listening sailors are dazzled by Theseus' bold words (48–50), but the speech is not well received by its primary audience: Minos re-sponds (52–66) with a challenge to Theseus that sets in motion the remaining action of the poem.

The extant corpus of Pindar, considerably larger than that of Bacchylides and remarkable in that it preserves four complete books of epinician odes, neverthe-less contains only a handful of speeches that depict persuasion attempts. Such direct speeches occur during the mythological portions of the odes, wherein Pindar turns from praising the victor in his authorial persona to recounting a narrative in the third person. By my reckoning, only the speeches of Pelops to Poseidon (*Olympian* 1.75–85), Jason to Pelias (*Pythian* 4.138–55), Pelias to Jason (*Pythian* 4.156–67), and Themis to the assembled Olympians (*Isthmian* 8.35–45) qualify as represented rhetorical persuasion within Pindar's odes. Although "Pindar's rhetoric" has been the subject of much scholarly attention, it is primarily the rhetoric of the authorial voice, rather than of character speech, that has been studied.[54] My examination of rhetoric in the Pindaric odes is, as usual, limited to the direct speeches of characters who are trying to persuade others to action within the poems' mythical narratives, for it is these speeches that provide the closest parallel to Homeric rhetorical speeches.

Of the four speeches mentioned above that employ rhetorical strategies to persuade an internal audience, I take Jason's speech in *Pythian* 4.138–55 as representative of Pindar's grasp of such strategies. This speech is reported as part of the Argonautic myth that dominates this uniquely lengthy Pindaric ode; it is an attempt to negotiate a peaceful distribution of power between Pelias (usurper of the throne of Iolchus) and Jason, the rightful and returning heir. As a stranger to Iolchus, Jason does not yet have the resources to reclaim the throne by force; instead, he must persuade Pelias to relinquish it. The narrative description of Jason's speech is rich with the vocabulary of persuasion: πραῢν δ' Ἰάσων / μαλθακᾷ φωνᾷ ποτιστάζων ὄαρον / βάλλετο κρηπῖδα σοφῶν ἐπέων ("In a soft voice Jason distilled soothing speech and laid the foundation of wise words," 136–38).[55] Jason begins by addressing Pelias respectfully as the son of Poseidon, and then offers a *gnômê* concerning human behavior: "The minds of mortals are all too swift to commend deceitful gain above justice, even though they are headed for a rough reckoning the day after" (139–40). Rather than emphasizing the inevitability of this gnomic outcome, however, Jason advocates moving beyond such commonplace behavior to a different, and nobler, course: "You and I, however, must rule our tempers with law and weave our future happiness" (141). Jason thus masks his first demand in a cloak of respect and cámaraderie. His contrast between "the minds of mortals" and the responsibilities of Pelias is intended to flatter the king, setting him apart from those he rules (*diathesis*). This strategy resembles Theseus' challenge to Minos in Bacchylides 17.23 ("restrain your arrogant might, hero"), which has a precedent in the antagonistic rhetoric between allied warriors of equal status in the *Iliad*. Jason simultaneously asserts himself as Pelias' equal by speaking about these kingly responsibilities as something necessary for "you *and I*." Jason continues to press his association with Pelias in the subsequent lines as he invokes their common ancestry from Enarea (142–45). These lines quite literally establish his *êthos*, as Jason identifies himself and his ancestry—and by implication his claim to the throne—for the benefit of Pelias and the members of Pelias' court to whom Jason is a stranger.

The central proposal of the speech is predicated on an appeal to propriety and reason, but the concluding lines mark a change in Jason's tone toward his rival:

> **It is not proper** (οὐ πρέπει) for the two of us to divide the great honor of our forefathers with bronze-piercing swords or javelins. For I give over to you the sheep, the tawny herds of cattle, and all the fields which you stole from my parents and administer to fatten your wealth—I do not mind if these overly enrich your house—but, as for the scepter of sole rule and the throne upon which Kretheus' son [Aison] once sat and rendered straight justice to his people of horsemen, these you must give up without grief on both sides, lest some more troubling evil arise for us from them. (*P.* 4.147–55)

Having established a bond between Pelias and himself, Jason now uses this bond as a reason to urge a peaceable transfer of rule. Within the **enthymeme** argument indicated by the reasoning that "it is not proper" for two kinsmen to resort to violence, Jason invokes the honor of their shared forefathers (μεγάλαν προγόνων τιμὰν) as both a premise and a *diathesis* strategy. The reminder of this familial bond is calculated to disarm Pelias' objections, as well as to provide a preemptive shaming device (*pathos*) should he respond with hostility. Jason's subsequent proposal of power distribution—couched as a demand more than a request—reveals a shift in his persuasive tactics. Up until this point, Jason has cultivated a friendly tone towards Pelias. Now he peppers his demands with accusations. He states the object of his persuasion in a concluding **enthymeme**, using as a premise the **topic of consideration of incentives and disincentives** in the form of a veiled threat: "These you must give up without grief on both sides, lest some more troubling evil arise for us from them."

Pelias responds "calmly" (ἀκᾷ) to this challenge, but he has no intention of complying with Jason: his ingratiating reply (156–67) includes the proposal that Jason recover the golden fleece before assuming kingship of Iolchus. On a rhetorical level, Jason's failure to persuade Pelias may be in part a result of what Charles Segal observes as the fundamental difference in the two men's "modes of utterance." Segal contrasts "Jason's frankness" with "Pelias' dissimulation"; they employ speech in ways that are respectively "open and closed, spontaneous and controlled."[56] In addition, the tone with which Jason ends his speech is perhaps too antagonistic to persuade an arrogant king (however valid his claim might be). As such, it follows in the tradition of persuasion attempts by Agamemnon, Polydamas, and others in the *Iliad* that fail through a disregard for their particular listener's sense of pride.

This brief examination of represented speech in Pindar only scratches the surface of the much larger subject of Pindar's attitude toward speech. One particular aspect of this attitude is relevant to my investigation of the connection between Homeric characters' practice of persuasion and the rhetorical theory of the Classical era. This is Pindar's frequent reflection on the capacity of speech (both his own and others') to promote both truth and falsehood.[57] In the famous meta-rhetorical passage in *Olympian* 1, for example, Pindar articulates the ambivalent power of speech (for which he uses three different terms in the space of four lines): "Wonders are many, but then too, I think, in men's talk (φάτις) stories (μῦθοι) are embellished beyond the true account (ἀλαθῆ λόγον) and deceive by means of elaborate lies" (28–29). Here and elsewhere, Pindar depicts speech as a tool which can be manipulated either in service of or in opposition to the truth, and this uneasiness about the combination of power and potential for deception foreshadows what will become the primary criticism of the discipline of rhetoric from the fifth century onward. In *Nemean* 7, Pindar links this notion of the convincingly deceptive power of speech to its prototypical perpetrator, Homer: "I believe that Odysseus' story (λόγον) has become greater than his actual suffering because of Homer's sweet verse, for upon his fictions and soaring craft (ψεύδεσί οἱ ποτανᾷ <τε> μαχανᾷ) rests great majesty, and his skill deceives with misleading tales (σοφία δὲ κλέπτει παράγοισα μύθοις)" (20–23). The clever efficiency of this densely meta-rhetorical passage is that its accusations apply equally well to the words of Homer—the ostensible though not unambiguous referent of the possessive oἱ—and those of Odysseus.[58] "Odysseus' story" could be either the λόγος told *about* Odysseus by Homer, or the λόγος told *by* Odysseus in the many versions of his life story that he offers to different audiences throughout the *Odyssey*; the σοφία that deceives with misleading μῦθοι could likewise characterize Homer's fictional narrative, or the cunning μῆτις of Odysseus, displayed so often in his Homeric speeches. Pindar's relationship with rhetorical direct speech thus might be summed up as nodding to Homer's prowess in this arena while placing his rhetorical emphasis elsewhere: namely, within the authorial voice, directed toward the single goal of praising victorious athletes. Where Homer's direct speeches display persuasive techniques covering a variety of subjects, situations, and audiences, Pindar prefers to reflect on speech as an abstract instrument, and above all to use this instrument in praise of victors and their communities.

Ultimately, lyric poetry—be it elegiac, iambic, or melic—does not have the structure or aim to support a narrative framework with lengthy persuasive speeches, which in turn allow for the diversity, complexity, and systematic deployment of rhetorical techniques found in Homeric epic. It is notable, however, that these lyric speeches all employ rhetorical techniques that mirror specific types of rhetoric—even specific speeches—within Homer. Stesichorus' Jocasta uses a *pathos* appeal in speaking to her sons that closely resembles Andromache's attempt to convince Hector to stay out of battle in *Iliad* 6. Theseus' address to Minos in Bacchylides 17 and Jason's speech to Pelias in Pindar's *Pythian* 4 combine acknowledgement of their rivals' birth and status with rebuke linked to the responsibilities conferred by this status—a strategy which finds a precursor in the rhetorical approaches of Nestor, Hector, Polydamas, and others in the *Iliad*. Thus on the rare occasions that a lyric speaking character tries to convince an internal audience, Homeric precedents seem to be close at hand.

_⌒ ⌒_

As chapter 2 demonstrated, many of the specific techniques identified and taught in Aristotelian rhetorical theory are present in Homeric speeches. As we have seen throughout this chapter, far fewer examples of this sort of technical level of rhetoric show up in non-Homeric Archaic poetry. Those Archaic compositions in which rhetoric *does* occur with more concentration and sophistication— such as the *Homeric Hymn to Hermes*, the exhortations of Callinus and Tyrtaeus, and speeches embedded in mythical narratives in choral lyric—tend to be those that bear the closest resemblance to Homer in their subject matter or their formal characteristics. The elegiac exhortations of Callinus and Tyrtaeus are similar to many of the speeches in the *Iliad* in terms of their battlefield context and occasion. The Homeric Hymns have formal similarities to Homer in terms of their hexameters, narrative structure, and represented direct speech. The lyrics of Stesichorus, Bacchylides, and Pindar have elements of both content and form in common with Homeric rhetoric, in that they treat mythical and heroic subjects and contain represented direct speech. It would seem, then, that Homer, whether through direct or indirect influence, showed the way for later authors in depicting rhetorical persuasion. Herodotus claimed that Homer and Hesiod, by means of their poems' pervasive cultural influence, "taught the Greeks their gods" (*Histories* 2.53); in much the same way, I am proposing that Homer taught the Greeks their rhetoric.

CHAPTER SIX

From Poetry to Theory

The fifth century BCE saw a burgeoning variety of literary and societal practices interacting with each other in Greece, and particularly in Athens. Competing with the Archaic poetic tradition were the new poetic forms of tragedy and comedy, the new prose forms of historiography and oratory, and the emerging disciplines of philosophy and rhetoric. In Athenian society, the institutions of radical democracy and the popular courts had, by the end of the fifth century, created a robust market in rhetorical skill. On the poetic front, the emergence of tragedy in fifth-century Athens supplied a dramatic increase in the body of pre-Aristotelian poetry that represented speech, and the cross-pollination between tragic *rhêseis* and the burgeoning sophistic movement increased toward the end of the fifth century. Euripides' language was thought by his own contemporaries to be influenced by sophistry, a reputation most famously caricatured in Aristophanes' *Frogs*. My aim throughout this study has been to trace the literary transmission of rhetoric from Homer to Aristotle, and to account for the rhetorical correspondences between these two authors. Examining how rhetoric moved from poetic representation into formal theory in the Classical era is the final step in this process.

I. TRAGEDY

Given its structural qualities, tragedy is a prime example of the phenomenon that I have highlighted in Homeric poetry: the poetic representation of rhetorical speech. Many tragic speeches have been the subject of analysis for their rhetorical qualities. The lawcourt scene in the *Eumenides* is tragedy's foremost example of judicial rhetoric, and other judicial / agonistic conflicts abound (e.g., the debate between Creon and Antigone in Sophocles' *Antigone*, or that between Helen and Hecuba in Euripides' *Trojan Women*). Euripidean plays in particular showcase argumentation and persuasion between characters, often with fatal consequences: Dionysus luring Pentheus into the Maenads' clutches in the *Bacchae*, for example, or the nurse tempting Phaedra into transgression in the *Hippolytus*.

Tragic rhetoric largely falls outside the purview of this project, however, for several reasons. First, Homeric poetry holds a unique place in this investigation because it contains the earliest (as well as the most extensive and elaborate) representation of speech in Greek literature. Tragic rhetoric is simply not as chronologically remarkable. A second and related reason is that most of the Greek tragedies that survive date to the mid- and late fifth century, meaning that their authors likely had contact with professional rhetorical instruction and theorization occurring in Athens at the same time; tragedy therefore lacks the pristine state of Archaic poetry with respect to theorized rhetoric. As Ober and Strauss have observed, "If political rhetoric makes use of the symbols and structures of tragedy, so too tragedy makes use of the symbols and structures of political rhetoric. . . . The rhetoric of politics in tragedy is largely the rhetoric of contemporary democratic Athens. Both tragic poets and political orators could see themselves as teachers: both aimed at the improvement of the citizen, both communicated through rhetoric."[1]

Third, the placement of speech within a narrative framework is the phenomenon in which I am particularly interested, since this "mixture" of dictions offers the reader opportunity to assess the ways that the narrator characterizes speakers, as well as audience reactions to those speakers. The generic and structural differences between epic and tragedy naturally affect their respective presentations of speech. Plato famously analyzes this fundamental difference between the genres in *Republic* 3.392d–394c, where he compares the diction (λέξις) of epic to that of tragedy by distinguishing between poetry that solely consists of "narrative" (διήγησις), such as dithyramb; poetry that solely consists of "imitation" (μίμησις), such as tragedy; and poetry that mixes the two (δι' ἀμφοτέρων), such as epic.

Finally, there is a structural aspect of tragedy that renders its persuasion attempts different, in many cases, from Homeric persuasion attempts (and, indeed, from "real" oratory): tragic persuasion often does not occur within a single, self-contained speech. More often, it comes about through an extended dialogue scene involving a series of challenges and responses by the interlocutors. Dialogue is integral to the rhetoric of tragedy in a way that it is not to the rhetoric of epic. For all of these reasons, I will defer to others on the subject of rhetorical speech in tragedy, since it has already been so amply and expertly treated.[2]

II. THE SOPHISTS AND PLATO

No survey of pre-Aristotelian developments in rhetoric would be complete without acknowledging the fifth-century rise of sophistic practices, for they represent the beginnings of a didactic and systematized treatment of rhetorical techniques. Both sophistic speeches and the Socratic dialogues of Plato fall outside the purview of my survey of direct speech in poetry, but they are an important link between the Archaic poetic tradition and the emergence of a formal discipline of rhetoric. It is within the sophistic writings of fifth- and fourth-century Athens that the first surviving instances of a "meta-vocabulary" of rhetoric emerge.[3] The word *rhêtorikê*, for example, is first attested in Plato's *Gorgias*, which dates to around 385 BCE. The argument from probability, which gained the label *eikos*, was purported to be an invention of Tisias or Corax (shadowy figures of the mid-fifth century).[4] Neil O'Sullivan articulates the widely accepted account of the origins of the argument from probability when he says that "the argument from εἰκός . . . goes back to Tisias and / or Corax, and its extensive use can be seen in what is perhaps our earliest rhetorical document, Antiphon's *Tetralogies*, as well as in tragedy and Thucydides."[5] Although O'Sullivan acknowledges the appearance of *eikos* in the literary genres of tragedy and historiography, he says nothing of its presence in Homeric speeches or the *Homeric Hymn to Hermes* (where the *eikos* argument features prominently, as noted in chapter 5). O'Sullivan's neglect of *eikos* in Homer is a telling example of a contemporary view of rhetoric that has written out the possibility that it might be found as far back as Homer—a view perhaps best summed up by Cole's assertion that "Greek literature before Plato is largely 'arhetorical' in character."[6] This attitude ultimately derives, I will suggest, from Aristotle's attitude toward Homer with regard to rhetoric (see section III below).

Among the relatively few sophistic writings that survive, there is one subgenre of sorts in which the influence of Homeric speech is particularly evident: model forensic speeches placed in the mouths of epic heroes, designed both to entertain and to enlighten their audience.[7] These hybrids of heroic myth and forensic oratory include Gorgias' *Defense of Palamedes* (late fifth / early fourth century), Antisthenes' *Ajax* and *Odysseus* (late fifth / early fourth century), and Alcidamas' *Odysseus: Against the Treachery of Palamedes* (early / mid-fourth century). In the *Defense of Palamedes*, Gorgias depicts the unlucky hero defending himself against a charge of treason brought by Odysseus. In the *Ajax* and *Odysseus*, Antisthenes depicts each speaker voicing his claim to the arms of Achilles. In the *Odysseus: Against the Treachery of Palamedes*, Alcidamas (a pupil of Gorgias) provides the prosecution speech in what is perhaps a response to his teacher's *Defense of Palamedes*. Allied in genre to these four "mytho-forensic" speeches, as I have labeled them elsewhere (Knudsen 2012), are Gorgias' and Isocrates' *Encomi[a] of Helen*. The latter speeches are better-known examples of sophistic oratory; but they are of less interest to this project than the mytho-forensic speeches because they praise Helen from an outside perspective, rather than assuming the identity of Helen herself. Although the four mytho-forensic speeches might seem to bear little resemblance to actual speeches in Homer because of their formal properties (such as length and didactic purpose), a closer examination of their argumentation reveals not only a mythological connection but also a rhetorical connection to Homeric epic. The speeches exhibit strategies of argumentation that are in the process of being crystallized into the genres of forensic oratory, philosophical debate, and rhetorical instruction, and as such they link the rhetoric of Homeric characters with formal theory and practice in Classical Athens. As Kathryn Morgan has observed, the sophists "occupy a position that mediates between what we consider the realm of philosophy and that of the poets and other public performers. . . . Their concerns with language, and their manipulations of myth to express these concerns place them in the philosophical camp, but they also display their expertise in a more freewheeling and extrovert manner, as befits the performers of public display orations."[8]

To explore this phenomenon in more depth, I turn to Antisthenes' antilogic pair of speeches, the *Ajax* and *Odysseus*.[9] Perhaps because Antisthenes is better known for his philosophical than for his rhetorical writings (he was a disciple of Socrates, and is credited with founding the Cynic school), these speeches have received relatively little scholarly attention.[10] This is regrettable, for the two speeches provide a brilliant example of the antilogy tradition in sophistic rhetoric (better known from Antiphon's *Tetralogies*, opposing speeches that depict invented Athenian court cases) while at the same time exploring the creative possibilities of poetic-rhetorical hybridization. The mythological inspiration for the speeches is the *hoplôn krisis* episode that had been depicted in the *Little Iliad*, alluded to in *Odyssey* 11, and exalted by Sophocles' *Ajax* (produced a generation before Antisthenes' speeches). Like Sophocles, Antisthenes is producing a creative reinterpretation of the epic version—in this case, a reinterpretation that exemplifies competing rhetorical strategies and philosophical ideologies.[11]

Antisthenes' verbal characterization of Odysseus and Ajax reinforces the traditional Homeric polarities between the two heroes. Ajax is the man of action, forthright and naïve, who bluntly and repeatedly champions deeds over words when speaking to the judges:

> You should not look at **words** (λόγους) when judging concerning heroic virtue (ἀρετή), but rather at **deeds** (ἔργα). For war is decided **not by word but by deed** (οὐ λόγῳ . . . ἀλλ᾽ ἔργῳ): we cannot **compete in debate** (ἀντιλέγειν) with our enemies, but must either conquer them by fighting or be slaves in silence.[12] (53.7)

This disdain for words recalls the sentiment that Ajax had voiced in his relatively laconic speech during the embassy to Achilles in *Iliad* 9.625–26: "I think that nothing will be accomplished **by** argument (μύθοιο) on this errand." In Antisthenes' speech, Ajax complains that Odysseus has the upper hand in any contest of words, particularly since those judging the case had not been present to observe "the deeds themselves" (τοῖς ἔργοις αὐτοῖς, 53.1), that is, the battle for Achilles' body and arms. Ajax disparages the judges throughout his speech, voicing many variants of the phrase "you judges who know nothing" (53.1, 4, 7, 8). Such an antagonistic attitude toward the audience that he is trying to persuade constitutes an extreme lack of *diathesis*, and thus an obvious rhetorical blunder. It is, however, in keeping with Ajax's familiar identity as a blunt and unvarnished speaker; he provides Antisthenes with a readily recognizable model of dysfunctional rhetoric, just as Odysseus will be a model of effective rhetoric.

Aside from his complaints about the injustice of the trial, Ajax makes three major rhetorical arguments for his case. The first concerns his own achievements with regard to the situation in question; he reminds the arbiters that he had rescued Achilles' body in battle, which (he claims) was a more valuable prize to the Trojans than the armor that Odysseus rescued (53.2). This reasoning leads to his second major argument, namely an attack on Odysseus as a man of cowardly and dishonorable character:

> I thought it right to take the armor so that I could hand it over to his friends; but he [wants it] so that he can sell it, since he would not dare to use it: for no coward would use distinguished armor, knowing that the armor would reveal his cowardice. (53.3)

This ad hominem strategy dominates the middle of Ajax's speech. "For there is nothing which he does in any way openly, while I would dare to do nothing secretly," Ajax asserts (53.5), simultaneously promoting his own *êthos* as a plain speaker while invoking Odysseus' epic reputation for obscuring the truth. After attacking Odysseus for caring more about profit than about honor and reputation, Ajax sums up his character assassination with the rhetorical question, "Then is this worthless and sacrilegious man (ὁ μαστιγίας καὶ ἱερόσυλος) worthy to possess the armor of Achilles?" (53.6).

Ajax's final argument is an **enthymeme**, premised on a threat in the form of the ominous *gnômê*, "Justice is to be dispensed even to the judges, if they do not judge rightly" (53.8). In the enthymeme conclusion, he seems to be hinting at actual violence against his audience: "look toward these things and consider: if you do not judge rightly, you will perceive that a word (λόγος) has no strength against a deed (ἔργον), and a speaking man will not be of any help to you" (53.7–8). Such a belligerent tone would surely ring true to an audience familiar with the prickly, defensive demeanor that Ajax displays in Homer, most notably in the underworld in *Odyssey* 11. For the purposes of rhetorical persuasion, however, it is the wrong note to strike; it does the opposite of disposing the audience favorably (*diathesis*). Ajax has stubbornly clung to his severe heroic idealism, and this does not win debates in a sophistic world.

Having provided an example of what not to do when arguing a case, Antisthenes supplies a counterpart speech exemplifying an effective way to argue (though not necessarily the morally superior one). Antisthenes' Odysseus is the consummate rhetorician, attuned to his audience and ruthlessly clever in his argumentation. From his very first words, Odysseus exudes expansive graciousness and a firm claim to the moral high ground: "This speech of mine is not to you [Ajax] only, because of whom I stand here; but also to all the others—for I have done more good for the encamped army than all of you have" (54.1). This opening launches Odysseus into one of the two major rhetorical thrusts of his speech: attesting his own benevolent *êthos*. Antisthenes' Odysseus employs the technique masterfully as he gives an account of his service to and sacrifice for the Greek cause at Troy. He reminds his audience that the role he played in the war was uniquely dangerous and uniquely important (54.2), and then mounts an impassioned defense against Ajax's claim that his methods of fighting are underhanded and ignoble. He combines arguments of necessity and pragmatism with a claim to piety as he defends his seizure of the statue of Athena from the Trojans (54.3), which Ajax had labeled as blasphemous. In countering this charge, Odysseus deftly pivots from another reminder of his virtuous *êthos* to an ad hominem attack on his opponent: "Even though you [Ajax] have been saved through my rebukes, you cannot be persuaded, and indeed you go so far as to threaten to do these men some harm if they vote to award the arms to me" (54.5). In a single stroke, while ostensibly addressing Ajax, Odysseus has reminded the judges both of his own role as savior of the Greek army, and of the most negative aspects of Ajax's character. This is no Iliadic battlefield; in the tamed context of a fifth-century court of justice, where (as Ajax rightly feared) *logoi* trump *erga*, Odysseus can manipulate not only his own *êthos* but that of his opponent as well.

Throughout Odysseus' speech there are allusions to the sophistic terminology of Antisthenes' age. During his extended attack on Ajax's character, for example, he observes, "if indeed it is necessary to form an opinion of something on the basis of likelihood (ἐκ τῶν εἰκότων), I would suppose that you might do yourself some evil by your bad temper" (54.5). The reference to "likelihood" is clearly a nod to the sophistic appropriation of *eikos* as a technical term. Such play with the boundaries between the speech's heroic setting and its rhetorically didactic function culminates in the closing lines, where Odysseus predicts his afterlife in poetry using a string of Homeric and quasi-Homeric epithets: οἶμαι δέ, ἄν ποτέ τις ἄρα σοφὸς ποιητὴς περὶ ἀρετῆς γένηται, ἐμὲ μὲν ποιήσει πολύτλαντα καὶ πολύμητιν καὶ πολυμήχανον καὶ πτολίπορθον ("I suppose if ever there should be born some poet who is wise concerning heroic virtue, he would depict me as endurance-full and plan-full and resourceful and city-sacking," 54.14). Antisthenes' choice of σοφός as a modifier for ποιητής (an obvious reference to Homer) slyly marks the confluence of Homeric tradition and sophistic practice here at the end of Odysseus' speech.

Unfortunately, the mytho-forensic subgenre that Antisthenes represents was a short-lived phenomenon, with surviving speeches confined to the period from the late-fifth to the early-fourth centuries BCE. (although a similar genre would resurface in the *progymnasmata* of the Second Sophistic under the designation of *êthopoiia*). As with the sophistic movement more broadly, the mytho-forensic phenomenon seems to have given way to the formal rhetorical and philosophical theories introduced by Plato and Aristotle in the fourth century.

A final link in the transmission of rhetoric from Homer to fully realized Aristotelian theory is the work of Plato, whose wide-ranging and complex relationship with rhetoric has been the subject of much scholarly work.[13] Unlike Aristotle's approach to rhetoric, which is patently systematic and as such can serve as a measuring stick for analyzing rhetorical technique in speech, Plato's treatment (most prominent in the *Gorgias* and *Phaedrus* dialogues) is diffuse, often critical, and ultimately aporetic. Aristotle is concerned with the nature of rhetoric only to a limited extent; once he has dispensed with a definition early in the

Rhetoric ("an ability, in each [particular] case, to see the available means of persuasion," 1.2.1), he spends the majority of his treatise discussing the components of rhetoric and how to practice it effectively. In contrast, the debates over rhetoric that Plato depicts have little to say about the mechanics of rhetorical practice, instead concerning themselves with what rhetoric is, and whether or not it leads its practitioners—and audience—closer to the truth. One further distinction I will mention (out of the many that could be noted) between Aristotle and Plato with regard to rhetoric is in their respective views on the relationship between rhetoric and dialectic. While Aristotle defines rhetoric as the *antistrophos*, or counterpart, to dialectic (*Rhetoric* 1.1.1), Plato sees these two pursuits as separate, even opposite. For Plato, dialectic is an essential component of the philosophical process (see *Phaedrus* 276a–278b) that produces a "living, breathing discourse" (276a). This stands in contrast to what Andrea Nightingale has termed the "alien discourse[s]" of memorized or written-down rhetorical speeches.[14] With such a perspective on rhetoric, Plato holds at arm's length the "conventional" understanding of rhetoric (i.e., a system of techniques and arguments to be exerted in persuasion of another)—an understanding shared by Iliadic speakers, the sophists, Aristotle, and modern society alike.

Jean Nienkamp has observed that "part of the difficulty in extracting positions on rhetoric from the *Gorgias* and the *Phaedrus* is that the dialogues are about much more than rhetoric—in fact, they situate rhetoric in larger philosophical, societal, and interpersonal contexts, a rendering that colors the specific positions on rhetoric offered in each. . . . These dialogues add an emphasis on ethics and language use."[15] Such an emphasis means that pinning down any notion of "Platonic rhetorical theory" is difficult, if not impossible: Plato's "views" on rhetoric, as expressed through the mouth of Socrates, have constant recourse to the broader requirements of his philosophical and ethical principles. Additionally, these views seem to unfold and evolve between dialogues, and even within a single dialogue, depending on the identity and opinions of Socrates' interlocutors and on the course of discussion. The early dialogue *Gorgias* (c. 385 BCE) contains Socrates' famous denotation of rhetoric as a "knack" (ἐμπειρία) rather than a "skill" (τέχνη). A "knack," according to Socrates, is something that mimics other subjects such as politics, medicine, and the like, but does not involve any actual expertise (*Gorgias* 462b–466a). In Socrates' view, a "knack" is no more than a type of flattery (κολακεία), in that it tells the listener whatever he wants to hear. This harsh view of rhetoric's nature is borne out in Socrates' subsequent evaluation: "for the person who has no intention of behaving unjustly it doesn't seem to me to have much use—if in fact it has any use at all" (481b).[16] Throughout most of the dialogue, Socrates argues that rhetoric stands in opposition to justice and virtue and the life of philosophy because it tends to be used unscrupulously by those who wish to exercise power unjustly. But near the end, he hints at the possibility that rhetoric might be practiced in an ethically acceptable fashion:

> But among so many arguments this one alone survives refutation and remains steady: . . . that every form of flattery, both the form concerned with oneself and that concerned with others, whether they're few or many, is to be avoided, and that oratory and every other activity is always to be used in support of what's just. (*Gorgias* 527b–c)

Plato continues to explore this more receptive attitude to rhetoric in the *Phaedrus* (c. 375–365 BCE). This is a complex dialogue encompassing a variety of types of discourse, as Nightingale has observed, including different literary genres and types of rhetoric.[17] In the *Phaedrus*, Socrates gives an account of rhetoric that links aspects of rhetorical practice that we see in Homeric speech to aspects of rhetorical theory that we see in Aristotle—albeit in a distinctly Platonic idiom. Socrates rests his case for a philosophically based rhetoric on the premise that "the nature of speech is in fact to direct the soul (ψυχαγωγία)" (*Phaedrus* 271d), and it is this concept of *psychagôgia* that constitutes an acceptable manner of practicing rhetoric for Socrates.[18] Toward the end of the dialogue (260a–262c), he builds the argument that to practice rhetoric successfully—as a τέχνη, not a τριβή (synonymous with ἐμπειρία)—it is necessary to know the truth about every subject upon which the course of persuasion touches. "There is no genuine art of speaking without a grasp of truth (τοῦ δὲ λέγειν . . . ἔτυμος τέχνη ἄνευ τοῦ ἀληθείας ἧφθαι οὔτ' ἔστιν)," Socrates argues, "and there never will be" (260e). This notion that persuasion must be grounded in truth leads Socrates to make a distinction between the formal properties of rhetoric (which are the sole concern of sophists and handbook-writers, and which Socrates calls "a little threadbare," 268a), and the content or subject matter of rhetoric. Along with possessing true knowledge of the subject under debate in any speech, Socrates says, the speaker must possess true knowledge of the souls of his audience:

> Anyone who teaches the art of rhetoric seriously will, first, describe the soul with absolute precision. . . . Second, he will explain how, in virtue of its nature, it acts and is acted upon by certain things. . . . Third, he will classify the kinds of speech and of soul there are, as well as the various ways in which they are affected, and explain what causes each. He will then coordinate each kind of soul with the kind of speech appropriate to it. (*Phaedrus* 271a–b)

Socrates had given attention to the nature and aetiology of souls earlier in the *Phaedrus*, during his so-called "Great Speech" on *erôs* (*Phaedrus* 244a–257b). This concept of different "kinds of soul" is complex and intertwined with the whole of Plato's philosophical thought. For the purposes of rhetoric, Plato sees it as essential for instructors to describe, and speakers to apprehend, the souls of those whom they are attempting to persuade. "Otherwise," argues Socrates, "all we'll have will be an empirical and artless practice (τριβῇ μόνον καὶ ἐμπειρίᾳ). We won't be able to supply, on the basis of an art (τέχνη) . . . a soul with the reasons and customary rules for conduct that will impart to it the convictions and virtues we want" (270b).

Focusing on the *souls* of the audience would seem to be a uniquely Platonic approach to rhetorical effectiveness, but it is worth comparing this approach to aspects of both Homeric and Aristotelian rhetoric. As we saw in chapter 2, Homeric speakers often tailor their rhetoric to the particular audience: Nestor attempts to appease Achilles and Agamemnon with individualized flattery, claiming that the former hero is "stronger," the latter "greater" (*Iliad* 1.280–81); Hera cannily approaches Zeus with arguments about the respect demanded by her status as queen of the gods and his wife, and with flattering words about his ultimate authority (4.51–67 and 15.36–45). Moreover, Homeric speakers make explicit reference to the effectiveness of such attention to the particular character of their audience, as when Nestor tells Patroclus that he is the only one who can persuade Achilles to return to battle, since "the persuasion of a friend is a strong thing" (11.793). Both the relationship between speaker and audience, and a speaker's knowledge of his audience, are crucial in determining the rhetorical approaches of characters in the *Iliad*. This is true whether the parties in question are acquainted with each other (as they are in most of the *Iliad*'s persuasive speeches) or not (as in the case of the speeches between Achilles and Priam). It is what I have been calling the rhetorical technique of *diathesis*. What we see represented in the *Iliad*, then, is a strategy for persuasion that looks not unlike Socrates' description of the well-trained orator:

> On meeting someone he will be able to discern what he is like and make clear to himself that the person actually standing in front of him is of just this particular sort of **nature** (φύσις) he had learned about in school—to that he must now apply speeches of such-and-such a kind in this particular way in order to secure conviction about such-and-such an issue.[19] (*Phaedrus* 271e–272a)

Likewise, Plato's theory has certain affinities with Aristotle's notion of "disposing the listener" favorably based on an assessment of the listener's character and points of susceptibility to emotional appeal (see *Rhetoric* 1.2.3, 2.12–17). As is his wont, Aristotle takes a pragmatic approach to assessing audience character and tailoring one's rhetoric accordingly. In *Rhetoric* 2.12–17, he details different types of audience character (the young, the old, those in the prime of life) and the effects on audience character of various circumstances (good birth, wealth, and power) in an attempt to create a calculus for *diathesis*. The young, for example, are "prone to desires," and "impulsive and quick-tempered and inclined to follow up their anger [by action]" (*Rhetoric* 2.12.3ff.). The implication of such an analysis is that an effective approach to persuading the young is to play upon their desires and stir them to anger (among other things), whereas the old will be persuaded by what is advantageous for themselves, and are susceptible to appeals to pity, since "they think that all kinds of sufferings are close to hand for themselves" (*Rhetoric* 2.13.15).

What becomes apparent in tracking rhetorical notions from Homer to Plato to Aristotle is a common awareness that a successful orator must understand the identity—variously termed the nature (φύσις), the soul (ψυχή), or the character (ἦθος)—of his audience, and must match his speech to that particular identity. Homeric characters represent this practice when they use *diathesis* in fictional deliberative contexts. Plato articulates an approach to the practice whereby philosophy and rhetoric intersect in the contemplation of the soul and in leading the soul towards the Good (*psychagôgia*). Aristotle presents the practice in terms of character classifications and applying persuasive strategies based on these classifications "to dispose the hearer in some way" (*Rhetoric* 1.2.3).

While the systematic nature of Aristotle's rhetorical theory makes it a useful measuring stick for analyzing Homeric speech practice, Plato's discursive style makes his work less suited to such a task. Plato does, of course, engage with Homer on numerous occasions throughout his work, but Homer does not come up in any significant way during the dialogues on rhetoric—with one interesting exception. There is a hint in the *Phaedrus* that Homeric speech may have provided some background—whether in a specific or a more broadly cultural sense—for Plato's rhetorical theory. That hint comes during Socrates' discussion of rhetoric as *psychagôgia*. As Socrates explains to Phaedrus, rhetoric understood in this way can occur not only in the conventional rhetorical contexts of the law court or the assembly, but also in private interactions, addressing any number of subjects (*Phaedrus* 261a–b). When Phaedrus expresses surprise at this broad notion of rhetoric, Socrates responds, "Well, have you only heard of the rhetorical treatises (τέχνας . . . περὶ λόγων) of Nestor and Odysseus—those they wrote in their spare time in Troy? Haven't you also heard of the works of

Palamedes?" (261b). Scholars have debated what exactly Socrates might be referring to in this unelaborated reference to τέχναι of Homeric heroes (see discussion of this passage in chapter 1, section II). Two explanations seem possible. First, Socrates could be referring to a contemporary tradition of putting "rhetorical treatises" in the mouths of Homeric characters for the purposes of instruction or display, such as the mytho-forensic speeches of Gorgias, Antisthenes, and Alcidamas discussed above. Alternatively, Plato could be invoking the example of Homeric speakers as models for the type of rhetoric that he is theorizing—namely, one whose definition and application reach beyond the formal and occasional strictures in which the handbooks of his day typically presented rhetoric. Indeed, Plato (like Aristotle) is dismissive of his rhetorical predecessors, the sophists and handbook-writers who by the late fifth century had begun to be associated with the invention of the discipline.[20] Rhetoric, as both Plato and Aristotle envision it, is comprised of far more than clever wordplay and stylistic tropes; it involves leading the soul (Plato), or finding the available means of persuasion for each case (Aristotle). In this sense, the two philosophers' perspectives on rhetoric have more in common with each other than either of them has with the handbook-writers. Cole comments on this fact, noting that despite their vast differences in method and approach,

> Aristotle's procedure makes sense as a consistent effort to develop some workable means of realizing the rhetorical program laid down by Plato—a program calling for knowledge of all the relevant facts and principles involved in a given case and all the potentially useful ways of presenting them as well. . . . Narrowed range and increased specificity and practicality do not, however, prevent the discipline set forth at length in the *Rhetoric* from being essentially the same one envisioned in the *Phaedrus*.[21]

I would propose an addition to Cole's insight: that both Plato and Aristotle, whether they recognized it or not, were drawing on a "rhetorical program" modeled by the speakers in Homeric poetry centuries earlier.

III: ARISTOTLE

In the course of examining Homeric speech as a locus for the origins of rhetoric, I have had frequent recourse to Aristotle's *Rhetoric*, since it is the earliest-surviving systematic and comprehensive theory of rhetoric from ancient Greece. As such, the *Rhetoric* is a useful tool for identifying the rhetorical content of speeches represented in literature both before and after it was written in the mid-fourth century. But Aristotle gives little credit to Homer for contributions to the art of rhetoric, although the persuasive strategies used by Homeric speakers often accord closely with Aristotle's descriptions of such strategies. This section will examine the relatively superficial ways that Aristotle engages with Homer in the *Rhetoric*, and explore the possible reasons for this treatment.

Homer serves a somewhat uneasy dual role within Aristotle's *Rhetoric*: he is both a larger-than-life cultural icon and a source of *exempla* and *gnômai* for very minor details within Aristotle's analytical study. The first role is apparent when, for example, Aristotle asserts that one way of identifying "the good" is to observe "what any of the wise or good men or women has shown preference for, as Athena [for] Odysseus and Theseus [for] Helen and the goddesses [for] Paris and Homer [for] Achilles" (*Rhetoric* 1.6.25); or when, speaking of invoking ancient witnesses in judicial rhetoric, Aristotle notes that "the Athenians used Homer as a witness in their claim to Salamis" (1.15.13). The second role—Homer as a source of textual *exempla* for the *Rhetoric*—is more complicated. Aristotle cites the Homeric poems with some frequency, but seldom are these citations significant to Aristotle's description of rhetorical argumentation. More often they serve as illustrations of minor stylistic figures or tangential matters, quoted to serve the philosophical groundwork that Aristotle lays for his rhetorical theory. Homer is one of many authors that Aristotle uses in this way throughout the treatise, including tragedians (most prominently Euripides, but also Sophocles, Aeschylus, and Agathon), lyric poets (Sappho, Pindar, Simonides, Stesichorus), political orators (Pericles, Demosthenes), and sophists (Gorgias, Alcidamas).

As a first step in examining Aristotle's relationship to Homer in the *Rhetoric*, I have made a survey of all references to Homer in the treatise. Aristotle quotes or refers to the Homeric epics 33 times in the *Rhetoric*.[22] Of these 33 references, however, only 8 are used to illustrate actual rhetorical arguments or techniques. The other 25 references to Homer are of peripheral or no relevance to rhetoric itself, as they concern either stylistic/linguistic phenomena or tangential discussions. Representative of Aristotle's citation of Homer in a tangential way is *Rhetoric* 1.11.9: while discussing pleasure as a strategy particularly useful in judicial rhetoric, Aristotle notes that "even anger is pleasurable as Homer also [said in the verse he] composed about anger, 'Which is much sweeter than honey dripping from the comb' [*Iliad* 18.109]." Representative of Aristotle's use of Homer to illustrate a minor stylistic device is *Rhetoric* 3.10.2: during a discussion of metaphor, he observes that "metaphor most brings about learning; for when he (Homer) calls old age 'stubble,' [*Od.* 4.213] he creates understanding and knowledge through the genus, since old age and stubble are [species of the genus of] things that have lost their bloom." Like the latter example, roughly half of the *Rhetoric*'s 33 references to Homer occur in Book 3, which deals with the more superficial speech qualities of style (*lexis*), arrangement (*taxis*), and delivery. Consequently they have little or nothing to do with the persuasive strategies of argumentation with which Aristotle is concerned in Books 1 and 2, and which comprise the essence of his theory of rhetoric.

The eight Homeric passages that Aristotle cites to illustrate actual rhetorical arguments are worth noting, however, as they are most likely to shed light on the philosopher's view of Homer with regard to the formal discipline of rhetoric. The first three such citations occur during Aristotle's discussion of "the good" as an ethical topic useful for persuasion:

1. In general, the opposite of what enemies want or [of] what makes them happy seems advantageous; thus, it was well said, "Yea, Priam would rejoice. . . ." [*Iliad* 1.255]. (*Rhetoric* 1.6.20)

2. and 3. And what has cost much labor and expense [is good]; for it is an apparent good already, and such a thing is regarded as an "end" and an end of many [efforts]; and the "end" is a good. This is the source of the following: "And it would be a boast left to Priam. . . ." [*Iliad* 2.160]. And "It is a disgrace for you to have stayed long. . . ." [*Iliad* 2.298]. (*Rhetoric* 1.6.22)

Passage 1, from Nestor's speech attempting to reconcile Achilles and Agamemnon (analyzed in chapter 2, speech I), illustrates how the notion of providing something "good" to the enemy serves as an argument to dissuade the addressees from quarreling. Passage 2, from a speech of Hera addressed to Athena (which does not figure into my analysis of rhetorical speeches in the *Iliad*), decries the possibility that the Greeks might leave Troy without the prize, Helen, for which they have expended so much effort, and which is therefore "good." Passage 3, from Odysseus' rousing speech to the Greek troops (analyzed as a "model passage" in chapter 2), expresses much the same sentiment as the second.

The fourth and fifth instances of Aristotle citing Homer to illustrate rhetorical argument occur during his discussion of the concepts of greater and lesser within the broader context of identifying persuasive topics:

4. And the same things when divided into their parts seem greater; for there seems to be an excess of more things present. As a result, the poet also says that [the following words] persuaded Meleager to rise up [and fight]:

> Whatsoever ills are to men whose city is taken:
> Folk perish, and fire levels the city to the dust,
> And others led off children [*Iliad* 9.592–4]. (*Rhetoric* 1.7.31)

5. And what is self-generated [is greater] than what is acquired. Thus, the
    poet, too, says, "But I am self-taught" [*Od.* 22.347]. (*Rhetoric* 1.7.33)

Passage 4 comes from Phoenix's great embassy speech to persuade Achilles to
rejoin battle (analyzed in chapter 2, speech X). Aristotle cites this speech to illustrate not any sort of logical argument, *pathos*, or *êthos* appeals, but rather the persuasive device of reciting a litany (in this case, a litany of the possible effects of
losing a war). Passage 5 is spoken by Phemius in his attempt to persuade Odysseus to spare his life at the end of the *Odyssey*, and though it could be classed as
an argument from *êthos*, Aristotle cites it as an example of the persuasive superiority of whatever is self-generated.

The next two instances occur during Aristotle's discussion of the appropriate uses for *gnômai* in rhetorical persuasion:

6. and 7. One should even use trite and common maxims if they are appli-
    cable; for because they are common, they seem true, as though everyone
    agreed; for example, [it is useful] for one who is exhorting [troops] to face
    danger without first sacrificing to the gods [to say,] "One omen [literally,
    one bird] is best, to fight for one's country. [*Iliad* 12.243]. And if they are
    outnumbered, [to say,] "The War God is impartial" [*Iliad* 18.309]. (*Rheto-
    ric* 2.21.11)

Hector is the speaker in both of these passages (analyzed in the appendix,
speeches X and XXIV); both speeches are addressed initially to Polydamas but
end with exhortations of the Trojan troops. These are indeed clear examples of
gnomic premises for enthymemes aimed at stirring the audience to fight.

The eighth and final instance of Homer being cited to illustrate rhetorical
technique occurs during Aristotle's discussion of dramatic narration (*diêgêsis*)
as an element of speech arrangement, and as a persuasive device:

8. Further, speak from the emotions, narrating both the results [of emotion]
    and things the audience knows and what are special characteristics of the
    speaker or the opponents. . . . Many such things are to be found in Homer:
    "Thus she spoke, and the old nurse covered her face with her hands" [*Od.*
    19.361]. For those who begin to cry place their hands over their eyes. (*Rheto-
    ric* 3.16.10)

Passage 8 quotes the narrator of the *Odyssey*, and cites not a verbal argument but the rhetorical gesture accompanying such argument (a phenomenon that I have discussed in relation to several rhetorical speeches in the *Iliad*, e.g., Patroclus to Achilles in *Iliad* 16.21–45 and Priam to Achilles in *Iliad* 24.486–506).

This completes the survey of instances where Aristotle invokes the Homeric poems to illustrate rhetorical *pisteis*—that is, the crafted or "artistic" (ἔντεχνος) methods of persuasion which he considers to be the most essential component of rhetoric (see *Rhetoric* 1.1.3, 1.1.9, 1.1.11, 1.2.2). What the survey seems to indicate is that while Homer provides Aristotle with a convenient store of culturally familiar quotations (just as Euripides and Pindar do), he does not come into Aristotle's purview as a model for rhetoric in any systematic way. Aristotle offers no speculation or comment upon the implications of finding examples of rhetorical *pisteis* in Homeric speech; he does not connect the few Homeric examples of rhetoric that he cites, or suggest that, taken together, they might reflect a systematic understanding of rhetoric. To Aristotle, Homer is simply one among many sources of *exempla* for his treatise. He is in no way conceived of as a rhetorical predecessor to Aristotle, or a contributor to the discipline.

What sources for rhetoric, then, *does* Aristotle acknowledge? Aristotle mentions certain rhetorical predecessors, though he is loath to give credit to any of them. At the beginning of his treatise, while introducing the state of rhetoric "as things are now," he discusses the work of earlier "handbook-writers" (1.1.3). He dismisses these predecessors as having produced unsatisfactory treatments of rhetoric, claiming that they

> have worked on a small part of the subject; for only *pisteis* are artistic [*entechnos*] (other things are supplementary), and these writers say nothing about enthymemes, which is the "body" of persuasion, while they give most of their attention to matters external to the subject. (1.1.3) . . . For example, why it is necessary to have the introduction [*prooemion*] or the narration [*diêgêsis*] and each of the other parts; for [in treating these matters] they concern themselves only with how they may put the judge in a certain frame of mind, while they explain nothing about artistic proofs; and that is the question of how one may become enthymematic. It is for this reason that although the method of deliberative and judicial speaking is the same and though deliberative subjects are finer and more important to the state than private transactions, [the handbook-writers] have nothing to say about the former, and all try to describe the art of speaking in a law court. (1.1.9–10)

It is Aristotle's intention to shift the focus of rhetorical instruction away from the handbook-writers' obsession with structure and toward "artistic" consider-

ations (that is, argumentative strategies); and to broaden its scope from techniques primarily relevant to judicial oratory to those relevant to deliberative as
well. Aristotle continues to make disdainful mention of the handbook-writers
and the inadequacy of their theories at various points in the *Rhetoric*.[23] Despite
acknowledging them as his forbears, he distances himself from them throughout the treatise. Indeed, his tendency to speak of them in monolithic and anonymous terms—as "those who have composed handbooks" (οἱ τὰς τέχνας τῶν λόγων
συντιθέντες, 1.1.3)—serves to distinguish his own rhetorical project all the more
starkly from what has come before.

This is a very different approach from the one that Aristotle takes in setting
out his theory of poetry in the *Poetics*. Both the *Poetics* and the *Rhetoric* give analytical accounts of their respective subjects in which they separate, classify, and
explain the components of each. But a significant part of the *Poetics* is also devoted to tracing the origins of poetry in Greece and to identifying the inventors
of tragedy and epic, whereas the *Rhetoric* is largely devoid of this sort of "archaeo-
logical" project. This may help to explain Aristotle's treatment of Homer within
the *Rhetoric*. The purpose of the *Rhetoric* is scientific, not historiographical; it is
a treatise intended to analyze and provide instruction in a technical skill. As
such, it is fully forward-looking. Aristotle refers to predecessors and sources—to
the history of rhetoric—only insofar as he can use the handbook-writers as
straw men, and stake his claim to an innovative and definitive presentation of
rhetoric. Aristotle's view of his own foundational place in the history of rhetoric
gains support in the recent works by Cole and Schiappa that I have discussed at
several points. Cole attributes to Aristotle and Plato a philosophical approach to
rhetoric that sets them apart as "the true founders of rhetoric as well as of philosophy."[24] Schiappa argues that there is little or no real evidence of a tradition
of "technical rhetoric," or rhetorical handbooks, before the fourth century, and
that the *technai* to which Aristotle refers were simply exemplary speeches by
sophists such as Gorgias and Antiphon.[25] In Schiappa's opinion, "the careful
development of logical theory, including the categorization (based on epistemo-
logical criteria) of genuine and spurious arguments from probability, originated
no sooner than Aristotle."[26] Aristotle's own treatise successfully downplays the
role of his rhetorical predecessors and sets the terms of the discourse. But even
highly technical rhetoric can be conceived of, learned, and practiced before being described in a theoretical treatise. The rhetorical speech and meta-rhetorical
language present in the *Iliad* indicate that the poem's narrator and characters
understood and cultivated effective persuasive speech. One could argue, then—
using Aristotle's own definition of rhetoric as "an ability, in each [particular]

case, to see (θεωρῆσαι) the available means of persuasion" (1.2.1)—that the true inventor of rhetoric in the ancient Greek world is Homer, whose speaking characters detect and employ an array of those very means of persuasion that Aristotle would later catalogue.

IV. CONCLUSION: THE SEPARATION OF POETRY AND RHETORIC

The particular methodological approach Aristotle takes in the *Rhetoric*, so different from that of the *Poetics*, suggests why Aristotle fails to note the similarities between Homeric persuasion and his own system, and is silent about the possibility that the Homeric epics informed the *technê* of rhetoric. It seems likely that Archaic poetry had no place in Aristotle's conception of the discipline of rhetoric—innovative, technical, and philosophical as it was. By the fourth century, Homer was firmly associated with a religious and mythical past, and though Aristotle might cite the *Iliad* or *Odyssey* for the odd example of a rhetorical trope, these associations would have made it difficult for him to see Homer as a contributor to the *technê* of rhetoric. The notion of a sociocultural shift in Greek views of language and authority from the Archaic to the Classical periods has been discussed by many authors, among them Detienne in *The Masters of Truth in Archaic Greece* and Simon Goldhill in *The Invention of Prose*.[27] Detienne posits a boundary between magico-religious speech in the Archaic era and the secularized, philosophized speech that arose in the Classical era:

> For philosophy to pose the problem of the relation between speech and reality, and for sophistry and rhetoric to construct a theory of language as an instrument of persuasion, it was first necessary for the Greeks to supersede the system of thought in which speech was intermeshed in a network of symbolic values and was itself regarded as a natural power or dynamic reality acting spontaneously on its listeners.[28]

According to Detienne, a "gradual secularization of speech" occurred along with the rise of the Greek city-state, in which *logos* took on an autonomous authority no longer moored to divine inspiration and to the figures of the seer, bard, and king.[29] Along the same lines, Goldhill speaks of a "profound shift in institutional and intellectual practice" centered around the rise of prose in fifth-century BCE Greece—a shift from viewing poetry as the locus for authoritative discourse to viewing prose treatments of philosophy, history, and science as authoritative:

This shift could be expressed in its most simple and dramatic form as the move from the scene of a divinely inspired bard singing the poetry of the Muses for a spell-bound audience, to the scene of two orators, arguing a legal case in front of an appointed group of judging citizens. . . . The invention of prose involves a *contest of authority* [with poetry]. . . . The new writers of the new form of prose need to compete for (discursive) space in the city.[30]

However limited and lacking in nuance the notion of a cultural transition "from myth to reason" might be (and I will turn to the problems with this account in a moment), it is undeniable that fifth-century Greece saw the emergence of new and different types of discourse that competed with the mythical and poetic discourse of the Archaic age. To judge by subsequent history, this "contest of authority" between prose and poetry was won by Aristotle and the philosophical / analytical tradition. Eric Havelock has observed that "the history of Greek political theory, as also of Greek politics, has been written in modern times exactly as Plato and Aristotle would have wished it to be written";[31] I would argue that the same can be said for the history of rhetoric. For Aristotle and the tradition that he inaugurated, poetry was cast as an object of analysis, rather than being itself a possible source of authoritative knowledge on any "technical" subject, such as rhetoric. Although strands of a more open-minded approach to the rhetorical possibilities of Homeric poetry continued to appear in the ancient world—particularly in the work of literary critics and grammarians such as those cited in chapter 1—these were ultimately drowned out by the Aristotelian narrative.

In conjunction with the philosophical and scientific investigations of the Classical era came a trend toward classification, encapsulated by the separation of discourse into categories of prose and poetry, and further subcategories of genre. Aristotle, of course, was the classifier par excellence. His *Rhetoric* alone contains 17 instances of the noun διαίρεσις ("division" or "classification") or the verbs διαιρέω / προσδιαιρέομαι ("to divide" / "subdivide"), most of them referring to his methodology. In fact, Aristotle identifies διαίρεσις as an enthymematic topic in and of itself (2.23.10). This fondness for categories and generic separation is yet another barrier to Aristotle viewing Homer as a rhetorical predecessor. While he draws upon poetry for occasional examples, he seems to conceive of the rhetorical techniques that he describes as applying strictly to the realm of contemporary oratory. He explicitly emphasizes the distinction between poetry and prose (which he refers to as "bare words," ψιλοὶ λόγοι) during his discussion of rhetorical style (*lexis*) in Book 3 of the *Rhetoric*:

Since the poets, while speaking sweet nothings, seemed to acquire their reputation through their *lexis*, a poetic style came into existence [in prose as well], for example, that of Gorgias. Even now, the majority of the uneducated think such speakers speak most beautifully. This is not the case, but the [proper] *lexis* of prose differs from that of poetry. (*Rhetoric* 3.1.9)

The problem with mixing poetry and rhetoric, according to Aristotle, is that effective persuasion requires clarity and natural-sounding language—two elements that generally do not characterize poetry (although he does cite Euripides as an example of tragedy's move toward using natural speech in 3.2.5):

Authors should compose without being noticed and should seem to speak not **artificially** (πεπλασμένως) but **naturally** (πεφυκότως). (The latter is persuasive, the former the opposite). . . . A word in its prevailing and native meaning and metaphor are alone useful in the *lexis* of prose. (*Rhetoric* 3.2.4–6)

A final difference that Aristotle identifies between poetry and rhetoric has to do with the relative suitability of speaking emotionally (λεγεῖν παθητικῶς, 3.7.11) in the two discourse modes. In oratory, he argues, impassioned utterances are appropriate only on rare occasions and when certain conditions have been met—namely, "when a speaker already holds the audience in his control and causes them to be stirred either by praise or blame or hate or love" (*Rhetoric* 3.7.11). By contrast, such an emotional style is more generally appropriate in poetry, "for poetry is inspired" (ἔνθεον γὰρ ἡ ποίησις, 3.7.11).

Poetry in Aristotle's *Rhetoric*, then, serves several purposes. First, it populates his store of (seemingly interchangeable) quotations from well-known sources, which can be inserted as practical illustrations of rhetorical devices, stylistic flourishes, and accepted truths at various points. Homer appears alongside Simonides, Pericles, Agathon, and others in this capacity. Second, poetry represents a category that may be contrasted with rhetoric, thus throwing into sharper relief the supposed distinctives of rhetorical diction (i.e., clear, plain speech; the absence of emotional style). What poetry does not do, in Aristotle's account, is embody or inform the *technê* of rhetoric. Only the handbook-writers are eligible for this role, since their genre and aims are roughly the same as his (though their execution falls short). The discontinuity between poetry and rhetoric that Aristotle perceives, and perpetuates, fits into the modern notion of a sociocultural shift in the Classical era as described by Detienne, Goldhill, and others. Such a shift—from locating authoritative discourse in "magico-religious" poetic utterance to locating it in philosophical and technical prose writings—

can of course be detected in certain texts from the centuries between Homer and Aristotle. But something has been lost in this "from *mythos* to *logos*" narrative, which places poetry on one side of the divide and rhetoric on the other. Homer's technically sophisticated persuasive speeches exemplify the fact that *mythos* and *logos* are often intertwined in ancient Greek discourse, and I would argue that the practice of rhetoric in fact represents an area of *continuity* between Homer and the developments of the fifth and fourth centuries. Homeric techniques of persuasion—although they appear within a mythic narrative—are often the same as the intricate techniques of persuasion used by speakers in the Athenian assembly and taught by the sophists, handbook-writers, and Aristotle himself. And by dint of Homer's ubiquity in the Classical world, Homeric speeches cannot help but have informed these more traditional examples of the earliest rhetoric. The disciplinary compartmentalization of Aristotle's *Rhetoric* has, through its influence on later histories of rhetoric, effaced this remarkable phenomenon. It is time to recover the view of that much more obscure ancient figure, Pseudo-Plutarch, who maintained that the earliest of Greek poets was also a τεχνίτης λόγων—an artificer of discourse.

Appendix

Analysis of Remaining Iliadic
Rhetorical Speeches

In addition to the catalogue of 19 speeches analyzed in chapter 2 (including Odysseus' speech at 2.284–332, used as a "model passage"), I have identified 39 other speeches in the *Iliad* that exhibit rhetorical argumentation. These speeches, along with my analysis of their rhetorical techniques, are presented in chronological order.

    I. Achilles makes an appeal to his mother Thetis at 1.365–412, although the attempted persuasion is limited to the end of the speech (393–412). After explaining his grievance against Agamemnon, Achilles begs Thetis for a favor. He begins with a command that forms the conclusion of the **enthymeme** that will follow: "You then, if you have power to, protect your own son, going to Olympos and supplicating Zeus" (393–94). Achilles' use of his own identity as a son to entail Thetis' pity and sense of obligation constitutes both an appeal to *êthos* and an exercise of *diathesis*. He then introduces the premise of the enthymeme (using the typical enthymematic marker, γάρ), which relies on presenting an argument that Thetis could in turn use to persuade Zeus to grant Achilles' request. Achilles recounts a claim that Thetis had made "many times" about an event from the mythical past:

> For (γάρ) . . . you said you only among the immortals
> beat aside shameful destruction from Kronos' son the dark-misted,
> that time when all the other Olympians sought to bind him. . . .
>   Then you,
> goddess, went and set him free from his shackles. . . . (396–406)[1]

Achilles, having used his own *êthos* to exert a claim on Thetis in his attempt to persuade her, suggests that she do the same to persuade Zeus (and thus achieve Achilles' object). Tying this premise to the enthymematic conclusion to end his speech, Achilles exhorts his mother to "sit beside him and take his knees and remind him of these things now, if perhaps he might be willing to help the Trojans . . . [so] that Atreus' son wide-ruling Agamemnon may recognize his madness, that he did no honour to the best of the Achaians" (407–12). The speech is successful: Thetis assents to Achilles' request (1.419) and later convinces Zeus (1.523–27).

II. Nestor addresses the Greeks—and Agamemnon in particular—at 2.337–68, a speech that follows up the elaborate speech of Odysseus (2.284–332) analyzed in chapter 2, section II. This is a relatively short speech by Nestor's standards; nevertheless, it incorporates several of the rhetorical devices later mentioned by Aristotle. Nestor begins with a vehement rebuke of his audience:

> Oh, for shame! You are like children when you hold assembly,
> infant children, to whom the works of war mean nothing.
> Where then shall our covenants go, and the oaths we have taken? . . .
> We do our fighting with words only, and can discover
> no remedy, though we have stayed here a long time. (337–43)

Such biting words are certainly indicative of the "shame culture" that is present in the *Iliad*,[2] but they also represent a calculated play on the emotions of the particular audience (**pathos**): these fighting men will abhor the thought of resembling infants and cowards, and will thus be inclined to listen to Nestor's rebuke (**diathesis**). (Aristotle explains the rhetorical efficacy of manipulating an audience's emotions in *Rhetoric* 2.1.8, focusing specifically on the emotion of shame at 2.6.1–2.)

In lines 2.344–49, Nestor directs several commands at Agamemnon in the imperative (ἄρχευ', ἔα φθινύθειν) concerning how to deal with any remaining stragglers. Then he resumes his address to the broader assembly once again, opening into an **enthymeme** argument. The enthymematic premise (signaled by the particle γάρ) comes first; it takes the form of an appeal to the promise of Zeus' favor in the past, and as such is reminiscent of an argument that Odysseus had made in his preceding speech:

> For (γάρ) I say to you, the son of all-powerful Kronos
> promised, on that day when we went in our fast-running vessels,
> we of Argos, carrying blood and death to the Trojans.
> He flashed lightning on our right, showing **signs** (σήματα) of favour. (350–53)

Nestor even mirrors Odysseus' technique as far as to invoke the vocabulary of signs; the lightning bolt he recalls parallels the omen of the snake and sparrow as an appeal to the persuasive power of divine authority. With Zeus' recalled promise as the premise, Nestor concludes the enthymeme with a command: "Therefore (τῷ, corresponding to the γάϱ of line 350) let no man be urgent to take the way homeward until after he has lain in bed with the wife of a Trojan to avenge Helen's longing to escape and her lamentations" (354–56). He then directs a threat toward anyone who attempts to turn back home ("before all others he may win death and destruction," 357–59), employing *pathos* by drawing upon the emotion of fear. This approach to creating a favorable disposition in his audience (*diathesis*) contrasts with Odysseus' more patient, sympathetic attitude toward the same demoralized warriors. These differences in rhetorical emphasis and priority are characteristic of the two speakers: Odysseus is adept at *diathesis*, or reading his audience; Nestor at appeals to *êthos*, or the credibility of his own venerable character and experience.

Nestor concludes his speech by again turning to Agamemnon with commands, this time of a practical nature: he must draw up his troops according to tribe (2.360–68). Embedded in the instructions to Agamemnon, however, is a barb directed at the Argive audience. This comes in the form of a final appeal to the army's sense of shame (*pathos*), as Nestor notes that the arrangement of troops will help to separate the bad soldiers (κακός, 365) from the good (ἐσθλός, 366). His parting line implies that the Greeks have failed to capture Troy thus far because of their "cowardice and ignorance of warfare" (368). Thus Nestor closes his speech on the same note on which he had opened: shaming. This completes a ring-composition structure within the speech: shaming; commands to Agamemnon; enthymematic exhortation to stay and fight followed by a threat; commands to Agamemnon; shaming. The result of Nestor's speech with regard to arousing the troops is obscured because it is immediately followed by another speech, namely Agamemnon's response. But in the eyes of his primary addressee, at least, Nestor has been effective; Agamemnon proclaims him a victor in the art of assembly-speaking (ἦ μὰν αὖτ' ἀγοϱῇ νικᾷς, 2.370) and implements his suggestions (371ff.).

III. Athena addresses Pandarus at 4.93–103 in the guise of the Trojan hero Laodocus, attempting to persuade him to break the tenuous treaty between the warring sides by shooting an arrow at Menelaus. Her opening address conveys flattery (*diathesis*), as she calls him "wise son of Lykaon" (93); she then commands him to "let me persuade you" (93) to shoot an arrow at Menelaus. This command serves as the conclusion to an **enthymeme** whose premise follows in the form of an appeal to the **topic of consideration of incentives and disincentives** (topic #20): "So you might dare send a flying arrow against Menelaos and win you glory and gratitude in the sight of all Trojans, particularly beyond all else with prince Alexandros" (94–96). This enthymeme argument is then repeated in reverse, with slight variation, to form a chiastic structure: "Beyond all beside you would carry away glorious gifts from him, were he to see warlike Menelaos, the son of Atreus, struck down by your arrow, and laid on the sorrowful corpse-fire" (97–99). Through this repetition, Athena emphasizes the incentives of both immortal glory and material gain, and this persuasive technique is effective for her particular audience. Hearkening back to Athena's opening command "let me persuade you" (μοί τι πίθοιο), the narrator informs us that the goddess "persuaded the fool's heart in him" (τῷ δὲ φρένας ἄφρονι πεῖθεν, 4.104).

IV. At 7.109–19, Agamemnon addresses Menelaus in an attempt to dissuade him from dueling with Hector, for fear that he will be killed. The main force of his argument comes from an **enthymeme** whose conclusion is stated as a command: "Hold fast, though it hurts you, nor long in your pride to fight with a man who is better than you are" (110–11). The premise draws on an argument from the **topic of greater and less** (topic #4): "There are others who shudder before him. Even Achilleus . . . trembles to meet this man, and he is far better than you are" (112–14). If the Achaeans' greatest warrior fears combat with Hector, Agamemnon argues, how much more should Menelaus, an inferior fighter, dread such an encounter. After this forceful premise, Agamemnon reiterates his conclusion ("Go back now and sit down," 115), and then ends his speech on a more reassuring note. He notes that Hector's challenge will not go unanswered, even though Menelaus is not the right candidate for the job: "The Achaians will set up another to fight against this man, and . . . I think he will be glad to leave off" (116–18). This assurance, by which Agamemnon shows sensitivity to Menelaus' valiant disposition and concern for honor (*diathesis*), proves convincing. The narrator reports that "the hero spoke like this and bent (παρέπεισεν) the heart of his brother since he urged wisely (αἴσιμα παρειπών)" (7.120–21).

V. Nestor addresses the assembled Greek army at 7.124–60 with an exhortation in response to Hector's public challenge of the Greek warriors to a duel (7.67–91).[3] No one save Menelaus had risen to the challenge; so after Agamemnon dissuades Menelaus from fighting (see speech IV above), Nestor attempts to stir up the spirits of better-qualified challengers. His opening move is an appeal to shame in several different manifestations, all designed to put his audience in a particular state of mind (*diathesis*). He addresses the audience as ὦ πόποι, then continues with the shame-inducing statement that "great sorrow settles on the land of Achaia" (124). Nestor elaborates upon the coupled ideas of sorrow and shame over the next seven lines, channeling them through the invoked presence of Peleus: "Surely he would groan aloud, Peleus, the aged horseman, the great man of counsel among the Myrmidons . . ." (125–26). Using the authority vested in Peleus' *êthos* to arouse the emotion of shame in his audience (*pathos*), Nestor projects from Peleus' joyful reaction to the noble men of the past what his response would be to the cowardly ones of the present:

> **Once** (ποτέ), as he questioned me in his house, he was filled with great joy
> as he heard the generation and blood of all of the Argives.
> **Now** (νῦν) if he were to hear how all cringe away before Hektor,
> many a time he would lift up his very hands to the immortals,
> and the life breath from his limbs would go down into the house of Hades. (127–31)

This appeal also serves as an **enthymeme** premise, a reason for acting on Nestor's implied conclusion to rise up and meet Hector's challenge. Embedded in this argument is Nestor's appeal to his own *êthos*: *he* is an authority on what Peleus' response would be, because he and Peleus were comrades and interacted in the past (127–28). Nestor's *êthos* is further reinforced by the fact that, as Keith Dickson notes, he possesses authoritative inventory of all the Greeks (128). Such "extradiegetic analepsis" (narration of events outside the scope of the poem), to use Dickson's term, is particularly remarkable considering that the *Iliad*'s narrator had been forced to rely on the Muses to produce a similar catalogue: "The old man draws on no source other than that of his own vast personal memory," Dickson observes. "His authority for what he says is grounded in what he himself has *seen*, not in some mediated access—e.g., hearsay—to the events in question."[4]

Nestor continues to leverage his own *êthos* in the next section of his speech, an extended recollection of a scene from the war between the Pylians and Arcadians. In that war, Nestor had himself played the role of hero in a duel against the Arcadian hero Ereuthalion—a duel with many parallels to the one Hector is currently proposing, including the fact that the "bravest" (ἄριστοι) of the Pylians "were all afraid and trembling: none had the courage" (7.151). Not only does Nestor employ the *êthos* technique with statements such as "my hard-enduring heart in its daring drove me to fight him. I in age was the youngest of all of them" (152–53), he also sets himself up as a *paradeigma* to be followed.[5] This recollection of a past feat turns into an **enthymeme**, beginning with a premise that argues from the **topic of greater and less** (topic #4) in lines 157–60. Nestor contrasts his own willingness to duel against Hector despite his old and feeble state—that is, less ability to fight (157–58)—with the reluctance of the Greek warriors, who are much younger and in better condition—that is, greater ability to fight (159–60). His final statement is not a typical enthymematic conclusion or command, but it does convey strong prescriptive implications: "But you, now, who are the bravest of all the Achaians, are not minded with a good will to go against Hektor" (159–60). Nestor's "scolding," as the narrator characterizes it in the aftermath of the speech (ὣς νείκεσσ' ὁ γέρων, 7.161), is successful: nine warriors immediately volunteer, and Ajax is chosen by lot for the duel.

VI. Odysseus' speech as part of the embassy to persuade Achilles to rejoin the Greek army (9.225–306) is, in large part, a vehicle for conveying Agamemnon's offer of lavish gifts to Achilles. But at the beginning and again at the very end of the speech, Odysseus uses his own persuasive arguments on Achilles in an attempt to augment—and even to counter—the potentially offensive nature of Agamemnon's offer. Odysseus' first and most extensive argument is one of **diathesis**, an attempt to dispose Achilles toward helping his fellow Greek warriors through an appeal to his pity (**pathos**). The Greeks face "a trouble all too great," Odysseus explains, "that we look on and are afraid. There is doubt if we save our strong-benched vessels or if they will be destroyed, unless you put on your war strength" (229–31). The *pathos* invoked by this account of the army's desperate straits serves as an enthymematic premise, one that Odysseus develops further in lines 232–46. He relates the Trojans' success, led by Hector, who "in the huge pride of his strength rages irresistibly" (237–38); and notes that Zeus is aiding the Trojans. A renewed emotional appeal in lines 244–46 ("All this I fear terribly in my heart . . . let for us it be destiny to die here in Troy, far away from horse-pasturing Argos") is followed by Odysseus' **enthymeme** conclusion: the command "Up, then! if you are minded, late though it be, to rescue the afflicted sons of the Achaians from the Trojan onslaught" (247–48). Another **enthymeme** follows on the heels of the first. In place of pity, Odysseus now uses a threat predicated on the emotion of fear (**pathos**) as his premise: "It will be an affliction to you hereafter, there will be no remedy found to heal the evil thing when it has been done" (249–50). This argument anticipates what will be a centerpiece of Phoenix's appeal to Achilles in the second embassy speech: that Achilles will regret it if he waits until it is too late to help. The conclusion to this second enthymeme is another command from Odysseus: "No, beforehand take thought to beat the evil day aside from the Danaans" (250–51).

Then Odysseus turns to a different argumentative tactic: an appeal to the authority (**êthos**) of one whom he knows Achilles respects, perhaps above all other mortals—namely, his father Peleus. The invocation of an external authority figure through direct quotation was discussed in relation to other speeches in chapter 2 (see especially the discussion of Nestor's speech to Patroclus in 11.656–803, in which Nestor quotes Menoitius). Here, Odysseus produces a strikingly apt quotation from Peleus that mirrors his own appeal to Achilles: " 'Be it yours to hold fast in your bosom the anger of the proud heart, for consideration is better. Keep from the bad complication of quarrel, and all the more for this the Argives will honor you' " (255–58). Although the **enthymeme** that the quoted Peleus uses is a simple formula reminiscent of wisdom literature (the **topic of consideration of incentives and disincentives** (topic #20) is presented in the form of honor from Achilles' colleagues), it is the speaker's identity that is the key to this persuasive tactic.

Odysseus ends the part of his speech that contains his own appeal with another **enthymeme**, whose conclusion—"Yet even now stop, and give way from the anger that hurts the heart" (9.259–60)—is followed by a premise comprised of the **topic of consideration of incentives and disincentives** (topic #20): "Agamemnon offers you worthy recompense if you change from your anger" (260–61). What follows is the ultimate offer of incentives, as Odysseus recites the long list of gifts and honors that Agamemnon has promised to Achilles if he returns to fight (262–99). But in the last lines of his speech, Odysseus returns to his own voice for one final appeal. His argument is a prime example of *diathesis*; he acknowledges Achilles' likely reaction to Agamemnon's gifts, hoping thereby to disarm Achilles and leave him open to persuasion by another route: "But if the son of Atreus is too much hated in your heart, himself and his gifts, at least take pity on all the other Achaians, who are afflicted along the host" (300–302). This returns Odysseus to his initial strategy of appealing to *pathos* in the service of an **enthymeme** argument. For good measure, he adds a final **topic of consideration of incentives and disincentives** (topic #20) by asserting that "[the Achaians] will honor you as a god. You may win very great glory among them. For now you might kill Hektor" (302–4). Odysseus' appeals are ineffectual in this case, however. As Achilles says in reply, "without consideration for you (ἀπηλεγέως, literally "bluntly") I must make my answer" (9.309). His majestic refusal speech that follows is of course no reflection on Odysseus' persuasive powers, but is rather a rejection of Agamemnon and his gifts.

VII. Nestor seeks volunteers for a nighttime ambush in an address to the assembled Greek army at 10.204–17. He opens with a mild appeal to shame, questioning whether there is any man who, "in the daring of his own heart" (ἑῷ αὐτοῦ / θυμῷ τολμήεντι, 204–5), will face the Trojans. His vocabulary emphasizes a bravery that his audience is not demonstrating, but that he wishes to evoke; he subtly plays on their sense of shame (an example of *diathesis*) by attributing to the rival Trojans the epithet "high-hearted" (μεγαθύμους, 205). An extended **enthymeme** comprises the bulk of the speech, employing as its conclusion suggestion instead of the more typical imperative command—an approach that is appropriate to the occasion (soliciting volunteers, rather than exhorting or rebuking soldiers on the battlefield). "So he might catch some enemy, who straggled behind them," Nestor suggests, "or he might overhear some thing that the Trojans are saying" (206–10). Nestor then states the enthymematic premise—the rationale for the action he is promoting—in the form of a future less vivid condition: "Could a man learn this, and then come back again to us unhurt, why huge and heaven-high would rise up his glory (κλέος) among all people, and an excellent gift (δόσις ἐσθλή) would befall him" (211–13). This premise, with its promise of future reward, employs the now-familiar **topic of consideration of incentives and disincentives** (topic #20). Nestor increases the appeal by elaborating on the nature of the incentive:

> For all those who hold by the ships high power as princes,
> of all these each one of them will give him a black sheep,
> female, with a lamb beneath; there shall be no gift like this one,
> one that will be forever by at the feasts and festivals. (214–17)

Such luxurious expansion of the single idea of a δόσις ἐσθλή (Nestor could have left it at that) constitutes the rhetorical technique of *auxesis*. By elaborating upon the virtues of the incentive, Nestor shows respect for the anticipated effort that will entail such a reward. This again demonstrates his subtle attention to the need for *diathesis*, and as such provides a contrast with Agamemnon's stingy reward-offer to Teucer at 8.281–91 (see chapter II, section III). Accordingly, Nestor's speech is successful in its object: the Greek warriors' first response is awed silence (πάντες ἀκὴν ἐγένοντο σιωπῇ, 10.218); then Diomedes volunteers, and a horde of other Greeks follow suit (219–32).

VIII. Polydamas attempts to persuade Hector and the Trojan chiefs to adopt his battle strategy at 12.61–79, after the Trojans have reached an impasse on the battlefield because of the difficulty of the terrain for their horses. The opening of this speech focuses on laying out a practical strategy: Polydamas urges the Trojans to dismount from their horses rather than trying to cross the Achaeans' ditch in chariots (61–64). This proposal forms the conclusion of an **enthymeme** for which the premise is Aristotle's **topic of the consequence** (topic #13): "There is no way to get down, no way again to do battle from horses," Polydamas warns, "for the passage is narrow and I think they must be hurt there" (65–66). If it is the will of Zeus to destroy the Achaeans, says Polydamas, so much the better; but the prudent strategy is to prepare for the worst:

> ... If they turn again and a backrush comes upon us
> out of the ships, and we are driven against the deep ditch,
> then I think no longer could one man to carry a message
> get clear to the city, once the Achaians have turned back upon us. (71–74)

Again here, Polydamas depicts the consequences to the Trojans of neglecting his advice, providing an uncomfortable vision of the future that he hopes will dissuade Hector and the army from their current course. He caps off this speech with another **enthymeme**. Its conclusion is comprised of a frank demand that the Trojans let themselves be persuaded (ἀλλ' ἄγεθ', ὡς ἂν ἐγὼ εἴπω, πειθώμεθα πάντες, 75), followed by practical instructions in the imperative and the hortatory subjunctive (76–78). The enthymeme premise closes the speech: "As for the Achaians, they will not hold, if the bonds of death are fastened upon them" (78–79). This is so obvious a statement as to form a kind of *gnômê*, but it does provide a reason for the action that Polydamas is exhorting. The response to the speech is favorable; Hector is pleased at what the narrator refers to as this "counsel of safety" (μῦθος ἀπήμων, 12.80), and the Trojans immediately implement its advice (81–87).

IX. The next two speeches in this catalogue are part of a dialogue between Polydamas and Hector, the first delivered by Polydamas at 12.211–29 in response to the portent of the eagle and snake that the Trojans have just witnessed. He begins with the complaint that Hector always opposes his plans, even though Polydamas is a good speaker (ἐσθλὰ φραζομένῳ, 211–12)—an explicit appeal to *êthos*. He then turns this self-attributed character quality into an insult of Hector, questioning his ability to speak skillfully: "There is no good reason for you, in your skill, to argue wrong (παρὲξ ἀγορευέμεν), neither in the councils nor in the fighting, and ever to be upholding your own cause" (212–14). Polydamas' characterization of Hector as an inferior rhetorician is supported elsewhere in the *Iliad*, most notably by the narrator himself when he comments on the respective strengths of Polydamas and Hector in 18.252: ἀλλ' ὁ μὲν ἄρ μύθοισιν, ὁ δ' ἔγχεϊ πολλὸν ἐνίκα ("But he [Polydamas] was better in words, the other [Hector] with the spear far better"). In the present context, however, it is a poor choice for the purpose of putting his audience in a favorable frame of mind.

Polydamas continues his argument with an **enthymeme**, the conclusion placed first in the form of a simple command: "Let us not go on and fight the Danaans by their ships" (12.216). The extended premise is Polydamas' interpretation of the eagle and snake omen in 216–27, which serves the function of a "sign" (σημεῖον) for his argument.[6] The interpretation of the omen, taken to apply to the Trojans' current situation, employs the correlative phrases ὧδε γὰρ ἐκτελέεσθαι ὀΐομαι (217) and ὡς ἡμεῖς (223), which Polydamas uses to frame his description of the portent, and which produce his interpretation (the enthymematic premise):

So [like the eagle who dropped the snake] we . . .
we shall not take the same ways back from the ships in good order;
since we shall leave many Trojans behind us, whom the Achaians
will cut down with the bronze as they fight for themselves by their vessels. (223–27)

Polydamas' closing statement, like the opening lines of the speech, refers to his own ability to persuade, as well as claiming knowledge of the gods' minds. He is only slightly more subtle here than he had been at the beginning of the speech in promoting his own *êthos*, using the figure of an interpreter of the gods (θεοπρόπος) as a stand-in for himself, and couching the confident statement in terms of a potential optative: "So (ὧδέ) an interpreter of the gods would answer, one who knew in his mind the truth of portents, and whom the people believed in [literally, "whom the people were persuaded by, οἱ πειθοίατο λαοί]" (228–29). The effectiveness of this speech suffers from the fact that Polydamas emphasizes his own character qualities (*êthos*) to the neglect of what will please or placate the audience (*diathesis*), and the result of such rhetorical imbalance is that it fails to persuade. Hector responds vehemently with reproof, disagreement, and persuasion of his own.

X. Hector's tirade at 12.231–50 is ostensibly addressed to Polydamas, but it is highly conscious of the audience of Trojan warriors that is present, and serves as an exhortation (and hence a persuasion attempt) to this broader audience. Disapproval and rebuke in response to Polydamas' challenge takes up the first half of the speech (231–40), and Hector picks up on Polydamas' focus on prowess in speech and argumentation. He uses the verb ἀγορεύω twice in the span of three lines (231, 233) as he questions Polydamas' capabilities at speaking in the assembly, and he chastises him with the line "Your mind knows how to contrive a saying (μῦθον) better than this one" (232). Hector sets up an opposition between Polydamas' counsel and the counsels of Zeus, with which he claims to be personally acquainted (ἅς τέ μοι αὐτὸς ὑπέσχετο καὶ κατένευσε,

236). In an attempt to outdo Polydamas, who had promoted his own *êthos* by claiming to be an interpreter of the gods, Hector invokes the greatest of the gods as his personal confidante. He follows with an **enthymeme** in lines 237–43 that draws on an argument resembling Aristotle's **topic of turning against the adversary the things said by the adversary against the speaker** (ἐκ τῶν εἰρημένων καθ' αὐτοὺς πρὸς τὸν εἰπόντα, topic #6, *Rhetoric* 2.23.7). Alluding to Polydamas' appeal to the omen of the eagle—an appeal that had invoked the gods by extension in its ending claim, "So an interpreter of the gods would answer" (12.228)—Hector issues a sarcastic dismissal: "You tell me to put my trust in birds, who spread wide their wings. I care nothing for these, I think nothing of them" (237–38). This leads to the enthymeme conclusion, in which Hector insinuates that to believe in bird signs is, in fact, to deny the promises of Zeus: "No, let us put our trust in the counsel of great Zeus, he who is lord over all mortal men and all the immortals" (241–42). The subsequent premise takes the form of a *gnômê*: "One bird sign is best: to fight in defence of our country" (243). This enthymeme appeals to two irrefutable values for Hector's Trojan audience: piety toward the gods, in implied contrast to the petty superstition of Polydamas; and courage in fighting to protect one's homeland, in implied contrast to Polydamas' cowardice.

Hector concludes his speech with an extended attack (12.244–50) on Polydamas' character, basing this attack on Polydamas' reluctance to press forward in battle. Clearly, Hector is no longer trying to persuade Polydamas himself—if that was ever his intent in this speech—since ad hominem attacks run counter to the strategy of *diathesis*. Instead, he is using his opponent as a straw man in order to incite the Trojan audience to favor his own cause. He ends by threatening Polydamas with death if he turns any soldier away from fighting by "beguiling him with your arguments" (παρφάμενος ἐπέεσσιν, 248–50). This reference to Polydamas' prowess in speaking brings full-circle not only Hector's speech (which had opened with reproaching Polydamas for his poor μῦθος), but also the entire dialogue: Polydamas had begun *his* speech by criticizing Hector's use of argumentation (12.212–13). In short, a significant component of these antagonists' rhetoric is impugning each other's rhetoric (and promoting their own). In this instance, Hector's persuasive strategy carries the day, and the Trojans follow his lead into battle: "He spoke, and led the way, and the rest of them came on after him with unearthly clamour" (12.251–52).

XI. A unique phenomenon occurs at 12.269–76, when Telamonian and Oilean Ajax deliver a simultaneous exhortation to Greek soldiers on the battlefield. For the purposes of rhetorical analysis, the speech is like any other, despite being attributed to dual speakers. The narrative introduction to the speech offers an unusually detailed commentary on the speakers' rhetorical strategy: "[They] stung them along, using kind words to one, to another hard ones, whenever they saw a man hang back from the fighting" (ἄλλον μειλιχίοις, ἄλλον στερεοῖς ἐπέεσσι / νείκεον, ὅν τινα πάγχυ μάχης μεθιέντα ἴδοιεν, 267–68). This is essentially a representation of the *diathesis* technique—a recognition of the need for different persuasive approaches depending on the individual addressed. The narrator's commentary is borne out in the speech itself, which opens with the Aiantes acknowledging through their vocative address the widely varied statuses of the men whom they hope to persuade: "Dear friends, you who are preeminent among the Argives, you who are of middle estate, you who are of low account . . ." (269–70). They then turn these stated differences into a concise **enthymeme**: "Since all of us are not alike in battle [gnomic premise], this is work for all now [conclusion]" (270–71). A second **enthymeme** immediately follows, this one with the hortatory conclusion preceding the premise: "Now let no man let himself be turned back upon the ships. . . . So may Olympian Zeus who grips the thunderbolt grant us a way to the city, when we beat off the attack of our enemies" (272–76). This premise, the ending note of the speech, is an appeal to **topic of consideration of incentives and disincentives** (topic #20); the Aiantes argue that the Greeks' ultimate goal of capturing Troy may result from heeding their exhortation. It is a short and relatively simple speech, appropriate for the battlefield context. But it is effective: "Such was their far cry, and they stirred the Achaians' war strength," observes the narrator (12.277).

XII. Sarpedon addresses Glaucus at 12.310–28 in a speech aimed at persuading his Lycian comrade to take the lead with him in the fighting. His opening argument is an **enthymeme** based on the *êthos* that he and Glaucus share: their identity as noblemen and, consequently, their leadership responsibilities. Sarpedon offers his enthymematic premise in the form of a rhetorical question: "Why is it you and I are honoured before others with pride of place, the choice meats and the filled wine cups in Lykia?" (310–14). His conclusion, linked to the premise by the conjunction τῷ, is simple: "Therefore (τῷ) it is our duty in the forefront of the Lykians to take our stand, and bear our part of the blazing of battle" (315–16). Although the enthymeme's premise does not perfectly correspond to any of Aristotle's topics, it is nevertheless a commonplace of persuasion across time and cultures, along the lines of *gnômai* such as the Biblical observation, "To whom much is given, much is required" (Luke 12:48), or Spiderman's guiding premise, "With great power comes great responsibility." A second, separate premise to the same enthymematic conclusion follows in lines 317–21, as Sarpedon appeals to Glaucus' desire for honor by means of a fictional interlocutor, who hypothetically would speak in praise of the two warriors if they "fight in the forefront of the Lykians" (321). Beck, who has analyzed the phenomenon of character-quoted direct speech in the *Iliad*, observes that Trojan speakers tend to "quote hypothetical, usually anonymous, future comments about their own reputations, mainly in order to add drama and vividness to expressive speeches about death on the battlefield."[7] This rhetorical gesture also exhibits Aristotle's **topic of consideration of incentives and disincentives** (topic #20), as it invokes a hypothetical future occurrence in order to motivate present action. Sarpedon closes his exhortation with another **enthymeme** in 326–28. The *gnômê* "No man can turn aside nor escape [the spirits of death]" (327) serves as the premise, while the conclusion reiterates Sarpedon's main persuasive object: "Let us go on and win glory for ourselves, or yield it to others" (328). Such bracing logic proves effective, as Glaucus complies (οὐδ' ἀπίθησε 12.329) and joins Sarpedon in leading the Lycians into battle.

XIII. Poseidon delivers three battlefield exhortation speeches to members of the Greek army in Book 13, assuming the guise of a fellow warrior each time. The first of these speeches is addressed to the Aiantes at 13.47–58. Its argumentation is simple, based on a single enthymematic argument that is repeated with slight variations. Poseidon (in the guise of Calchas) begins with an imperative command: "Aiantes, you two, remembering the spirit of warcraft and not that of shivering panic, must save the Achaian people" (47–48); this forms the conclusion of the first **enthymeme**. Its premise is an appeal to the **topic of consideration of incentives and disincentives** (topic #20) as Poseidon invokes the fearsome threat of Hector: "But I fear most terribly disaster to us in the one place where that berserk flamelike leads them against us, Hektor" (52–54). This incentive doubles as an appeal to the emotion of fear (*pathos*) as he imagines the consequences to the army if the Aiantes do nothing to stop Hector. A second, similar **enthymeme** follows, this time with more specific instructions for action. The enthymeme conclusion is conveyed by Poseidon's suggestion that a god is prompting them to "stand fast strongly yourselves, urge the rest to stand also" (56). Its premise consists of another **topic of consideration of incentives and disincentives** (topic #20), and offers the hope of victory against Hector rather than the fear of defeat: "Thus (τῷ), hard though he sweeps on, you might stay him beside the fast-running ships. . . ." (57–58). Poseidon's exhortation is effective in concert with his act of filling the Aiantes with fighting strength; they lead the Greeks' stand against Hector (13.59–80).

XIV. Poseidon's second Book 13 exhortation is addressed to a small group of Greek warriors at 13.95–124. Beginning with what will be a prominent strategy within the speech, he invokes the emotion of shame (*pathos*) in order to dispose the men to his purpose (*diathesis*):

> Shame (αἰδώς), you Argives, young fighting men, since I for my part
> have confidence that by fighting you can save our ships from destruction;
> but if you yourselves are to go slack from the sorrowful fighting
> now is seen your day to be beaten down by the Trojans.
> Oh for shame (ὢ πόποι)! . . .
> that the Trojans could come against our ships, they who in time past
> were like fugitive deer before us. . . . (95–102)

In addition to the strategy of shaming, Poseidon employs an **enthymeme** based on a conditional sentiment. Its conclusion is contained in the brief participial phrase "by fighting"; its premise is conveyed by an appeal to the **topic of consideration of incentives and disincentives** (topic #20), and encompasses both an incentive to fighting ("you can save our ships from destruction") and a disincentive to slacking ("now is seen your day to be beaten down").

Poseidon continues to elaborate on the theme of the Trojans' weakness and the corresponding shame for the Greeks through the middle portion of his speech (13.102–110). Toward the end of the speech, his rhetorical strategy shifts from emphasizing the negative qualities of shame and weakness that have beset the Greek army (and its leader Agamemnon) to emphasizing the positive counterparts of these qualities: honor and glory. "But you can no longer in honor (καλά) give way from your fighting valor being all the best men (ἄριστοι) along the host," Poseidon argues (116–17). He contrasts this flattering reminder of his audience's elite status and attendant responsibility (*diathesis*) with a statement that he would not blame a weak man for reluctance to fight (117–19)—another version of the sentiment that Sarpedon had expressed to Glaucus in Book 12 (see speech XII above). A final **enthymeme** ties together the themes of this exhortation, beginning with a premise that appeals to the **topic of consideration of incentives and disincentives** (topic #20): "soon you will bring to pass some still greater evil with this hanging back" (120–21). The conclusion comes in the form of the command "let every one of you plant in his heart's depth discipline and shamefastness (αἰδῶ)" (121–22), and a second premise to this enthymeme—"for Hek-

tor of the great war cry is fighting beside our vessels in his power. . . ." (123–24)—
ends the speech. Poseidon's exhortation achieves its desired effect, as the men
join ranks to hold off the Trojans (13.125–35).

XV. Poseidon's final exhortation in this series is delivered in the guise of the
Aetolian warrior Thoas to Idomeneus at 13.232–38. The speech opens with a
threatening wish that "that man who this day willfully hangs back from the
fighting" would "never win home again out of Troy land, but stay here and be
made dogs' delight for their feasting" (232–34). An **enthymeme** follows, its conclusion stated first in the form of a simple command: "Take up your armour and
go with me. We must speed this action together" (234–35). As a premise, Poseidon argues that he and Idomeneus, by joining forces, would have an advantage
over a single person working alone: "since we, being two (δύ' ἐόντε), might
bring some advantage" (236). He reinforces this notion of strength in numbers
with the **gnômê** "The warcraft even of sad fighters combined turns courage"
(237). A final expression of the possibility for advantageous collaboration comes
in Poseidon's closing line: "You and I would have skill to fight even against good
men" (238). By touting his own and Idomeneus' ability to match "good men"
(ἀγαθοί) in battle, this line serves both as an appeal to the speaker's *êthos*, and as
an instance of **diathesis** in that it compliments Idomeneus for his skill and courage. The speech is a success; Idomeneus arms himself and then relays a battle
exhortation in turn to his comrade Meriones (13.249–53).

XVI. Polydamas' speech to Hector at 13.726–47 finds him in the familiar role
of urging caution in battle strategy. He also resumes his antagonistic tone toward Hector and his recurring complaint that Hector's prowess in warfare is
not matched by skill in the βουλῆ (cf. 12.211–14). After making this complaint at
some length (726–34), Polydamas turns to the persuasive portion of his speech,
a strategic proposal (735–47). This proposal takes the form of an **enthymeme**,
with premises preceding and following the conclusion. The first premise is a
description of the situation (736–39), drawing upon visual evidence (Aristotle's
τεκμήριον) to highlight the difficulties currently encountered by the Trojan soldiers, who are "fewer men against many, being scattered among the vessels"
(739). The conclusion-command follows: "Draw back now, and call to this place
all of our bravest. . . ." (740–44). The second premise follows, an argument
from the **topic of consideration of incentives and disincentives** (topic #20):
"Since (γάρ) I fear the Achaians might wreak on us requital for yesterday; since
(ἐπεί) beside their ships lurks a man insatiate of fighting and I think we can no

longer utterly hold him from the fighting" (744–47). Despite a lack of conciliatory language, Polydamas' argumentation—aided by the evidence of battlefield conditions—is convincing to Hector: the formula ἄδε δ' Ἕκτορι μῦθος ἀπήμων (13.748) is the same one that the narrator had used at 12.80 in the aftermath of an earlier speech by Polydamas (see speech VIII above).

XVII. Diomedes' speech at 14.110–32—addressed primarily to Agamemnon, secondarily to the assembled Achaeans—contains both rhetorical and meta-rhetorical persuasion. It is an argument for the right to make an argument, the right to be considered an orator. Diomedes makes the speech in response to Agamemnon's proposal to desert the campaign against Troy and sail home, and specifically to the challenge Agamemnon had posed at 14.107–9, "Now let someone speak who has better counsel (ἀμείνονα μῆτιν) than this [Odysseus' preceding rebuke] was; young man or old; and what he says will be to my liking." The bulk of Diomedes' speech is comprised of a defense of his own qualifications for taking an authoritative stance counter to the sentiments of his commander-in-chief. Diomedes bases his defense on an argument from *êthos*, although his claims to nobility and trustworthiness derive largely from his father's character and reputation. In an attempt to legitimize himself among his aristocratic and older peers, Diomedes asserts that "I also can boast that my generation is of an excellent father" (113). An elaboration of Tydeus' ancestry, exploits, and wealth follows (115–25). This expanded appeal to *êthos* is not unprecedented among Iliadic speakers—it is a technique most notably employed by Nestor at 1.259–73 and 7.133–58—but Nestor recounts his own past, whereas Diomedes (who is too young to have a past) lays claim to his family history to prove his own worth.[8]

The rhetorical use to which Diomedes puts his family history is clear from the transition to the argumentative portion of his speech. He transforms the authority gained from his father's reputation into the premise of an **enthymeme** with the statement "He surpassed all other Achaians with the spear. If all this is true, you must have heard of it" (14.124–25). The enthymeme's conclusion makes clear that Diomedes is leaning on his father's *êthos* to make his argument, and extending that *êthos* to apply to himself: "Therefore (τῷ) you could not, saying that I was base and unwarlike by birth, dishonor any word that I speak, if I speak well. Let us go back to the fighting wounded as we are. We have to" (126–28). The defiant claim "You could not . . . dishonour any word that I speak, if I speak well" (οὐκ ἄν με . . . μῦθον ἀτιμήσαιτε πεφασμένον, ὅν κ' ἐῢ εἴπω) opens up a new dimension to the argument. Thus far, Diomedes has been parlaying his father's reputation into an assertion of his own *êthos*; now he hazards his honor on his own speaking ability (an ability that has received external affirmation from Nestor, 9.54–56). Having thus asserted his right to be heard and heeded, Diomedes issues a string of simple commands and strategic instruction (128–32) to end his speech. These instructions take into account both the need to preserve the leaders' well-being ("We must hold ourselves . . . clear of missiles, so that none will add to the wound he has got already," 129–30), and the need for the leaders to be present on the battlefield to uphold their soldiers' morale ("But we shall be there to drive them on, since even before this they have favoured their anger," 131–32). Diomedes' arguments have the desired effect; we are told that the Achaeans "listened well to him, and obeyed (ἐπίθοντο) him" (14.133).

XVIII. Hera addresses Aphrodite at 14.198–210 in an attempt to gain her help in seducing Zeus, part of Hera's plot to provide an advantage to the Greeks by distracting Zeus from his will (*boulê*) for the war. Perhaps the most cannily manipulative of Iliadic speakers, Hera is not above incorporating deception into her rhetoric. She structures her argument as an **enthymeme**, beginning with the conclusion / command, "give me loveliness and desirability" (198), and adducing as a premise the false mission to resolve a quarrel between Oceanus and Tethys (200–207). Hera crafts her story so as to arouse Aphrodite's sympathy and to negate her view of Hera as an aggressive rival. Elaborating on the figures of Oceanus and Tethys allows Hera to recount her own youth and vulnerability, when the two ancient gods "brought me up kindly in their own house, and cared for me and took me from Rheia, at that time when Zeus of the wide brows drove Kronos underneath the earth" (202–4). Hera's manipulation of her own *êthos* in this way lulls Aphrodite into trusting her tale. She also employs the technique of *diathesis* as she tailors her request to Aphrodite's susceptibilities: she claims that she needs Aphrodite's specialty, an aphrodisiac, to settle Oceanus' and Tethys' marital quarrel (205–7). In this, Hera has correctly calculated what will be an irresistible prospect for her listener. As she concludes her speech, Hera speaks of her desire to use persuasion (παραιπεπιθοῦσα) on Oceanus and Tethys (208–10). Such an awareness of persuasion—and mentioning persuasion as part of a larger scheme designed to persuade the unsuspecting addressee—demonstrates Hera's skill at using rhetorical tools.

As an additional method of favorably disposing her listener, the goddess of love, Hera uses derivatives of the word φίλος in each of the four final lines of the speech (*diathesis*):

ἀλλήλων ἀπέχονται
εὐνῆς καὶ **φιλότητος**, ἐπεὶ χόλος ἔμπεσε θυμῷ.
εἰ κείνω γ' ἐπέεσσι παραιπεπιθοῦσα **φίλον** κῆρ
εἰς εὐνὴν ἀνέσαιμι ὁμωθῆναι **φιλότητι**,
αἰεί κέ σφι **φίλη** τε καὶ αἰδοίη καλεοίμην.

> They have stayed apart from each other
> and from the bed **of love**, since rancour has entered their feelings.
> Could I win over with persuasion the **dear** heart within them
> and bring them back to their bed to be merged **in love** with each other
> I shall forever be called honoured by them, and **beloved**. (14.206–210)

This passage also introduces a source of motivation that lends plausibility to Hera's deception. As a second premise to her enthymematic conclusion (stated in line 198) that Aphrodite should give her desirability, Hera confesses a hope to "be forever called honoured by [Oceanus and Tethys], and beloved" (210). This use of the **topic of consideration of incentives and disincentives** (topic #20) is, of course, an atypical one: instead of promising advantage to the addressee, Hera feigns candor about her own selfish motives. The true rhetorical ploy at work here is an unexpressed invocation of likelihood (**eikos**) that plays on Aphrodite's expectations about and knowledge of Hera's character: proud and vain as she has many times shown herself to be, Hera is indeed likely to desire the honor and love of the senior gods. As this reflects somewhat unfavorably on Hera's character, it is perhaps also intended to exploit the latent antagonism between the two goddesses, and represents yet another use of *diathesis*. Hera is calculating that her admission of weakness will lull Aphrodite into complacency by giving her a false sense of power and superiority over her rival. This combination of argument and deception works exactly as it was intended to do, and Aphrodite happily gives Hera an aphrodisiac girdle (14.211–21).

XIX. Although Hera famously manipulates Zeus through seduction to achieve her own will in Book 14, the actual seduction does not entail a persuasive speech from Hera. Instead, she effects one of the great persuasive maneuvers of the epic by making Zeus think that he must persuade *her* to go to bed with him. Enticed by the charms of Aphrodite's girdle, now worn by Hera, Zeus begs his wife to postpone her spurious errand to Oceanus and Tethys with a rhetorical speech at 14.313–28. The first two lines contain a carpe diem sentiment: "Hera, there will be a time afterwards when you can go there as well," Zeus pleads; "But now let us go to bed and turn to love-making" (313–14). The rest of the speech consists of a single **enthymeme** construction, based upon the argument that Zeus feels more desire for Hera now than he has felt for any woman ever. The conclusion of Zeus' first enthymeme ("Now let us go to bed . . .") doubles as the conclusion to this second one. The premise which follows begins promisingly: "For (γάρ) never before has love for any goddess or woman so melted about the heart inside me, broken it to submission, as now" (315–16). This sentiment seems designed to flatter Hera and thus render her receptive to her husband's advances (*diathesis*). But then Zeus begins to elaborate on his feelings, employing *auxesis* to unintentionally comical effect: "Not that time when I loved the wife of Ixion . . . nor when I loved Akrisios' daughter, sweet-stepping Danaë . . . nor when I loved the daughter of far-renowned Phoinix, Europa . . . not when I loved Semele, or Alkmene . . . not when I loved the queen Demeter . . . not when it was glorious Leto, nor yourself, so much as now I love you, and the sweet passion has taken hold of me" (317–28). For the omniscient audience of the *Iliad*, Zeus' seduction rhetoric is doubly comical: for one thing, his words must have an effect on Hera opposite to *diathesis* in that they remind her of all his extramarital dalliances; for another, this persuasion attempt, abysmal as it is, is exactly the response Hera wanted. After a bit of calculated resistance from Hera at 14.330–40, Zeus has his way with her—and thus she has her way with him.

XX. The *Iliad*'s next rhetorical speech follows up on the seduction-of-Zeus episode in Book 14. Hera delivers a defense speech of sorts at 15.36–45, aiming to appease Zeus' anger and to persuade him not to punish her. She begins by swearing an oath that she is not responsible for the Achaeans' successes. This oath expands to fill six lines, invoking as witnesses first the realms of earth, heaven, and the underworld (36–38), and then Zeus himself: "The sanctity of your head be witness, and the bed of marriage between us: a thing by which I at least could never swear vainly" (39–40). Hera displays both *diathesis* and *êthos* techniques in these two lines. The flattering and deferential reference to Zeus constitutes *diathesis*, as does the mention of the marriage bed; Zeus, as we have seen in Book 14—and as Hera is well aware—is highly susceptible to the appeal of the marriage bed. Hera invokes her own trustworthy *êthos* with the phrase "I at least could never swear vainly." Her claim to take the marriage oath seriously also provides a veiled reproach of her husband (who has not been so faithful to his oaths in this matter)—a subtle psychological manipulation that contributes to putting him in an acquiescent frame of mind (another instance of *diathesis*).

The *logos* component of Hera's speech occurs in the second half, and consists of a claim of innocence and ignorance in the matter of the Greeks' recent success against the Trojans. She employs an argument from likelihood (*eikos*) to protest her innocence and Poseidon's culpability, seamlessly shifting the blame onto another god based upon that god's *êthos*: "It is not through my will that the shaker of the earth Poseidon afflicts the Trojans . . . but it is his own passion that urges him to it and drives him" (41–43). Finally, she returns to *diathesis* in the closing lines of the speech, expressing a demure submission to Zeus' authority and guidance: "No, but I myself also would give him counsel to go with you, o dark clouded, that way that you lead us" (45–46). The speech achieves Hera's desired result, as Zeus is appeased: "The father of gods and men smiled on her" (15.47).

XXI. Hector delivers a battlefield exhortation to the Trojans and their allies at 15.486–99, incited by his observation that Teucer's arrows have missed their intended target—himself—by divine intervention (15.458–83). He opens with a common exhortation formula that acts as the conclusion to an **enthymeme**: ἀνέρες ἔστε, φίλοι, μνήσασθε δὲ θούριδος ἀλκῆς / νῆας ἀνὰ γλαφυράς ("Be men now, dear friends, remember your furious valour along the hollow ships," 487–88). The premise that follows is an appeal to evidence (Aristotle's τεκμήριον), in that Hector claims to have been an eyewitness to Zeus' partiality to the Trojans: "since (γὰρ) I have seen with my own eyes how by the hand of Zeus their bravest man's arrows were baffled" (488–89). A second **enthymeme** follows in lines 490–94, similar in argumentation to the first but reversed in structure, so as to form a chiasm with the first one. Here the premise comes first, in the form of a *gnômê* which picks up on the notion of visual evidence: "Easily seen (ῥεῖα δ' ἀρίγνωτος) is the strength that is given from Zeus to mortals either in those into whose hands he gives the surpassing glory, or those he diminishes and will not defend them" (490–92). The premise continues by applying this *gnômê* to current situation: "as now he diminishes the strength of the Argives, and helps us" (493). The second enthymeme's conclusion, an exhortation to "fight on then by the ships together" (494), ensues. As a final premise for his exhortation, Hector offers an appeal to the **topic of consideration of incentives and disincentives** (topic #20)—in this case, the incentives of honor and family: "He has no dishonour when he dies defending his country, for then his wife shall be saved and his children afterwards, and his house and property shall not be damaged" (496–98). The speech is successful in its object, as we learn from the formulaic narrative comment following it: "So he spoke, and stirred the spirit and strength in each man" (Ὣς εἰπὼν ὤτρυνε μένος καὶ θυμὸν ἑκάστου, 15.500).

XXII. Hector addresses the Trojan allies with another battlefield exhortation at 17.220–32. His first argument is an assurance that he has not called them to fight for selfish reasons, but so that they could "defend the innocent children of the Trojans, and their wives, from the fighting Achaians" (221–24). This appeal to pity is calculated to evoke in his addressees the memories of their own families and thereby put them into a favorable frame of mind (*diathesis*). It puts into practice Aristotle's discussion of the rhetorical effectiveness of appeal to emotions (*Rhetoric* 2.2–11), in particular his observation that the basis of pity is the nearness in "age, in character, in habits, in rank, in birth" of the sufferer to oneself, so that one can plausibly imagine the misfortune happening to oneself (*Rhetoric* 2.8.13). Hector exploits this tactic here, evoking the allies' pity (and, he hopes, their aid) by inviting them to identify with the Trojans' suffering. He also relies heavily in this speech on an appeal to his own *êthos* and that of the people he represents. In particular, he emphasizes the qualities of selflessness, sacrifice, and courage: "With such a purpose I wear out my own people for presents and food, wherewith I make strong the spirit within each one of you" (225–26), he argues as an enthymematic premise for the argument that his audience *should* aid the Trojans. The conclusion to this **enthymeme** is a command: "Therefore (τῶ) a man must now turn his face straight forward, and perish or survive" (227–28). Hector closes the speech with an appeal to the **topic of consideration of incentives and disincentives** (topic #20) in lines 229–32, a straightforward offer of reward—half the spoils and κλέος equal to Hector's—for any man who can retrieve Patroclus' body from Ajax and the Greeks. The speech is successful, as the allies take immediate action (not even pausing to give verbal affirmation) on Hector's exhortation (17.233–34).

XXIII. The next two speeches in this catalogue are in dialogue with each other: the alternate proposals of Polydamas and Hector for dealing with the reappearance of Achilles on the battlefield. Polydamas speaks first, addressing the Trojan forces at 18.254–83 with a counsel of caution. It is worth noting the narrator's lengthier-than-usual introduction of the speaker, which remarks that ὁ μὲν ἄρ μύθοισιν, ὁ δ' ἔγχεϊ πολλὸν ἐνίκα ("He [Polydamas] was better in words, the other [Hector] with the spear far better," 18.252). This comment (which is discussed at greater length in the collection of meta-rhetorical passages in the introduction) is consistent with other clues throughout the *Iliad* that point to the poem possessing an evaluative notion of what it means to speak effectively. Polydamas' first argument is that the Trojans should go on the defensive now that Achilles is again fighting for the Greeks. This multifaceted **enthymeme** begins with the conclusion "I myself urge you to go back into the city and not wait for the divine dawn in the plain" (254–56). Its premises are several, beginning with an argument resembling Aristotle's **topic of induction** (ἐξ ἐπαγωγῆς, topic #10, *Rhetoric* 2.23.11), which draws conclusions based on the evidence of other situations that may have some bearing on the question at hand. "While this man was still angry with great Agamemnon, for all that time the Achaians were easier men to fight with" (257–58), Polydamas observes, inviting the audience to infer that Achilles' reinstatement into the Achaean forces will make them more formidable opponents. Polydamas combines this premise with arguments from his own experience and from the **topic of consideration of timing** (topic #5), according to which different behavior occurs or a different judgment is made before and after some signal event: "For (γὰρ) I also used then to be one who was glad to sleep out near their ships. . . . But now I terribly dread the swift-footed son of Peleus" (259–61). A third premise takes the form of a warning: Achilles' wrath is so violent that he will threaten the very city of Troy and its women (262–65). This threat to the things that the Trojans hold most dear is both an argument from the **topic of consideration of incentives and disincentives** (topic #20) and an appeal to the emotion of fear to make the audience receptive (*diathesis*). The conclusion to this extended enthymeme is restated following the litany of premises: "Let us go into the town; believe me; thus it will happen" (266).

In the second half of his speech, Polydamas largely repeats his arguments from the first half. If the Trojans stay where they are, he warns, Achilles will drive them back to the city with heavy casualties; the strategic move would be to preempt him by withdrawing now (18.267–83). The speech ends with practical instructions and an optimistic picture of the results of the recommended course of action ("His valour will not give him leave to burst in upon us nor sack our town," 282–83). Polydamas demonstrates his awareness of the audience's state of mind by conceding that his counsel may pain them for the moment (εἰ δ' ἂν ἐμοῖς ἐπέεσσι πιθώμεθα κηδόμενοί περ, 273), calculating that such sympathy will dispose them more favorably toward him (*diathesis*). His prowess in speaking, however, is for naught on this occasion. Whether he has miscalculated his audience's state of mind, is defeated by Hector's subsequent counterproposal, or is simply the victim of the inexorable will of Zeus, Polydamas' arguments fail to win over the Trojans.

XXIV. Hector's response to Polydamas at 18.285–309 is aimed not so much at persuading Polydamas himself, but at persuading the entire Trojan audience at hand to take a different course of action than the one Polydamas had advocated. His opening line repeats the formula with which he had begun his antagonistic address to Polydamas at 12.231 (Πουλυδάμα, σὺ μὲν οὐκέτ᾽ ἐμοὶ φίλα ταῦτ᾽ ἀγορεύεις), again targeting for criticism Polydamas' supposed expertise at speaking. Hector then employs *diathesis* by strongly identifying himself with the Trojans and their concerns and frustrations:

Have you not all had your glut of being fenced in our outerworks?

There was a time when mortal men would speak of the city

of Priam as a place with much gold and much bronze. But now

the lovely treasures that lay away in our houses have vanished. (287–90)

Rather than arousing the emotion of fear, as Polydamas had done, Hector stirs up anger and indignation in his audience with these sentiments. An **enthymeme** follows, pointing to the evidence of the recent improvement in the Trojans' fortunes. Drawing its premise from the **topic of consideration of timing** (topic #5), Hector notes that the changing favor of Zeus over time has made all the difference. The Trojans *had* been doing badly, so long as Zeus was angry with them (ἐπεὶ μέγας ὠδύσατο Ζεύς, 292); *now*, however, Zeus' favor has returned (νῦν δ᾽ . . . μοι ἔδωκε Κρόνου πάϊς ἀγκυλομήτεω / κῦδος ἀρέσθ᾽ ἐπὶ νηυσί, 293–94). The conclusion of this enthymeme—"why, fool, no longer show these thoughts to our people" (295)—is directed at Polydamas alone. For the benefit of the wider audience, however, Hector hints at the cowardice of a man who would withdraw from battle even when the gods are favorable.

In the transition to the second half of his speech, as he turns from Polydamas to address the Trojans directly, Hector issues brute commands rather than persuasive arguments. The vocabulary of persuasion, however, persists: "Not one of the Trojans will be persuaded (ἐπιπείσεται) by you," he taunts Polydamas; "I shall not allow it. Come, then, do as I say and let us all be persuaded (πειθώμεθα)" (18.296–97). A series of practical instructions follows that includes an **enthymeme** construction. In the conclusion to the enthymeme, Hector suggests that if any Trojan fears for the safety of his possessions, he should donate them to the people (300–301). As the premise, Hector invokes the **topic of consideration of incentives and disincentives** (topic #20), noting that "it is better for one of our own people to partake in them than for the Achaeans to" (302). It is not until the last lines of the speech that Hector addresses the major point of Polydamas' argument: the threat of Achilles. He employs an appeal to his own *êthos* to inspire his men not to fear the Greek champion: "If it is true that brilliant Achilleus is risen beside their ships, then the worse for him if he tries it, since I for my part will not run from him" (305–8). He supports this bluster with a *gnômê* designed to preempt the argument that he is no match for Achilles in battle: "The war god is impartial. Before now he has killed the killer" (309). These bold words drown out Polydamas' cautions, however grounded in reality and experiential evidence they had been, and the Trojans roar their approval (310). In a rare narrative gesture, the narrator comments on this persuasive victory, voicing the opinion that although Hector's rhetoric is successful, it is not good counsel:

> Fools, since Pallas Athene had taken away the wits from them.
> They gave their applause to Hektor **in his counsel of evil** (κακὰ μητιόωντι),
> but none to Poulydamas, **who had spoken good sense before them** (ὃς ἐσθλὴν
> φράζετο βουλήν). (18.311–13)

This narrative observation also provides an ironic symmetry to the passage, which had begun with a similar comment on these two speeches: that Polydamas has the skill to "win" (ἐνίκα) with μύθοι, Hector the skill to win with the ἔγχος (18.252). As is clear on several occasions in the *Iliad*, however, excellence in speaking and strength of argumentation are no guarantee of rhetorical success—a disquieting truth that will haunt the debate over rhetoric in the Classical era and beyond. Hector's proposal is exactly what his audience wanted to hear, and on this occasion, *diathesis* trumps all other strategies.

XXV. Odysseus at 19.155–83 delivers a speech directed primarily to Achilles, though he briefly addresses Agamemnon at the end. The speech is a counterproposal to Achilles' call for the Greek army to begin fighting immediately now that he has decided to rejoin the battle (19.146–53). Odysseus employs *diathesis* from the start, taking a respectful and flattering tone even while disagreeing with Achilles: "Not that way, good fighter that you are, godlike Achilleus. . . ." (155). He then makes his proposal in the form of two **enthymeme**s, the first consisting of a negative command ("Do not drive the sons of the Achaians on Ilion when they are hungry, to fight against the Trojans") plus a premise ("since [ἐπεὶ] not short will be the time of battle, once the massed formations of men have encountered together, with the god inspiring fury in both sides") (155–59). The second **enthymeme** is a positive command ("Rather tell the men of Achaia here by their swift ships, to take food and wine") plus a premise ("since [γὰρ] these make fighting fury and warcraft") (160–61). The latter gnomic premise is expanded with practical observations about the body's need for sustenance in order to perform well in battle (162–70). Odysseus then restates his enthymematic conclusion: "Come then, tell your men to scatter and bid them get ready a meal" (171–72).

In the second half of this speech, Odysseus encourages reconciliation between Agamemnon and Achilles, suggesting that Agamemnon offer gestures of good faith (19.172–78). Ever mindful of the need for *diathesis* when speaking to Achilles, Odysseus is attentive to what will please him ("Let the lord of men Agamemnon bring [the gifts] to the middle of our assembly . . . so your own heart may be pleasured," 172–74); and he acknowledges Agamemnon's earlier insult to Achilles' honor by calling upon Agamemnon to "stand up before the Argives and swear an oath to you that he never entered into [Briseis'] bed and never lay with her" (175–76). Odysseus concludes his speech with an **enthymeme** ostensibly directed at Agamemnon; it is clear, however, that he retains an awareness of Achilles in the audience. The enthymeme conclusion comes first: "And you, son of Atreus, after this be more righteous to another man" (181–82). It is followed by the premise in the form of a *gnômê*: "For there is no fault when even one who is a king appeases a man, when the king was the first one to be angry" (182–83). Odysseus' speech is persuasive to Agamemnon; the king voices his approval of the μῦθος (185) and proceeds to take his advice by giving a speech of instruction to his chiefs (185–97). Achilles, however, is not convinced. Rather than responding directly to Odysseus, he addresses Agamemnon's response to Odysseus; and although he does not try to thwart the king's decision to feed his troops, he makes known his disagreement with the plan (19.205–14).

XXVI. At 19.216–37, Odysseus delivers another speech incorporating rhetorical persuasion. It has the same general aim as speech XXV above: to convince Achilles of the need to rejuvenate the troops before resuming battle. It is a more sincere and personalized appeal, however. Odysseus does not *need* Achilles' permission or agreement for his plan, since Agamemnon has already given his support to Odysseus. Ostensibly he has nothing to gain from this appeal. The fact that he even makes it shows his concern with accord among the Greeks, and his recognition of the importance of winsome speech in the midst of the power manipulations that have occurred between the chief players (particularly Agamemnon and Achilles). Odysseus, unlike Agamemnon, understands that persuasion is concerned not only with achieving what one wants in the immediate circumstance, but also with winning over the heart and mind of the audience—a longer-term, and ultimately more effective, rhetorical strategy.

Odysseus begins with a flattering salutation to Achilles, using the same formula that Patroclus had used at 16.21: ὦ Ἀχιλεῦ, Πηλῆος υἱέ, μέγα φέρτατ' Ἀχαιῶν (19.216). The adjective φέρτατος is repeated in comparative form in the next line, as Odysseus continues his exercise of *diathesis* by comparing himself unfavorably to Achilles in matters of strength: "You are stronger (κρείσσων) than I am and greater (φέρτερος) by not a little with the spear" (217–18). He then suggests one area of his own *êthos* in which he "might" surpass Achilles, couching this notion in the potential optative to maintain a deferential tone: "Yet I in turn might overpass you in wisdom (σεῖο νοήματί γε προβαλοίμην) by far, since (ἐπεὶ) I was born before you and have learned more things" (218–19). Odysseus' appeal to his trustworthy *êthos* based on the understanding gained through age and life experience doubles as the premise of an **enthymeme**, for it is followed by the conclusion "therefore (τῶ) let your heart endure to listen to my words" (220). A second **enthymeme** addresses the specific case that Odysseus is making. It begins with the *gnômê* "when there is battle men have suddenly their fill of it" (221), then applies this commonplace to the particular situation at hand with the premise, "there is no way the Achaians can mourn a dead man by denying the belly" (225–27). His conclusion is a command: "No, but we must harden our hearts and bury the man who dies . . . and all those who are left about from the hateful work of war must remember food and drink" (228–31). An additional premise follows this conclusion: "so that afterwards all the more strongly we may fight on forever relentless against our enemies" (231–32). The entire argument is based on the **topic of the consequence** (topic #13), as it depicts the potentially disastrous consequences of following Achilles' counsel (men tiring of battle), and the good consequences of following Odysseus' advice (men having the strength to fight more strongly). As a capping conclusion to this multifaceted enthymeme, Odysseus ends his speech with something that he knows will appeal to Achilles, namely a battle cry: "Therefore let us drive on together and wake the bitter war god on the Trojans, breakers of horses" (236–37). The narrator records no response from Achilles to this speech. It would seem that the *Iliad*'s preeminent hero is as impervious to persuasion as ever.

XXVII. Achilles delivers a battlefield exhortation to his Greek comrades at 20.354–63, a relatively short speech that relies heavily (but not exclusively) on arguments from *êthos*. The speech opens with three stark imperative commands (μηκέτι νῦν Τρώων ἑκὰς ἕστατε . . . ἀνὴρ ἄντ' ἀνδρὸς ἴτω, μεμάτω δὲ μάχεσθαι, 354–55) as Achilles forgoes any attempt to soften his audience through *diathesis*. His premise for issuing these commands is an argument from the **topic of greater and less** (topic #4): "It is a hard thing for me, for all my great strength, to harry the flight of men in such numbers or to fight with all of them. Not Ares, who is immortal, not even Athene could take the edge of such masses of men and fight a way through them" (356–59). If not even Ares and Athena could take on such odds, how much less can mortal Achilles hope to do so without assistance? Achilles embeds within this argument some elements of an appeal to his own *êthos* as a means of garnering legitimacy for his request. He reminds the audience of both his extraordinary abilities in warfare, and his willingness to engage in battle however impossible the odds. As such, he sets himself up as a **paradeigma** for his audience to follow.[9] He develops this line of argumentation further in the final lines of the speech:

> But what I can do with hands and feet and strength I tell you
> I will do, and I shall not hang back even a little
> but go straight on through their formation, and I think that no man
> of the Trojans will be glad when he comes within my spear's range. (360–63)

If Achilles himself is willing to spare no effort, it follows that the least his comrades can do is stand fast in support of him. He offers the example of his own behavior both to inspire action and to inspire confidence in the Greek warriors. But the result of this "urging" (ἐποτρύνων), as the narrator characterizes his speech (20.364), is unspecified: the narrative shifts immediately to the other side of the battlefield and to Hector's corresponding exhortation to the Trojans.

XXVIII. Hector exhorts his men at 20.366–72 with a rhetorical speech that is an **enthymeme** in its entirety, beginning with the conclusion in the form of the speech-opening command "Do not be afraid of Peleion" (366). The premise is built on an appeal to a common **gnômê** about the gods: "since (ἐπεί) they are far stronger than we are" (368) and give unmitigated success to no man. "Even Achilleus will not win achievement of everything he says," Hector observes; "Part he will accomplish, but part shall be baulked halfway done" (369–70). Hector ends the speech by invoking his own *êthos,* as he, like Achilles before him, attempts to inspire his men by example: "I am going to stand against him now, though his hands are like flame, though his hands are like flame, and his heart like the shining of iron" (371–72). The exhortation is successful; the Trojans lift their spears to fight (20.373–74).

XXIX. After Priam begs Hector not to go out to face Achilles in a speech at 22.38–76 (see chapter 2, section III), Hecuba delivers her own emotional appeal to her son at 22.82–89. In hopes of convincing Hector to stay behind the walls of Troy, Hecuba's rhetoric incorporates a dramatic gesture, as do several other rhetorical speeches in the *Iliad* (e.g., Patroclus "stood by Achilles and wept warm tears" as an accompaniment to his plea at 16.21–45; and Priam draws attention

to his own gesture of kissing "the hands of the man who has killed my children" as part of his appeal to Achilles at 24.486–506). Hecuba's gesture—"his
mother in tears was mourning and laid the fold of her bosom bare and with one
hand held out a breast" (22.79–80)—is closely linked to her *êthos* appeal to her
son. She begins her speech by indicating her breasts as part of an enthymematic argument: "Hektor, my child, show respect for these (τάδε τ' αἴδεο), and take
pity on me (μ' ἐλέησον), if ever I gave you the breast to quiet your sorrow" (82–83).
The **enthymeme** conclusion, expressed as the two commands "show respect" and
"take pity," is followed by a premise that not only draws upon Hecuba's *êthos* as
the mother who gave Hector life and nourishment, but also makes an explicit
appeal to the emotion of pity (**pathos**) in order to make him sympathetic to her
(**diathesis**). The remainder of Hecuba's short speech focuses on the likely consequences of the confrontation between Hector and Achilles. She employs another **enthymeme** in lines 85–89, beginning with the command "Do not go out
as champion against him" (85), and then offering as a premise a glimpse of the
pitiable grief that she and Andromache will experience with Hector dead: "For
(γάρ) if he kills you I can no longer mourn you on the death-bed, sweet branch,
o child of my bearing, nor can your generous wife mourn you, but a big way
from us beside the ships of the Argives the running dogs will feed on you" (86–
89). This argument invokes the **topic of consideration of incentives and disincentives** (topic #20); Hecuba presents the bereavement of his wife and mother,
as well as his own gory demise, as disincentives to Hector's proposed course
of action. For good measure, she adds another reminder of her relationship to
Hector with the aside "O child of my bearing," thus invoking *êthos* for a final
time. Despite the rhetorical strategies packed into this short speech, however,
Hecuba is unable to dissuade her son from going to his fated death; she and
Priam, we are told, "could not move the spirit in Hektor" (22.91).

XXX. Book 23 provides a number of short persuasive speeches in the context of
Patroclus' funeral. The first is Achilles' exhortation to the Myrmidons at 23.6–11
to keep their horses harnessed to their chariots so that they can perform ritual-
ized mourning for Patroclus. Achilles' opening address to his men—"Myrmidons,
you of the fast horses, my steadfast companions (ἐμοὶ ἐρίηρες ἑταῖροι)"
(6)—exhibits *diathesis* in its reminder of the bond between them, and his respect for them. The exhortation itself consists of a single **enthymeme** comprised
of the conclusion "we must not yet slip free of the chariots our single-foot horses,
but . . . drive close up to Patroclus and mourn him," supported by the premise
"since (γάρ) such is the privilege of the perished" (7–9). Achilles' argument rests

on the commonplace that it is the "privilege of the perished" to receive such a mourning ritual. In response, the Myrmidons assent and drive their chariots three times around Patroclus' body as Achilles leads the lament (23.12–15).

XXXI. The ghost of Patroclus pleads with Achilles to bury him in a rhetorical speech at 23.69–92. The plea draws primarily on the technique of *diathesis*, as Patroclus attempts to stir up his friend's sympathetic emotions and dispose him favorably. The speech opens with a reproach ("You sleep, Achilleus; you have forgotten me," 69), contrasting Achilles' current behavior with a reminder of the past ("but you were not careless of me when I lived, but only in death," 70). The command to bury him and let him pass through the gates of Hades is followed by an appeal to pity (*pathos*), as Patroclus chronicles his miserable liminal existence (71–74). He then moves on to a recollection of shared memories, calculated both to invoke pity in Achilles and to remind him of the bond that had existed between them: "No longer shall you and I, alive, sit apart from our other beloved companions and make our plans, since the bitter destiny that was given me when I was born has opened its jaws to take me" (77–79). Patroclus makes a second request in 82–84 (repeated in 91–92), begging that his ashes be laid in the same urn as Achilles' ashes when *he* dies. His persuasion tactic for this request uses *êthos*—a reminder of his friendship with Achilles and their shared past—in order to engender favorable feeling (*diathesis*):

> . . . just as we grew up **together** (ὁμοῦ) in your house,
> when Menoitios brought me there from Opous, when I was little . . .
> There the rider Peleus took me into his own house,
> and brought me carefully up, and named me to be your henchman. (84–90)

Patroclus' mention of Peleus represents yet another deployment of *diathesis*. It is a technique frequently used by speakers attempting to persuade Achilles (see also Phoenix at 9.434–605, Patroclus at 16.21–45, and Priam at 24.486–506). Those who know Achilles well realize that, for persuasive purposes, invoking his father is one of the only ways of putting him in a favorable—or at least susceptible—frame of mind. The pathetic memories that Patroclus recounts at 84–90 serve as an **enthymeme** premise. He expresses the conclusion at 91–92: "Therefore (ὣς), let one common (ὁμή) vessel, the golden two-handled urn the lady your mother gave you, hold both our ashes." The ὁμή of this image of ashes mingling in the urn picks up on the ὁμοῦ of line 84, where it had referred to the two heroes' childhood together—a linguistic linking of the enthymematic premise and conclusion. Patroclus ends his speech with the word μήτηρ, thus

invoking both Achilles' parents over the course of the appeal. He is successful in his persuasion attempt; Achilles responds, "I shall do as you tell me"
(πείσομαι ὡς σὺ κελεύεις, 23.96).

XXXII. Nestor addresses his son Antilochus at 23.306–48 with a speech that
is part exhortation and part instruction in how to win the chariot race during
Patroclus' funeral games. Nestor begins his speech with *diathesis* in the form of
flattery, conceding that, although Antilochus is young, "Zeus and Poseidon have
loved you and taught you horsemanship in all of its aspects. Therefore there is no
great need to instruct you; you yourself know well how to double the turning-
post" (306–9). He notes that Antilochus' slower horses put him at a competitive
disadvantage; but this can be counteracted by "strategic thinking" (μητίσασθαι,
312). Nestor uses an enthymematic argument to exhort his son on this point,
beginning with the **enthymeme** conclusion, "Remember then, dear son, to have
your mind full of every resource of skill (μῆτις), so that the prizes may not elude
you" (313–14). The first premise consists of a series of *gnômai* regarding the superiority of skill to brute strength:

> The woodcutter is far better for **skill** (μῆτις) than he is for brute strength.
> It is by **skill** (μῆτις) that the sea captain holds his rapid ship
> on its course, though torn by winds, over the wine-blue water.
> By **skill** (μῆτις) charioteer outpasses charioteer. (315–18)

Nestor reinforces this argument with a second premise, this time using the
classic wisdom-literature device of a contrast between the foolish and the wise
man (319–25). The charioteer who drives "recklessly" (ἀφραδέως), Nestor observes, "finds his horses drifting out of the course" (321); while the one who
drives skillfully, watchfully, and steadily has the advantage, even if his horses
are slower.

Lines 23.326–42 are dedicated to pure technical instruction on how Antilochus may gain a logistical advantage in the race; but as he closes, Nestor makes
a final enthymematic argument that sums up both the hortatory and instructional aspects of the speech. "So, dear son, drive thoughtfully and be watchful"
(343), he commands in the **enthymeme** conclusion, reiterating his emphasis on
skill. The premise offers an argument from the **topic of consideration of incentives and disincentives** (topic #20): "For (γάρ) if you follow the others but get first
by the turning post, there is no who could sprint to make it up, nor close you,
nor pass you" (344–45). Never content with brief arguments, Nestor ends his
speech with confident elaboration of this incentive (*auxesis*): "not if the man

behind you were driving the great Arion, the swift horse of Adrestos, whose birth is from the immortals, or Laomedon's horses, who were the pride of those raised in this country" (346–48). Although the narrator marks no immediate response to this speech from Antilochus, the young man does implement his father's advice and rides to a second-place finish in the race, "not by speed but by taking advantage" (κέρδεσιν, οὔ τι τάχει, 23.515).

XXXIII. Antilochus delivers a speech at 23.403–16 that has an unusual addressee: his father's horses, who are carrying him in the chariot race for Patroclus' funeral games. It is undoubtedly odd that Antilochus would address animals as though they could understand argumentative reasoning, but it is not unprecedented in the *Iliad*: Achilles addresses his horses at 19.400–403 and 420–23 (with commands, not persuasion), and Menelaus attempts to persuade his horses at 23.443–45 (see below, speech XXXV). Antilochus' speech comes in the heat of the race, as he strives to catch the chariot of Menelaus for second place. After opening the speech with short, vigorous commands ("Come on, you two. Pull, as fast as you can!"), he acknowledges the horses' slowness and assures them that he will not push them beyond the limits of their capabilities—an extension of sympathy calculated to dispose them favorably (*diathesis*): "I am not trying to make you match your speed with the speed of those others. . . ." (404). He then introduces an **enthymeme** whose conclusion, "Make your burst to catch the horses of the son of Atreus nor let them leave you behind" (407–8), is supported by a premise based on the emotion of shame (*pathos*): "for fear Aithe who is female may shower you in mockery" (408–9). In case the prospect of losing to a mare (Aithe was one of the horses driven by Menelaus) is not enough to motivate his horses, Antilochus puts forward a second **enthymeme**, this one based on the emotion of fear (*pathos*). Reversing the structure of the first enthymeme, he begins with the premise: "There will be no more care for you from the shepherd of the people, Nestor, but he will slaughter you out of hand with the edge of bronze, if we win the meaner prize because you are unwilling" (411–13). This threat leads to the enthymeme conclusion, Antilochus' command to "keep on close after him [Menelaus] and make all the speed you are able" (414). The speech ends on a note of *êthos*, as Antilochus assures the horses that they can have confidence in his skill and knowledge: "I myself shall know what to do and contrive it, so that we get by in the narrow place of the way. He will not escape me" (414–15). Antilochus' harangue produces the desired results in his horses; they run faster and eventually overtake Menelaus' chariot. As the narrator notes, however, their response is spurred by "fearing the angry voice of their master" (23.417) rather than by heeding his rhetorical arguments.

XXXIV. Menelaus delivers two short rhetorical speeches during the chariot race, the first to Antilochus at 23.426–28 and the second to his own horses. He opens his address to Antilochus with a brief rebuke ("This is reckless horsemanship," 426), and then proceeds to make a single enthymematic argument. The **enthymeme** conclusion comes in the form of the command "Hold in your horses" (426); it is followed by a premise based on the **topic of consideration of incentives and disincentives** (topic #20): "For (γάρ) the way is narrow here, it will soon be wider for passing. Be careful not to crash your chariot and wreck both of us" (427–28). By raising the possibility of a disastrous crash, Menelaus attempts to motivate his rival to yield the right-of-way. The argument is unsuccessful, however; Antilochus presses forward and it is Menelaus who ultimately gives way (23.429–37).

XXXV. After Antilochus passes him in the chariot race, Menelaus addresses his horses at 23.443–45 in a short persuasive speech designed to spur them to greater speed. Once again, the rhetorical content is a single **enthymeme** that spans the entire speech. His argument begins with the conclusion-command "Never hold back now, never stop" (443). The conclusion is then supported with an appeal to the **topic of consideration of incentives and disincentives** (topic #20)—"The feet of these and their knees will weary before yours do, seeing that the youth is gone from those horses" (444–45)—which holds forth the promise that Menelaus' horses are likely to overtake those of Antilochus if they keep pressing. The horses' response to Menelaus is described with the same formula that had been used after Antilochus' speech to his horses in 23.417–18: "they fearing the angry voice of their master ran the harder" (23.446–47).

XXXVI. Achilles delivers a speech of persuasion and rebuke to Ajax and Idomeneus at 23.492–98 after they have quarreled over whose observation of the leading horses in the chariot race is correct. The opening lines of the speech introduce an enthymematic argument, starting with Achilles' command (the **enthymeme** conclusion), "No longer now, Aias and Idomeneus, continue to exchange this bitter and evil talk" (492–93). The premise is twofold: first, Achilles appeals to the emotion of shame (*pathos*) with the statement, "for (ἐπεί) it is not becoming" (493); then he raises a hypothetical situation to demonstrate to the men their folly: "If another acted so, you yourselves would be angry" (494).

Having thus used emotion and imagination to dispose his audience in a certain way (*diathesis*)—namely, toward more measured behavior—Achilles proposes an alternative course of action. Idomeneus and Ajax should sit and wait for the victor to emerge in plain view; "then you each can see for himself, and learn which of the Argives horses have run first" (498). The speech ends on this note, and although the narrator does not record a response from the quarreling heroes, the lack of further incident suggests that Achilles' attempt to appease them is successful.

XXXVII. With Achilles persisting in his campaign to defile Hector's body, Apollo delivers a speech to the assembled Olympians at 24.33–54 in an attempt to persuade them to preserve the body of the Trojan hero. This speech employs elements of forensic oratory in its digression into a sort of prosecution of Achilles, though its overall function is deliberative. Apollo begins with a harsh address of the other gods as "hard" (σχέτλιοι) and "destructive" (δηλήμονες) because of their failure to stop Achilles' defilement of Hector (33). He then poses an **enthymeme** whose premise is a rhetorical question reminding the gods of Hector's piety toward them in life: "Did not Hektor burn thigh pieces of oxen and unblemished goats in your honour?" (33–34) As the enthymeme conclusion, Apollo offers a rebuke instead of the more usual command ("Now you cannot bring yourselves to save him, though he is only a corpse," 35). The intent of his sentiment (the object of the enthymematic argument) is clear, however: the gods *should* save Hector's body. The reminder of Hector's piety serves as an attempt to dispose the gods favorably (*diathesis*), as does Apollo's subsequent appeal to pity (*pathos*): he invokes Hector's wife, child, parents, and people, who are deprived of both the man himself and the opportunity to give him a proper burial (36–38).

For the remainder of the speech, Apollo turns his attention to Achilles, attacking his character and actions as though he were on trial and indicting the gods for supporting him: "No, you gods; your desire is to help this cursed Achilleus within whose breast there are no feelings of justice, nor can his mind be bent. . . . So Achilleus has destroyed pity, and there is not in him any shame" (39–45). Continuing his prosecution of Achilles, Apollo then draws upon the **topic of greater and less** (topic #4) to argue that Achilles is indulging in excessive revenge out of grief over the death of Patroclus:

For a man must some day lose one who was even closer
than this; a brother from the same womb, or a son. And yet

he weeps for him, and sorrows for him, and then it is over. . . .
But this man, now he has torn the heart of life from great Hektor,
ties him to his horses and drags him around his beloved companion's
tomb. (24.46–52)

The force of this argument is all the more keen considering that the generic
situation it pictures—a man who grieves the loss of a family member—is embodied in Hector's case; but Hector's family *cannot* weep for him in the appropriate manner because of Achilles' disproportionate grief for Patroclus. Apollo
does not tie this topic explicitly to any exhortation to action so as to form a
proper enthymeme, but in making a case that Achilles is acting in violation of
divine laws of justice and proportion, he again implies that the gods should in-
tervene. This implication looms over the final lines of the speech, in which
Apollo combines a warning with a final charge against Achilles: "Great as he is,
let him take care not to make us angry; for see, he does dishonour to the dumb
earth in his fury" (53–54). Apollo's appeal appears to be effective; Zeus agrees to
force Achilles to return Hector's body to his people, citing one of Apollo's arguments (that Hector always offered pleasing sacrifices to the gods) in his speech
at 24.65–76.

    XXXVIII. After Priam has entered Achilles' tent and pled with him for the
return of Hector's body at 24.486–506 (see chapter 2, section III), the two enemies pause for a period of mourning together. Achilles then offers a lengthy
response to Priam at 24.518–51, only a small part of which is devoted to rhetorical persuasion: most of the speech is a reflection on the unhappy life of mortals,
expanding upon Priam's lament over his own and Peleus' misfortunes. In this,
Macleod notes, it resembles the later genre of *consolatio*: "Just as the sufferings
of legendary heroes are invoked to console ordinary men, so here the sufferings
of ordinary men are invoked to console a legendary hero."[10] Achilles turns from
consolation to exhortation of Priam at two points within the speech, however,
both of which involve enthymematic argument. In 522–23, he urges Priam,
"Come, then, and sit down upon this chair, and you and I will even let our sorrows lie still in the heart for all our grieving." Following this **enthymeme** conclusion is a ***gnômê*** that functions as its premise: "For (γάϱ) there is not any advantage to be won from grim lamentation. Such is the way the gods spun life for
unfortunate mortals, that we live in unhappiness" (524–26). At the end of the
speech, Achilles employs another **enthymeme** to encourage Priam, again with a
gnômê as a premise: "But bear up, nor mourn endlessly in your heart [conclu-

sion], for (γάρ) there is not anything to be gained from grief for your son; you will never bring him back [premise]" (549–51).

XXXIX. Priam ignores Achilles' attempt to placate him, and responds at 24.553–58 by persisting in his original request for Hector's body. This brief speech contains an **enthymeme** comprised of the command (the enthymematic conclusion) that Achilles release Hector's body, followed by a premise drawn from the **topic of consideration of incentives and disincentives** (topic #20): "Accept the ransom we bring you, which is great. You may have joy of it, and go back to the land of your own fathers, once you have permitted me to go on living" (555–58). This perfunctory argument reveals the emotional strain and impatience in Priam; short imperative commands have replaced the more nuanced rhetorical techniques of his first speech (such as recollection of the past and appeals to emotion and *êthos*). The incentive that he offers—Achilles will be able to enjoy the ransom back in his homeland—betrays a lack of sensitivity to his listener (*diathesis*), ignorant as he is of the fact that Achilles is destined never to return home and has never been one to care much for ransom. (It is a moment of dramatic irony: the Iliadic narrator and audience, and indeed Achilles himself, know that Priam's offer holds no weight; only Priam remains unaware.) In addition, Priam displays presumption—a quality that Achilles despises—with the expectant participle ἐάσας ("once you have permitted me," 557). This anti-*diathesis* not only renders the speech ineffective, it undoes some of the goodwill that Priam's earlier speech had engendered. Achilles nearly retracts his intention to grant Priam's request in his fierce response at 24.559–70.

Notes

INTRODUCTION

1. Plato, *Phaedrus* 261a (trans. Nehamas and Woodruff); Aristotle, *Rhetoric* 1.2.1 (trans. Kennedy); Quintilian *Institutio Oratoria* 2.15.34 (trans. Butler).

2. Vickers (1988) 26.

3. In investigating the origins of rhetoric, I am leaving aside non-Greek traditions for the most part. For one thing, the term "rhetoric" is a Greek invention, and the theoretical framework surrounding that term even to this day is derived from the ancient Greek understanding, which cannot be equated with the understanding of eloquence or persuasion in other ancient cultures (on this last point, see for example Garrett 1993, "*Pathos* Reconsidered from the Perspective of Classical Chinese Rhetorical Theories"). Also, the investigation of rhetoric in non-Greek traditions is beyond the scope of this project. Finally, Kennedy has already made an excellent foray into the subject with his *Comparative Rhetoric*. Kennedy collects enough comparative data to observe that while ancient China, India, and the Near East all have literary traditions that depict persuasive speech, these rely for the most part on commands, aphorisms, and the speaker's authority (*êthos*), rather than venturing into logical argumentation. In employing argumentation, and other related rhetorical categories, Greek rhetoric is unique. Kennedy also notes that none of the ancient non-Western traditions has transmitted a "fully developed system of rhetorical terminology" to modern culture in the way that Greco-Roman rhetoric has done (Kennedy 1998 5). I will return to the question of whether rhetoric is present in ancient non-Western literature in chapter 4, but the definition and conception of the term "rhetoric" that I use for this project can be traced back to ancient Greece.

4. Schiappa (1999) 4–6 provides a summary of this traditional account and its modern adherents.

5. On Corax and Tisias as the traditional inventors of rhetoric, see among others Kennedy (1963) 58–61, (1994) 30–34, and (2007b); Usher (1999) 2–4; and Pernot (2005) 10–12.

6. Kennedy (2007b) provides a survey of the early development of rhetoric via these semilegendary figures and the technical handbooks that preceded the rhetorical works of Plato and Aristotle.

7. See Cole (1991) 28–29.

8. See Schiappa (1999) 10–13.

9. Struck (2004) 11.

10. Text of Pseudo-Plutarch from Kindstrand (1990); translation from Keaney and Lamberton (1996).

11. Dentice di Accadia Ammone's 2012 book *Omero e i suoi oratori: Techniche di per-suasion nell'*Iliade unfortunately appeared too late for me to take fully into account. Its overall contention is similar to my own (calling for a reexamination of the view that Homeric speeches are devoid of conscious rhetoric), although the author takes a different approach to analyzing Iliadic speeches and places little emphasis on Aristotelian rhetorical theory.

12. Redfield (1994) 7.

13. Walker (2000), whose work I will discuss in chapter 1, promotes the idea that rhetoric has origins in the poetic tradition; he deals only peripherally with Homer, however. Karp (1977), Toohey (1994), and Frobish (2003) have touched on certain aspects of rhetoric in Homer, but all of them have done so in article form. A book-length treatment of rhetoric in Homer necessarily allows for a deeper and more systematic exploration, supported by a greater accumulation of textual examples.

14. Pernot (2005) 6.

15. For a more extended discussion of this passage, see Martin (1989) 15–17, 95–96.

16. All citations of Homer are from the text of Allen and Munro (1920); all translations of the *Iliad* are taken or lightly adapted from Lattimore (1951).

17. Bakker (1997), for example, sees a connection between Homeric poetry and ancient rhetoric, but is clearly referring to Homer's narrative voice when he observes that "both Homeric poetry and classical rhetorical prose are, each in their own specific and very different ways, the rhetorical enhancement and manipulation of the basic properties of ordinary speech. Both are special speech, based on strategies that are reserved for special performance occasions and meant, in a truly rhetorical sense, to have a special effect on an audience" (129). Likewise Scodel's (2002) discussion of what she calls the "rhetorics" or "rhetorical positions" of Homer—namely, traditionality and disinterestedness—are concerned with the narrative voice, not character speech (65ff.); and Ford (2002) speaks of "rhetoric" and "rhetorical elements" in early Greek literature in terms of a literary work's total strategy—its persuasiveness or effectiveness in the face of its listening or reading audience (3 passim).

18. Pernot (2005) 3.

19. For an analysis of the particularly conversational aspects of speech in the *Odyssey*, see Beck (2005a) and (2012).

20. Beck (2005a) 149.

21. Although the dating of the Homeric epics is subject to debate, the period at which they began to be circulated in written versions is perhaps more relevant to the question of Homer's influence on rhetorical theory, and Aristotle's theory in particular. Even the relatively late date that Nagy (2003) posits in his "evolutionary model" for the textualization of Homeric epics locates a "definitive period, centralized in Athens, with potential texts in the sense of *transcripts*, at any or several points from the middle of the sixth century BCE to the later part of the fourth" (2). That Aristotle quotes Homer at numerous points in the *Poetics* and the *Rhetoric*, following the precedent of Plato, Isocrates, and other sophists (who in the generation(s) before Aristotle quoted and commented on aspects of the Homeric poem), indicates that these poems had achieved the status of "transcript" by the fifth century.

22. Kennedy (1998) 3.

23. Pernot (2005) x.

24. All citations of Aristotle's *Rhetoric* are from the text of Kassel (1976); all translations are taken or lightly adapted from Kennedy (2007a).

25. Martin (1989) 95.

26. Pernot (2005) offers a somewhat similar catalogue (3–4), which includes passages from both the *Iliad* and *Odyssey* and which, he says, "leave[s] no doubt as to [Homer's] critical awareness with regard to discourse" (3). He is dismissive of the possibility that Homer represented rhetoric in any technical sense, however: "Homer did not anticipate the laws of rhetoric, but he established, in accord with the ideas of his own time, the importance of the spoken word" (7).

27. Martin (1989) 22–23.

28. See Hainsworth (1993) 103: "ἀηλεγέως is 'forthrightly' (<ἀπό in a negative sense + ἀλεγ-ω)."

29. For a more extended discussion of this passage, see Mackie (1996) 71–74. Mackie observes that "Aeneas talks about versatility in language in a speech that suggests the diversity of his own linguistic abilities" (74).

30. Schol. A ad *Il.* 20.249.

CHAPTER 1: RECONSIDERING THE ORIGINS OF RHETORIC

1. Cole (1991) 40.

2. Pernot (2005) 6.

3. Ibid., 7.

4. Kennedy (1963) 35–36.

5. See Solmsen (1954): "Effective speech is for Hesiod not one of the two outstanding excellences of man [as it is in Homer, according to *Iliad* 9.443] but one of the two gifts of the Muses" (5). The differences between Homeric and Hesiodic conceptions of speech will be discussed further in chap. 5, section III.

6. Kennedy (1963) 39.

7. "Written eloquence [is] the prerequisite for an analysis of the working of eloquence in general." Cole (1991) 112.

8. Ibid., 41.

9. Ibid., 40.

10. Schiappa (1999) 11ff. In constructing this argument, he cites among others the work of Havelock (1986), who has asked, "May not all logical thinking be a product of Greek alphabetic literacy?" (39). But Halverson's (1992) critique of Havelock applies to Schiappa and Cole as well: "The problem is that [Havelock] seems to want to make alphabetic literacy the *sole* cause of the change [in Greek thought during the classical period], as if written language in and of itself created thought. As is so often the case, Havelock's arguments rest on a *post hoc propter hoc* fallacy: if writing preceded logical thought it must have caused it. . . . He observes, astutely enough, that written texts permitted reflective perusal and retrospective topicalization that led, or could lead, to the development of logical categories; but then he leaps to the conclusion that this would be impossible under acoustic conditions. This is certainly a false conclusion, for it is quite possible to reflect in the same way on an oral presentation" (160).

11. Schiappa (1999) 21–22.

12. Searle (1975) 355.

13. Walker (2000) viii.

14. Ibid., 12–13.

15. Ibid., x.

16. Kennedy (1957) 23.

17. Keaney and Lamberton (1996) 2.

18. Text of Pseudo-Plutarch from Kindstrand (1990); translation from Keaney and Lamberton (1996).

19. The language Pseudo-Plutarch uses to describe Homer's speech-craft here resembles that of Thucydides' famous statement at the beginning of his *History* (1.22.1) that he represents the characters in his history as saying "the things that were necessary/appropriate for the circumstances" (ὡς δ' ἂν ἐδόκουν ἐμοὶ ἕκαστοι περὶ τῶν αἰεὶ παρόντων τὰ δέοντα μάλιστ' εἰπεῖν . . . οὕτως εἴρηται). (Text of Thucydides from Jones and Powell 1942; translation is my own.)

20. Keaney and Lamberton (1996) 133.

21. Russell (1981) 137 provides a list of the instances of this opinion in ancient critics.

22. Buffière's (1973) comment on passage 170 of the *Essay* recapitulates in more explicit terms Pseudo-Plutarch's contention that Homer recognized rhetoric as a τέχνη: "Homère est un incomparable professeur de rhétorique. Et son art n'est pas purement intuitif, il est conscient et étudié. Homère sait que la parole est une science qui s'apprend: Phénix était chargé d'en instruire Achille, il devait faire du fils de Pélée, selon sa propre expression, 'un bon diseur de paroles'" (352).

23. See Keaney and Lamberton (1996) 10ff. for elaboration of this insight. For further discussion of the philosophical contributions of Pseudo-Plutarch, see De Lacy (1948); for general but less exhaustive overviews of the *Essay* than that of Keaney and Lamberton, see Buffière (1973) 72–77 and Kindstrand's introduction (1990). What little scholarship exists on this work has focused heavily on the identity of the author, perhaps because of the difficulty of pinning down its content in a way that sustains comment (e.g., Buffière, "[L'auteur] combat Aristippe et Epicure, énonce souvent les positions stoïciennes sans rien blâmer ni louer, mais donne en maint endroit la palme de la vérité à Platon et à Pythagore, notamment pour la croyance à l'immortalité de l'âme. . . . Ces données composent un portrait assez flou; et l'on comprend l'hésitation des critiques sur le nom de l'auteur" 74).

24. Buffière (1973) 75; cf. Keaney and Lamberton (1996): "His is an unpretentious but voracious intellect, unencumbered by any commitment to a particular philosophical school, engaged in a work that is essentially a popularization—a doxographer who focuses his doxography on the glorification of Homer" (12).

25. Text of the *Cratylus* from Duke et al. (1995); translation from Reeve (1998). For scholarly treatment of the *Cratylus*, see among others Barney (2001), who provides a broad interpretive (re-)reading of the dialogue, addressing the question of Plato's seeming oscillation between conventional and naturalistic accounts of naming; as well as Baxter (1992) and Sedley (2003), both of whom focus more particularly on the extensive section in the dialogue devoted to etymologies (often viewed as incongruous with the rest of the dialogue), in order to defend it as important to and consistent with Plato's larger philosophy of language.

26. Text of the *Phaedrus* from Burnet (1903); translation from Nehamas and Woodruff (1995). Ferarri (1987) provides an excellent discussion of the strains of thought at play in the *Phaedrus*, especially the interplay between philosophy and rhetoric in the dialogue.

27. Palamedes, though not mentioned in the Homeric epics, figures in the cyclic poem *Cypria* and is the subject of plays by Aeschylus, Sophocles, and Euripides. He is also the purported speaker in a model defense speech by Gorgias (DK B11a), and the imagined adversary in Alcidamas' response to that speech, *Odysseus: Against the Treachery of Palamedes*. Hyginus' *Fabulae*, a second-century CE handbook of mythology, reports Palamedes' two most well-known achievements: he was responsible for revealing Odysseus' true identity when the latter was feigning madness to avoid the Trojan expedition; and he was credited with inventing the letters of the Greek alphabet. This reputation for cleverness, reflected in the etymology of his name, is likely what made Palamedes a natural candidate for the practice of putting rhetorical speeches in the mouths of mythical figures, to which Plato here refers.

28. A tradition of placing exemplary speeches in the mouths of mythical figures arose in the rhetorical instruction of the fifth and fourth centuries, for example Gorgias' *Defense of Palamedes* and Antisthenes' *Ajax* and *Odysseus* (see discussion in chap. 6, section II). This suggests that actual Homeric speeches may have been viewed as (or, at any rate, adapted into) instructional treatises (*technai*). Even earlier, the lost poem Χείρωνος Ὑποθῆκαι, attributed to Hesiod, purportedly contained the centaur Chiron's wisdom and instructions for Achilles. Kurke (1990) explains that the Χείρωνος Ὑποθῆκαι belonged to a genre known as *hypothēkai* in Archaic Greece (at times treated as synonymous with the later category of *parainesis*); citing the work of Friedländer (1913), she writes that "The genre of *hypothēkai* would be characterized by a proem, an address to a specific addressee, sometimes by mythological material, but mainly by a collection of injunctions and traditional wisdom, loosely strung together with gnomic material" (90). The connection between Greek wisdom literature and the development of rhetoric will be explored further in chap. 5, section III.

29. White (1993) 195–96.

30. For further scholarship on Philodemus' rhetorical work, see Chandler (2006), a translation of *On Rhetoric* accompanied by exegetical essays; and Obbink's (1995) collection *Philodemus and Poetry*, particularly Blank's "Philodemus on the Technicity of Rhetoric." Chandler notes that one of Philodemus' aims seems to be to refute the view—common in his time among both Epicureans and others—that Epicurean philosophy was incompatible with rhetoric (13–17). He also observes that, in keeping with the Epicurean approach, Philodemus believes that of the three branches of rhetoric laid out by Aristotle, only epideictic (which he calls "sophistic") counts as a τέχνη: "Philodemus systematically and repeatedly denies that forensic and political rhetoric have any efficacy at all" (16).

31. See Chandler (2006) 13–15.

32. Text of Philodemus from Radermacher (1951), following and emending Sudhaus (1896); translation is my own.

33. See e.g., Gutzwiller (2007) 202–7.

34. Text of the *Brutus* from Malcovati (1970); translation from Hendrickson (1971).

35. Text of Strabo from Meineke (1877); translation is my own.

36. Text of Quintilian from Winterbottom (1970); translation from Butler (1921).

37. On the subject of Homer's reception in the Second Sophistic, see Kindstrand (1973), who argues that the movement drew on Homer more for his themes, plotlines, and even philosophical implications than for rhetorical instruction. Kindstrand examines in particular the work of Dio Chrysostom, Maximus of Tyre, and Aelius Aristides, and what each has to say on the subject of "Homer als Philosoph, Lehrer, und Rhetor." Of Dio, he remarks: "Wenn es sich um Homer als Rhetor handelt, kann man die Zurückhaltung Dions bemerken, da für ihn andere Aspekte seines Homerbildes erheblich wichtiger sind" (128). Maximus acknowledges no rhetoric in Homer whatsoever, which Kindstrand postulates is due to the conflict that Maximus perceives between viewing Homer as a philosophical exemplar (for which he makes strong claims), and as a rhetorician (171–72). Aristeides acknowledges the rhetorical ability of Homeric characters, but presents this as a natural gift or divine inspiration—an attitude that Kindstrand summarizes as follows: "a) die Rhetorik ist bei Homer vorhanden, und b) sie ist nicht eine τέχνη, was jedoch ihren Wert nicht verringert" (200–201).

38. Text of Hermogenes from Rabe (1969); translation from Wooten (1987).

39. Text of Sopatros from Radermacher (1951), following Walz (1832–36); translation is my own.

40. Aristotle uses the adjective ἀποδεικτικός seven times (and the adverb ἀποδεικτικῶς once) in the *Rhetoric*, applying it to speech (λόγος), proofs (πίστεις), and enthymemes (ἐνθυμήματα).

41. Roisman (2007) 431.

42. Kennedy (1957) 23.

43. Text of this anonymous *prolegomenon* from Rabe (1931); translation is my own.

44. Buffière (1973) is a partial exception, although his focus is on ancient views of Homer in general. His brief survey of what he calls "l'art oratoire" within Homer (349–54) is the most sustained attention given to the subject that I have found in modern scholarship. Kim (2001) has commented on the narrow scope of modern scholarship on ancient literary criticism. He attributes this to the "incompatibility between ancient and modern ways of treating poetry," with the result that the ancients' "much broader range of interpretive techniques and concerns—engaging with and reading Homer in the light of extra-literary interests—is effaced" (13–14).

45. Kennedy (1957).

46. Ibid., 23.

47. Pernot (2005) 6.

CHAPTER 2: INVESTIGATING HOMERIC RHETORIC

1. Kennedy (1963) provides an example of the conventional usage: "Aristotle's second kind of proof, that resulting from putting the audience into a certain state of mind, is known as pathos." (93)

2. Schiappa and Timmerman (2010) 75.

3. Fingerle (1939); Searle (1975).

4. For a detailed look at the function of enthymeme in Aristotle, see Burnyeat (1994).

5. These first-order parameters resemble, to some extent, Searle's (1975) category of directives as described in his taxonomy of speech acts. All of the speeches that I have

identified as rhetorical in the *Iliad* would qualify as directives in that they are, to use Searle's words, "attempts . . . by the speaker to get the hearer to do something" (355).

6. It could be argued that even a speech such as this one exhibits persuasion, in that it invites the audience to identify with the speaker in a common cause and shared experience, highlighted by the use of first-person plural verb at the end of the speech ("we shall fight again," αὖτε μαχησόμεθ'). But since Priam makes no actual statement of identification with his audience, it is difficult to argue that this represents anything more than an incidental effect of his sentiments about the uncertainty of war. In order to be classified as "rhetorical" in my analysis, speeches must demonstrate specific persuasive elements (confirmed by their codification in Aristotle's *Rhetoric*).

7. This phenomenon of multiple-audience persuasive speech occurs frequently in the assembly context; cf. Nestor to the Greek army and Agamemnon more specifically at 2.337–68; Zeus to Hera and the other gods at 4.7–19; Nestor to Diomedes, Agamemnon, and the Greek army at 9.53–78; Pandarus to Hector and the Trojan chiefs at 12.61–79; and Odysseus to Agamemnon and Achilles at 19.155–83.

8. For the notion of gesture as rhetorical, see Kennedy (1998) 36 passim; for the performative significance for Homeric heroes of holding the scepter, see Martin (1989) 96.

9. See de Jong (1987) 168–79; Beck (2008) and (2012) 25–47. Of this passage, de Jong notes, "By quoting verbatim the words spoken by Calchas on that occasion, Odysseus maximally reactivates the memory of the soldiers and also reckons that these words will again have a positive and stimulating effect" (173).

10. The difficulty of creating meaningful subcategories can be attributed to the fact that so many variables are at play in each speech. Many of the longer speeches, although they contain more techniques than do the shorter speeches, also contain long stretches in which no rhetorical techniques appear because other things are happening: for example, Achilles spends the first two-thirds of his speech to Thetis in 1.365–412 complaining and narrating past events, and only begins his persuasion attempt toward the end of the speech; and Nestor, among others, often takes lengthy digressions from his persuasive arguments into pure narrative of his past exploits. Thus the ratio of rhetorical techniques per number of lines tends to be lower in very long than in very short speeches that contain just one or two techniques. Such a ratio does not, then, say very much about the relative sophistication of the rhetoric used or the rhetorical ability of the speaker.

11. The diction of Nestor has received considerable scholarly attention: see for example Dickson (1995) on the narrative authority and the mediating powers of Nestor, Toohey (1994) on the rhetorical structure of Nestor's speeches, and Martin (1989) on Nestor as the *muthos* speaker par excellence. Dickson has noted that, along with Nestor's longevity, his "command of persuasive speech" is the most prominent feature of his characterization; that "he is also the speaker whose counsel is most often styled 'best' (ἀρίστη) in the *Iliad* (*Il.* 2.370–72; 7.324–25 = 9.93–94)"; and that his advice "most consistently earns the respect, approval and obedience of his fellow Akhaians." (10) According to Martin, Nestor is presented as the "ideal speaker in the *Iliad*" based on his mastery of authoritative speech (*muthoi*); Nestor "directs the greatest number of muthoi to others, but is himself never the recipient of such commands." (59) Toohey's analysis of this particular speech identifies formal rhetorical elements, although he focuses more on structure than content. He identifies in the speech an *exordium* (1.254–58), *prothesis*

(1.259–61), *paradeigma / pistis* (1.261–71), second *prothesis* (1.271–74), and *epilogue* (1.275–84) (154–55).

12. Martin (1989) gives a different name to this strategy (recollection), but likewise identifies it as a persuasive technique based on a claim to authority: Nestor "uses the device of recalling the past in order to legitimate his claim on authority in the present (I.259–74)" (80).

13. For a convincing interpretation of Agamemnon's impulse to test his men, see Knox and Russo (1989): "At this moment [after Agamemnon's dream, which had contained an imperative from Zeus to fight] it becomes a Holy War, and a fundamental rule of Holy War imposes itself: the dismissal in shame of any cowards, of any who have no heart for the battle or no faith in the god commanding it" (353).

14. See Martin (1989) for a more detailed analysis of Agamemnon's rhetorical weakness, indicated by the form and ineffectiveness of his commands. "As Agamemnon's speaking power wanes" over the course of the poem, Martin observes, "Achilles' waxes. . . . The control of authoritative speech passes like the Achaean scepter from the 'owner,' Agamemnon, to his young competitor" (62–63).

15. See especially *Rhetoric* 2.18.4: ἔτι δὲ περὶ μεγέθους κοινὸν ἁπάντων ἐστὶ τῶν λόγων· χρῶνται γὰρ πάντες τῷ μειοῦν καὶ αὔξειν καὶ συμβουλεύοντες καὶ ἐπαινοῦντες ἢ ψέγοντες καὶ κατηγοροῦντες ἢ ἀπολογούμενοι ("Further, a common feature of all speeches is the matter of magnitude; **for all use diminution and amplification** when deliberating and when praising or blaming and when prosecuting or defending themselves"). *Rhetoric* 1.9.38–40 describes the technique of *auxesis* in more detail, primarily in connection with epideictic oratory.

16. Achilles uses a similar argument to indict Agamemnon at 1.152–60 and 9.328–47.

17. See Martin (1989), Gill (1990), and Friedrich and Redfield (1978) for further exploration of the relationship between speech and characterization in the *Iliad*.

18. Nagy's discussion of this passage (1990b) points out that this wish is not a contrafactual one, but rather represents Hector's hubristic and deluded belief that being honored as a god is within the realm of possibility (294–99); see also Nagy (1999) 148.

19. I do not include Diomedes' speech of 9.32–49 in this catalogue because, although it has the effect of rousing the Greek troops' spirits after Agamemnon had proposed returning home, it does not contain rhetorical argumentation. Instead, it contains a strident rebuke of Agamemnon, an expression of petulant indignation, and a declaration of intent to remain and fight even in the absence of support from the rest of the army. As such, it does not qualify as *persuasion*.

20. Dickson (1995) sees Nestor's advanced age as the key factor in his rhetorical prowess, remarking that, in the world of the *Iliad*, "the kind of mastery needed in order to identify and reach the τέλος μύθων . . . belongs to older men, next to whom even an accomplished warrior is at best like a son" (13–14).

21. See Martin (1989) 24–26.

22. Hainsworth (1993) 67.

23. Martin (1989) 25.

24. Ibid., 138; see also 102–3 for a discussion of the positive connotations in the *Iliad* of Nestor's loquacity, and support for such prizing of speech-length from comparative studies.

25. Rosner (1976) 315.

26. See Nagy (1999) 104–5.

27. Scodel (2002) 170. Scodel also postulates that Phoenix's character and speech are largely unique to the *Iliad*, a product of the narrative context. (165ff.)

28. See Held (1987).

29. White (1984) 49.

30. Scodel (1982) notes that this autobiographical portion of Phoenix's speech involves a negative exemplum for Achilles (Phoenix's decision to flee those near and dear to him after a quarrel) that is cleverly sidelined by rhetorical sleight-of-hand, and replaced by the portion of his autobiography that is relevant to his appeal to Achilles. "An example which, if given as a negative paradigm, would embarrass the teller, is placed within his assertion of his special claim on his hearer's respect. It is not logical, but a rhetoric which in skill and discretion is more effective than the reasonable arguments the last portion of the speech employs" (136).

31. Held (1987) observes that only three speeches in the *Iliad* that include both a parable and a *paradeigma* are this one, Agamemnon's to Achilles and the Agaean assembly at 19.78–144, and Achilles' to Priam at 24.518–51. He sees significant parallels between these speeches (especially Phoenix's and Achilles') for this reason, arguing that they illustrate an educational process by which Achilles is instructed by Phoenix and then in turn instructs Priam of the same lesson (252–54).

32. Nagy (1999) points out that these two superlatives, "best of the Acheans" and "most dear [to Achilles]," do not aptly apply to all three of the embassy members (Phoenix is hardly among the ἄριστοι; Odysseus is hardly φίλτατος to Achilles). On this basis, then, "the ethical stance of the Embassy may well be undermined—from the heroic perspective of Achilles" (57–58). This would explain, at least partly, why Phoenix's speech is rhetorically ineffective.

33. For further discussion of the relationship between speeches and plot demands, see chapter 3, section III.

34. Despite Phoenix' failure to persuade Achilles, Whitman (1958) notes the evidence that Achilles is deeply moved by this speech, citing the words of his response to Phoenix at 9.612–13: "Stop confusing my heart with lamentation and sorrow for the favour of great Atreides" (178). White (1984) observes that Achilles manages to sidestep the demands of Phoenix's ethical appeal by extending a counteroffer of hospitality and refuge to Phoenix (49–50).

35. Martin (2000) 52. Martin discusses the digressive qualities of the speech, exhibited particularly in Nestor's *paradeigma* at 11.670–762, and identifies elements that mark it as unique (such as Nestor's "backward-moving style of exposition") and archaizing (such as the fact that, in lines 677–81, Nestor "is speaking exactly in the manner of Bronze Age Pylian palace officials") (58). Toohey (1994) provides an analysis of the rhetorical structure of this speech, as he had with Nestor's speeches in 1.254–84 and 7.124–60 (158–61).

36. Hainsworth (1993) 296.

37. Martin (1989) 61–62. See also Willcock (1977) 46–47 and de Jong (1987) 174–75 on the debate over the quotation's veracity.

38. Beck (2008) 165, 167. See also Dickson (1995), who observes that Nestor uses quotation "implicitly to establish the dominance of his own perspective; even when he 'impersonates' another speaker, his quotation is selective, governed not only by a certain viewpoint but also a definite rhetorical aim" (69).

39. I have chosen to treat the rhetorical arguments of these lines at the point when they are used on their intended audience, rather than when they are first suggested in Book 11. The credit for inventing these arguments, of course, belongs to Nestor rather than to Patroclus.

40. See Nagy (1999) 104–9.

41. Moulton (1981) analyzes this speech for its thematic similarities with other rebuke speeches in the *Iliad*—particularly Sarpedon's rebuke of Hector at 5.472–92 (discussed above, speech V)—and for its foreshadowing of Achilles' return to battle. "The speeches of Sarpedon in 5 and Glaukos in 17 are obviously connected," Moulton observes, but "the second rebuke is at almost every point an intensified version of the first" (3).

42. Macleod (1982), in his commentary on *Iliad* 24, remarks that this speech "begins straightaway with its main point; supplications in Homer are normally introduced in a more elaborate way; see 15.662–63, 22.338; *Od.* 11.67–68, 15.261–62. The abruptness betokens intense feeling" (127). I would add that there is calculation as well as emotion in this strategy: Priam knows the importance of Peleus to Achilles, and wastes no time in creating the association between himself and Peleus which will be the basis for his supplication.

43. Macleod (1982) 128.

44. Ibid., 128–29.

45. Ibid., 139–40.

46. For further discussion of the Niobe paradigm, see Willcock (1964) and Held (1987). Willcock defines *paradeigma* as "a myth introduced for exhortation or consolation" (142). This definition is more specific than the one Aristotle gives, namely that a paradigm is "to speak of things that have happened before" or "to make up [an illustration]" (*Rhetoric* 2.20.2). Willcock, following Kakridis (1949), focuses his attention on the *ad hoc inventio* of Achilles' *paradeigma*, as demonstrated by the unique detail of Niobe's refusal to eat in this account of the myth; Held discusses the similarities between Achilles' use of the Niobe myth and Phoenix's use of the Meleager myth in Book 9.

CHAPTER 3: PATTERNS OF ARISTOTELIAN RHETORIC IN THE *ILIAD*

1. Dickson (1995) 14.

2. For an in-depth analysis of Hector's speaking style and tendencies in the *Iliad*, see Mackie (1996). She considers Hector to be "the most 'poetic' performer of all" Iliadic characters, because "his inwardness is extreme, and his highly formal language instances the essential reflexivity of Jakobson's 'poetic' function, exemplified when a message's orientation toward its own form exercises the 'aesthetic function' of language" (66–67). Contributing to the poetic qualities of Hector's diction, Mackie observes, his speeches are highly concerned with praise (rather than blame), *kleos*, death, and memory (85–106).

3. Martin (1989) 48.

4. I apply the "deliberative" category to Homeric speeches that are addressed to only one person as well as those to a larger public audience because the deliberative aim—trying to persuade the listener(s) to take some action or attitude—is the same in both cases. Although Aristotle's "deliberative" category seems to have had in mind public

speeches addressed to a large audience, his definition of deliberative rhetoric as "either hortatory or dissuasive" (*Rhetoric* 1.3.3) and "exhorting what is expedient" (*Rhetoric* 1.3.5) applies to Homeric hortatory speeches whether they are addressed to one person or many.

5. On Achilles' value system and its relation to the heroic code, see among others Claus (1975), Friedrich and Redfield (1978), Redfield (1994), Nagy (1999). As Claus says regarding Achilles' speech in Book 9, "his rejection of the gifts, his threats to leave, and his concern for his life have a basis in patterns of *aidôs* and the heroic code" (25).

6. Much has been made of the uniqueness of Achilles' speech in the *Iliad*; less scholarly attention has been given to the speech and persuasion techniques directed toward Achilles, asking what common qualities link the attempts that fail, and the rare ones that succeed. Mackie (1996) discusses the failing attempts, observing that Odysseus, Phoenix, and Agamemnon all "talk to and treat Achilles as though he had no father, no property, and consequently no status" (146), and that such strategies are unsuccessful at moving Achilles. My aim in this coda is to identify the few productive or successful approaches to persuading Achilles.

CHAPTER 4: EXPLAINING THE CORRESPONDENCE BETWEEN HOMERIC SPEECH AND ARISTOTELIAN THEORY

1. West (1983) 7. See West (1983) on the Orphic Poems generally.

2. See West (1983) 39–44.

3. See Plett (1985) 62.

4. Kennedy (1998) 2–3.

5. Ibid., 3.

6. Ibid., 3–5.

7. On Nestor as rhetorical instructor for Diomedes, see Martin (1989) 23–26. In his speech at *Iliad* 9.53–78, Nestor corrects Diomedes' impetuous, incomplete challenge to Agamemnon with what Martin characterizes as "explicit instruction for the younger hero in how one reaches the 'perfection of speeches (*telos muthôn*).'" This instruction is a success; "having witnessed such expert teaching, Diomedes grows in rhetorical ability through the rest of the poem" (25).

8. Tigay (1982) provides a comprehensive treatment of the composition history of the *Epic of Gilgamesh*; see especially pp. 10–13 for Tigay's summary of the dating of the different versions.

9. Wills (1970) identifies several rhetorical strategies preserved in both literary and historical documents from ancient Mesopotamia, including systematic vituperation, the stylistic device of anaphora, and what he calls "logical speech organization" (403–5). He uses these findings to support his contention that there were assemblies in early Mesopotamian history that "seem to have had both deliberative and judicial functions and to have served as arenas for public address" (405). Only a few of the rhetorical examples Willis offers, however, are specific to persuasion (as opposed to criticism, instruction, etc.), and none of them approach the level of argumentative complexity found in Homeric rhetorical speeches.

10. Denning-Bolle (1987) 225–26.

11. Ibid., 226–27.

12. Translation of the *Epic of Gilgamesh* from George (1999).

13. Kennedy (1998) 122.

14. Denning-Bolle (1987) does, however, note the importance of dialogue in Near Eastern wisdom literature. She observes that "in Sumerian literature, the ancients termed one particular genre, *adaman-dug-ga*, which refers specifically to the contest literature. In this literature, two or more parties engage in a dispute, vying with each other over which is the superior object or creature." (225) Although this term is relatively rare in lexical lists, Denning-Bolle sees it as a parallel to ancient Greek phenomena: "The Mesopotamian enjoyed the art of verbal sparring as much as the Greeks reveled in the debater's techniques of the *agora*" (225).

15. Kennedy (1998) 124.

16. Ibid., 124.

17. Fox (1983) 16.

18. See Kennedy (1998) 118, 130–31.

19. Watson (1962) 34.

20. For this dating, see Giles (1967) 7.

21. Kennedy (1998) 151.

22. Garrett (1993) 22.

23. Watson (1962) 28.

24. Translation of the *Shūjīng* from Legge (1865).

25. On the authorship and dating of the *Mahābhārata*, see van Buitenen (1973) xxiii–xxv.

26. Kennedy (1998) 177.

27. McGrath (2004) 3, 144.

28. Translation of the *Mahābhārata* from van Buitenen (1973).

29. McGrath (2004) 162.

30. Ibid., 159–67.

31. Ibid., 133–77.

32. For discussion of ancient Greece as a uniquely debate-oriented culture, see (among others) Lloyd (1979) 59–125, Buxton (1982) 5–27, Griffith (1990), and Kennedy 1998 (197–99).

33. Buxton (1982) 26–27.

CHAPTER 5: RHETORIC IN ARCHAIC POETRY

1. The dates proposed by various scholars for the long Hymns range from the late eighth century to the early fifth century BCE. (see among others Richardson 2010, West 2003, Janko 1982, and Görgemanns 1976). Richardson gives an up-to-date and thorough overview of the considerations in dating three of the Hymns; he locates the *Hymn to Aphrodite* in the early seventh or even late eighth century (see p. 30), the *Hymn to Apollo* in the early sixth century (15), and the *Hymn to Hermes* in the mid- to late sixth century (24). In his 1974 commentary on the *Hymn to Demeter*, Richardson identifies the (late) seventh century as the most likely date for that Hymn (5–11). Although it is not necessary for the purposes of this project to resolve questions surrounding the Hymns' dating, the end of this section does offer some speculation about how the depiction of rhetoric in the long Hymns may shed light on their relative dating.

2. *Nemean* 2.1–3 reads: Ὅθεν περ καὶ Ὁμηρίδαι / ῥαπτῶν ἐπέων τὰ πόλλ᾽ ἀοιδοί / ἄρχονται, Διὸς ἐκ **προοιμίου** . . . ("Just as the sons of Homer, those singers of verses stitched together, most often begin with a prelude to Zeus. . . .") (Text of Pindar from Snell and Maehler 1987; translation from Race 1997). See also Thucydides' *History of the Peloponnesian War* 3.104, δηλοῖ δὲ μάλιστα Ὅμηρος ὅτι τοιαῦτα ἦν ἐν τοῖς ἔπεσι τοῖσδε, ἅ ἐστιν ἐκ **προοιμίου** Ἀπόλλωνος. . . . ("It is very clear that these practices were mentioned by Homer in the following verses, which are taken from the prelude [hymn] of Apollo. . . .") (Text of Thucydides from Jones and Powell 1942; translation is my own.)

3. West (2003) 5. See Cantilena (1982) and Janko (1982) for differing views on whether these shared formulas represent chronological development from Homer to the Hymns (Janko), or simply independent formular traditions (Cantilena).

4. I follow Clay (1989) 18–19 and Richardson (2010) 10–13 in viewing the *Hymn to Apollo* as a unified whole. I find their arguments for the poem's unity persuasive; beyond this, my analysis of the Hymn's direct speeches would not be materially affected by considering the Delian and Pythian portions separately. The question of the Hymn's unity has been amply treated elsewhere: Janko (1982) 99–100 passim makes the case for the Delian and Pythian halves as separate poems, and West (2003) 9–12 summarizes the controversy, operating from the assumption that the Hymn is a composite of two separate poems.

5. The 59-line *Hymn to Dionysus* (Hymn 7) does contain direct speech (an exchange between the Tyrsenian pirates' helmsman and captain concerning the treatment of the captured god, lines 17–31), but the exchange is simply a disagreement without any attempt at persuasion.

6. Text and translation of all *Homeric Hymns* from West (2003).

7. Miller (1986) 76.

8. Ibid., 79.

9. Clay (1989) 86.

10. For a fuller discussion of the rhetoric of Hermes in this hymn, focusing particularly on the similarities between his speech and sophistic argumentation, see Knudsen (2012b).

11. Speech comprises 39 percent of the *Hymn to Demeter*, 32 percent of the *Hymn to Apollo*, and 57 percent of the *Hymn to Aphrodite* (in only 6 speeches).

12. The rhetorical features of the *Hymn to Hermes* have been noted by several scholars. Kennedy (1963), in his overview of pre-Classical persuasion in Greece, speaks of Hermes' rhetorical sophistication and use of the *eikos* argument (40–41); Clay (1989) speaks in broad terms about the rhetoric of Hermes and how that relates to his particular domains of influence as a fledgling Olympian; Richardson (2010) in his commentary notes the rhetorical arguments and stylistic features of Hermes' two defense speeches (190–91, 199); and Görgemanns in his 1976 article "*Rhetorik und Poetik im homerischen Hermeshymnus*" examines how the *Hymn to Hermes* engages with its historical and cultural context, particularly with regard to the emergence of formal rhetoric. In addition, discussions of Hermes' sophistry in the matter of oaths can be found in Callaway (1993), Gagarin (2007a), and Fletcher (2008).

13. Clay (1989) 106, 110–11.

14. In addition to the rhetorical techniques present in this speech, Hermes' offer to swear an oath is a devious means of persuasion, for—as Callaway (1993) and Fletcher

(2008) have discussed—Hermes never actually swears the oath. The offer is a diversionary tactic; it makes Hermes look as though he has sworn the oath, but his use of the future tense (ὀμοῦμαι, "I will swear") and that the oath is never actually executed allow him to avoid perjury.

15. Clay (1989) 136.

16. Ibid., 141–42.

17. Ibid., 174.

18. Ibid., 178.

19. Walcot (1991) 152.

20. See Richardson (2010), West (2003), Janko (1982), and Allen et al. (1936). Görgemanns (1976) is the foremost proponent of the fifth-century date, based on his investigation into the relationship between the *Hymn to Hermes* and the fifth-century development of rhetoric under the sophists.

21. Richardson (2010) 30. Faulkner (2008) asserts that it has become the "*opinio communis*" that the *Hymn to Aphrodite* is "post-Homeric, but prior to the sixth century and the earliest of the *Hymns*" (47). West (2003) and Janko (1982) concur.

22. See Richardson (1974 and 2010). Janko (1982) and West (2003) also roughly follow this relative chronology, but split the *Hymn to Apollo* into two separate poems. Janko's chronology is *Hymn to Aphrodite, Delian Hymn to Apollo, Hymn to Demeter, Pythian Hymn to Apollo,* and *Hymn to Hermes.* West's chronology is *Hymn to Aphrodite,* either *Pythian Hymn to Apollo* or *Hymn to Demeter, Delian Hymn to Apollo,* and *Hymn to Hermes.*

23. The word "lyric" is, of course, merely a cover term for poetry that has immense variety in form, occasion, and subject matter. I use it as a convention for referring to all nonhexametric poetry of the Archaic period (elegiac, iambic and melic), but I acknowledge the unsatisfactory nature of the term.

24. Walker (2000) 206.

25. Latacz (1977).

26. On the dating and historical context of Callinus and Tyrtaeus, see Gerber (1997) 99–105.

27. Text of Callinus from West (1992); translation from Gerber (1999).

28. Gerber (1997) 100.

29. Hesiod's *Theogony* contains only a handful of direct speeches, of which two are attempts to persuade using rhetorical argument: Gaia's plea to her children to take revenge on Ouranos for sequestering them all in a cavern (*Theogony* 163–66); and Zeus' appeal to the hundred-handed monster children of Gaia and Ouranos to be allies in the Olympians' fight against the Titans (*Theogony* 643–53). Although both of these speeches succeed in their object, represented persuasion clearly has limited scope within the *Theogony.* Gaia's brief speech is framed as a conditional sentence ("if you wish . . ."), and its rhetorical content consists of a tentative **enthymeme** in which the conclusion—"we would avenge your father's evil outrage (πατρός γε κακὴν τεισαίμεθα λώβην)"—is supported by a premise that offers Ouranos' evil behavior as an incentive: "for (γὰρ) he was the first to devise unseemly deeds" (165–66). (Text and translation of Hesiod from Most 2006.)

Zeus' appeal to the hundred-handed, although lengthier than Gaia's speech, is still relatively short and simple in its rhetorical argumentation. His argument also centers on an **enthymeme**; its conclusion-command "manifest your great strength and your untouchable hands, facing the Titans in baleful conflict" (649–50) is followed by a premise that invokes the past and relies upon the audience's sense of obligation to the speaker (*diathesis*): ". . . mindful of our kind friendship, how after so many sufferings you have come up to the light once again out from under a deadly bond, by our plans" (651–53). By mentioning the Olympians' "faithful friendship" in the past, Zeus is also emphasizing his own trustworthiness (*êthos*).

30. For an extended discussion of the Near Eastern and Greek traditions of wisdom literature, see West (1978a) 3–30. West argues that, in all likelihood, "the Hesiodic poem stands in a tradition cognate with or influenced by oriental wisdom literature," and he cites evidence for "an Ionian tradition of paraenetic poetry" as a possible link (26–27).

31. West (1978a) 1.

32. Text and translation of Hesiod from Most (2006).

33. West (1978a) 47.

34. See Martin (2004).

35. West (1978a) notes that "The elegiac metre was widely used for admonitory poems of modest compass (up to a hundred lines or so). The advice might be for a particular political situation, or of general and lasting applicability. . . . [A] feature common to Hesiod and paraenetic elegy is the combination of injunctions with reasoning, complaints about the existing state of affairs, and warnings that the gods punish wickedness." (23–24).

36. Text of Theognis from West (1989); translation from Gerber (1999).

37. See West (1978a) 3–30.

38. See Solmsen (1954) 7ff.

39. Several phrases in this passage have parallels in Homer, as Solmsen (1954), West (1966), and others have noted. The image of "honeyed words" flowing from the mouth of a king (τοῦ δ' ἔπε' ἐκ στόματος ῥεῖ μείλιχα, 84) recalls the first description of Nestor in *Iliad* 1.249: τοῦ καὶ ἀπὸ γλώσσης μέλιτος γλυκίων ῥέεν αὐδή. This description introduces Nestor's speech of conciliation and arbitration between the disputing Achilles and Agamemnon, which places him in much the same role as is described in this Hesiodic passage: that of an arbiter-king. The phrase μαλακοῖσι παραιφάμενοι ἐπέεσσιν (90) also resembles a Homeric formula denoting the beguiling power of speech (e.g., παρφάμενος ἐπέεσσιν in *Iliad* 12.248–49 and *Od.* 2.188–89; ἐπέεσσι παραιφάμενος in *Iliad* 24.771).

40. See Detienne (1996) 70ff.

41. Cole (1991) 41; Kennedy (1963) 39; Detienne (1996) 70ff.

42. Detienne (1996) 88.

43. Robbins (1997) 233.

44. A spate of excellent scholarship has emerged on this relatively recently discovered fragment, first published in 1977 by Meillier, Boyaval, and Ancher. Among others, see Parsons' edition (1977), which establishes the arrangement of the papyrus fragments and provides a fundamental guide to the formal characteristics of the poem; West (1978b) on the argument for Stesichorean authorship; Haslam (1978) on the fragment's formal structure and particularly its use of the dactylo-epitrite, the first extant instance of this meter; Bremer et al. (1987) and Hutchinson (2001) for commentaries; and Burnett (1988) for extensive interpretive analysis of the surviving lines, speculation about

the poem's lost stanzas, and discussion of Stesichorus' treatment of the Theban mythic cycle.

45. Burnett (1988) has denied that this speech is rhetorical, arguing that it is, instead, "a full ethical portrait" of Jocasta, "a woman engaged in making a crucial decision while under the pressure of strongest emotion" (113). But the qualifiers "rhetorical," "ethical," and "emotional" need not be mutually exclusive when describing persuasive speech (after all, ethical and emotional expression are essential components of rhetoric in Aristotle's framework).

46. Text of Stesichorus from Davies (1991); translation from West (1993).

47. Bremer et al. (1987) 145–46.

48. Burnett (1988) 119.

49. Robbins (1997) 241.

50. Robbins (1997) notes that "The longer poems of Pindar and of Bacchylides in particular show the same fondness [as Stesichorus] for dramatic confrontation and for speeches," and identifies Bacchylides 5 and Pindar's Pythian 4 as primary examples of these phenomena (242). (While Bacchylides 5 does represent an exchange between Heracles and Meleager, neither character is exerting persuasion on the other, so it does not figure in my analysis.)

51. On the view that this poem might be a paean instead of a dithyramb, given its address to Apollo (130) and its description of the Athenian youths "singing a paean" (παιάνιξαν, 129), see Maehler (2004) 172, 188–89 (following Jebb) and Burnett (1985) 15–37. On the interrelated evidence for the dating of the poem and the idea that its subject matter is Bacchylides' invention, see Maehler (2004) 173–75.

52. Text of Bacchylides from Snell and Maehler (1970); translation from Campbell (1992).

53. See Maehler (2004) 180.

54. On the "rhetoric" of Pindar's authorial voice, see (among others) Bundy (1962), the classic treatment of Pindar's overarching rhetorical strategy, i.e., praising athletic victors; Race (1990), who is solely concerned with rhetoric in the sense of Pindar's poetic style, analyzing features such as "climactic elements," "break-offs," and "negative expressions" in the odes; Pratt (1993), who takes on Pindar's treatment of truth, lies, praise, and slander in epinician speech; and Pelliccia (1995), who focuses on Pindar's appropriation of bodily organs as "devices that will make some kind of dialogic interplay possible within this first-person structure" (288). Morgan (1993) provides an insightful contribution to the heated debate over whether the odes were performed chorally or by the poet alone when she discusses Pindar's "rhetoric of performance." She views Pindar's first- and second-person self-references, and references to the κῶμος, as "rhetorical" (that is, a product of his own purposefully constructed professional persona) rather than literal. None of these uses of the term rhetoric corresponds to the specific definition of rhetoric (involving persuasive argumentation) with which I am at present concerned.

55. Text of Pindar from Snell and Maehler (1987); translation from Race (1997). Braswell (1988) notes that the metaphor of "distilling" speech has its origins in Homer's introductory description of Nestor (Iliad 1.249) (222).

56. Segal (1986) 36–37.

57. On truth and falsehood in Pindar, see especially Pratt (1993), who connects Pindar's concern for truth with his epinician mission to praise the victor in an accurate and

reliable manner. Conversely, Pratt notes, "most liars that appear in Pindar's poetry [such as Odysseus in *Nemean* 7 and 8] are envious slanderers, because Pindar is particularly anxious to condemn and reject this type of lying" (122).

58. See Lloyd-Jones (1973) 130 and Carey (1981) 146 on the interpretive ambiguities of this passage.

CHAPTER 6: FROM POETRY TO THEORY

1. Ober and Strauss (1990) 248.

2. On rhetoric and tragedy, Buxton (1982) provides a classic treatment; Pelling (2005) gives a more recent overview, dealing with social and literary aspects of this relationship, discussing the role of rhetoric within a of individual number tragedies, and providing a review of scholarship on the subject; see also Bers (1994) and Goldhill (1997) on specific types of rhetorical language in tragedy. On the rich connection between tragic speech and fifth-century Athenian civic practice and performance, see among others Goldhill (1986) and (1990), Ober (1989) 152–55, Ober and Strauss (1990), Hesk (2007), and Martin (2007). On rhetoric in Euripides, who for obvious reasons has attracted the most attention of all the tragedians for his characters' rhetorical language, see among others Dale (1954) xxvii–xxviii, Conacher (1981), and Croally (1994).

3. In dating this so-called "First Sophistic" era, I include the productive years of the traditional figures as collected in Diels-Kranz under the designation "Ältere Sophistik," as well as the so-called "second generation" of sophists working in the fourth century, a group that includes Isocrates and Alcidamas (see Dillon and Gergel 2003, xiv). The "First Sophstic" thus extended from roughly 430 to 340 BCE. For scholarship on the sophists and the sophistic movement, see Gagarin (2002) 9–36, Kennedy (1994) 17–35, de Romilly (1992), Kerferd (1981), and Guthrie (1971).

4. On the origins and development of the concept of *eikos*, see Schiappa (1999) 35–39, Gagarin (1994), and O'Sullivan (1992) 28. Plato credits Tisias with the invention of this technique in *Phaedrus* 267a and 273a–c.

5. O'Sullivan (1992) 28.

6. Cole (1991) x, cf. 41.

7. For a fuller discussion of this sophistic phenomenon, see Knudsen (2012a). See also references to this practice in Morgan (2000) 101–31, Worman (2002) 149–92, and Gagarin (2002) 103–4.

8. Morgan (2000) 11.

9. This discussion of Antisthenes' *Ajax* and *Odysseus* is modified from a section of my 2012a article "Poetic Speakers, Sophistic Words."

10. See Radermacher (1892) and Lulofs (1900) for discussion of various textual and metrical considerations in the *Ajax* and *Odysseus*. Rankin (1986) is interested in the way that the speeches reflect Antisthenes' philosophical outlook, Focardi (1987) in the relationship between the speeches and later forensic practice. See also a brief discussion in Worman (2002) 185–88.

11. For more on the philosophical implications of the two speeches, see Rankin (1986). Gagarin (2002) observes that these speeches also explore general issues "such as the true nature of courage and cowardice, the value of traditional virtues in contrast to a more flexible 'situational ethics,' the value of appearance, and even the ability of *logoi* to rewrite and thus reinterpret the story of the past" (103–4).

12. Text of the *Ajax* and *Odysseus* from Giannantoni (1990); translation is my own.

13. To name just a few: McCoy (2007), Schiappa (1999) and (2003), White (1993), and Ferrari (1987). For further bibliography on Plato and rhetoric, see Nienkamp (1999) 215–17.

14. See Nightingale (1995) 133–71 on "alien and authentic discourse" in the *Phaedrus*. This refers to Plato's notion that the philosopher must not simply passively assimilate, but must actively engage with, "alien discourse"—such as rhetorical speeches or writings— and make them "authentic" by "measuring them against the truths he has discovered by dialectical investigation." (134)

15. Nienkamp (1999) 13.

16. Text of the *Gorgias* from Burnet (1903); translation from Zeyl (1987).

17. See Nightingale (1995) 133–71. In the course of Plato's wide-ranging treatment of different types of discourse in the *Phaedrus*, Nightingale notes, he makes the characters of Phaedrus and Socrates perform contemporary genres of rhetoric (especially encomiastic) within the three speeches embedded in the dialogue. Each of the speeches is intended to be persuasive in its own right, but each speech progressively changes and challenges the internal audience's (Phaedrus') interpretation of the speech(es) that preceded it—thus enacting the process of what Nightingale calls "authentic discourse" that Plato is striving for (154ff.).

18. Text of the *Phaedrus* from Burnet (1903); translation from Nehamas and Woodruff (1995).

19. I have adapted Nehamas' and Woodruff's translation in one regard here, substituting the word "nature" where they have "character" to translate φύσις. In my opinion this is a necessary change to avoid confusion with the Greek word more frequently translated as "character," namely ἦθος.

20. In the *Phaedrus*, Socrates gives a litany of sophistic figures associated with the invention of various (mostly minor) rhetorical devices: Thrasymachus (266c), Theodorus (266e), Evenus of Paros (267a), Tisias (267a, 273a–c), Gorgias (267a), Prodicus (267b), Hippias (267b), Polus (267b), Licymnius (267c), and Protagoras (267c). Rather than crediting these men with the invention of rhetoric, Socrates calls their art "a little threadbare" (268a); he cautions Phaedrus that they "teach these preliminaries and imagine their pupils have received a full course in rhetoric" (269c).

21. Cole (1991) 11–12.

22. In addition to these instances, there are three mentions of Homer the person (as opposed to his poems) in the *Rhetoric*: 1.6.25, 1.15.13, and 2.23.11. These mentions have no relevance to Homeric rhetoric, however. For example, Aristotle writes (when explaining arguments from induction), "[another example is] as Alcidamas [argued], that all honor the wise; at least, Parians honored Archilochus despite the nasty things he said [about them]; and Chians Homer, though he was not a citizen" (2.23.11).

23. See 1.2.4–5, 1.2.15, and 2.23.21 (referring to the τέχνη of Callipus), 2.23.28 (referring to the τέχνη of Theodorus), 2.24.11 (referring to the τέχνη of Corax), 3.1.7 (referring to the Ἔλεοι, a treatise on the emotions of Thrasymachus), and 3.13.3–5 (a more extended criticism of the handbook-writers' practice of making "laughable divisions," διαιροῦσι γελοίως, into detailed categories under the heading of τάξις).

24. Cole (1991) 29.

25. See Schiappa (1999) 45–47.

26. Ibid., 39.

27. I mention only these two authors out of many that could be cited on this idea, often expressed in the shorthand of "from *mythos* to *logos*" (a phrase coined by Wilhelm Nestle in his 1940 work, *Vom Mythos zum Logos*). The intellectual history of this idea, as well as more recent scholarly moves to problematize it, receives extensive and diverse treatment in Buxton's *From Myth to Reason? Studies in the Development of Greek Thought* (1999).

28. Detienne (1996) 88.

29. Ibid., 15–17.

30. Goldhill (2002) 4–5.

31. Havelock (1957) 18.

APPENDIX: ANALYSIS OF REMAINING ILIADIC RHETORICAL SPEECHES

1. Although Willcock (1964) sees this myth as an example of the use of a *paradeigma*, I agree with Held (1987) that it does not make sense in that function. Rather, Achilles is suggesting the use of this myth as persuasive for Zeus because it will remind him of his obligation to Thetis.

2. For the classic treatment of "shame-culture" in the *Iliad*, see Dodds (1951); for a more recent treatment of shame as a societal value in the *Iliad*, see Adkins (1997) 699–700.

3. Toohey (1994) offers an in-depth analysis of the rhetorical elements he finds in this speech, similar to his analysis of Nestor's speech in 1.254–84. In this case, as in the earlier speech (which I treat in chapter 2, section III), Toohey's analysis focuses primarily on the formal structure of the speech rather than on its argumentation.

4. Dickson (1995) 73–75.

5. Toohey (1994) notes that "the logic of the *paradeigma* is identical to that of the first of Nestor's speeches [1.254–84]. It makes its claim for persuasion on that most popular of rhetorical tropes, an appeal to the past—specifically Nestor's. The speech also evinces the paratactic, oral compositional mode of ring form (ABCBA), stressed also by Kirk. . . . But at the same time the technique used by this speech—the reminiscence—is totally in keeping with the ethos of old Nestor" (157–58). Regarding the technique of recollection used in the service of persuasion, Martin (1989) remarks that "the master of this genre is of course Nestor" (80).

6. See Aristotle *Rhetoric* 2.25.8, Ἐπεὶ δὲ τὰ ἐνθυμήματα λέγεται ἐκ τεττάρων . . . εἰκὸς παράδειγμα τεκμήριον σημεῖον. ("Enthymemes are drawn from four sources and these four are probability, paradigm, *tekmerion* [or necessary sign], and *semeion* [or fallible sign].") Aristotle further explains *tekmêrion* as a sign based on that which is necessary and everlasting, and a *sêmeion* as a sign based on that which is generalized or partial.

7. Beck (2008) 164.

8. This may reflect the familiarity of the *Iliad*'s composer and audience with the Cyclic tradition (for which see Burgess 2001)—in this case, Tydeus' role in the *Thebais* and Diomedes' in the *Epigonoi*.

9. A common usage of the term *paradeigma* in discussing the *Iliad* is articulated by Willcock (1964), who observes that "the mythical example is commonly used in speeches

in the *Iliad* when one character wishes to influence the actions of another. Usually it is a matter of exhortation or consolation. This is what is meant by a paradeigma" (147). Following Aristotle, my usage of *paradeigma* does not require it to be "mythical"; as in this instance, it can be used to describe any admirable or cautionary example, including that of the speaker's own behavior.

10. Macleod (1982) 131–32.

Bibliography

Abbenes, J. G. J., S. R. Slings, and I. Sluiter, eds. 1995. *Greek Literary Theory after Aristotle: A Collection of Papers in Honour of D. M. Schenkeveld.* Amsterdam.

Adkins, A. W. H. 1997. "Homeric Ethics." In *A New Companion to Homer,* edited by I. Morris and B. Powell, 694–713. Leiden.

Allen, T. W., W. R. Halliday, and E. E. Sikes, eds. 1936. *The Homeric Hymns.* 2nd ed. Oxford.

Allen, Thomas W. and David B. Munro, eds. 1920. *Homeri Opera.* 3rd ed. Oxford.

Apfel, Henrietta V. 1938. "Homeric Criticism in the Fourth Century B.C." *Transactions of the American Philological Association* 69, 245–58.

Austin, J. L. 1962. *How to Do Things With Words.* Cambridge, MA.

Bakker, Egbert. 1997. *Poetry in Speech: Orality and Homeric Discourse.* Ithaca.

Barney, Rachel. 2001. *Names and Nature in Plato's* Cratylus. New York.

Baxter, Timothy M. S. 1992. *The* Cratylus: *Plato's Critique of Naming.* Leiden.

Beck, Deborah. 2005a. *Homeric Conversation.* Washington, DC.

———. 2005b. "Odysseus: Narrator, Storyteller, Poet?" *Classical Philology* 100, 213–27.

———. 2008. "Character-Quoted Direct Speech in the *Iliad.*" *Phoenix* 62, 162–83.

———. 2012. *Speech Presentation in Homeric Epic.* Austin.

Bers, Victor. 1994. "Tragedy and Rhetoric." In *Persuasion: Greek Rhetoric in Action,* edited by I. Worthington, 176–95. London.

Blank, David. 1995. "Philodemus on the Technicity of Rhetoric." In *Philodemus and Poetry: Poetic Theory and Practice in Lucretius, Philodemus, and Horace,* edited by D. Obbink, 178–88. Oxford.

Braswell, Bruce Karl. 1988. *A Commentary on the Fourth Pythian Ode of Pindar.* Berlin.

Bremer, J. M., A.M. van Erp, T. Kip, and S. R. Slings, eds. 1987. *Some Recently Found Greek Poems.* Leiden.

Brown, Christopher G. 1997. "Iambos." In *A Companion to the Greek Lyric Poets,* edited by D. Gerber, 11–88. Leiden.

Buffière, Félix. 1973. *Les Mythes d'Homère et la Pensée Grecque.* Paris.

Bundy, Elroy. 1962. *Studia Pindarica.* University of California Publications in Classical Philology 18, Berkeley.

Burgess, Jonathan S. 2001. *The Tradition of the Trojan War in Homer and the Epic Cycle.* Baltimore.

Burnet, John, ed. 1903. *Platonis Opera,* vol. 2. Oxford.

Burnett, Anne Pippin. 1985. *The Art of Bacchylides.* Cambridge, MA.

———. 1988. "Jocasta in the West: The Lille Stesichorus." *Classical Antiquity* 7, 107–54.

Burnyeat, M. F. 1994. "Enthymeme: Aristotle on the Logic of Persuasion." In *Aristotle's* Rhetoric: *Philosophical Essays*, edited by D. Furley and A. Nehamas, 3–55. Princeton.

Butler, H. E., ed. and trans. 1921. *The Institutio Oratoria of Quintilian*. Cambridge, MA.

Buxton, R. G. A. 1982. *Persuasion in Greek Tragedy: A Study of* Peitho. Cambridge.

———, ed. 1999. *From Myth to Reason? Studies in the Development of Greek Thought*. Oxford.

Càffaro, Luca, ed. 1997. *Gorgia: Encomio di Elena, Apologia di Palamede*. Florence.

Caizzi, Fernanda Decleva, ed. 1966. *Antisthenis Fragmenta*. Milan.

Caldwell, Richard S. 1987. *Hesiod's Theogony*. Newburyport, MA.

Callaway, Cathy. 1993. "Perjury and the Unsworn Oath." *Transactions of the American Philological Association* 123, 15–25.

Campbell, David A., ed. and trans. 1992. *Greek Lyric IV: Bacchylides, Corinna, and Others*. Cambridge, MA.

Cantilena, Mario. 1982. *Ricerche sulla Dizione Epica I*. Rome.

Carey, Christopher. 1981. *A Commentary on Five Odes of Pindar: Pythian 2, Pythian 9, Nemean 1, Nemean 7, Isthmian 8*. New York.

———. 1994. "Rhetorical Means of Persuasion." In *Persuasion: Greek Rhetoric in Action*, edited by I. Worthington, 26–45. London.

Chandler, Clive. 2006. *Philodemus* On Rhetoric *Books 1 and 2: Translation and Exegetical Essays*. New York.

Claus, David B. 1975. "*AIDÔS* in the Language of Achilles." *Transactions of the American Philological Association* 105, 13–28.

Clay, Jenny Strauss. 1989. *The Politics of Olympus: Form and Meaning in the Major Homeric Hymns*. Princeton.

Cole, Thomas. 1991. *The Origins of Rhetoric in Ancient Greece*. Baltimore.

Conacher, D. J. 1981. "Rhetoric and Relevance in Euripidean Drama." *American Journal of Philology* 102, 3–25.

Connors, Robert J. 1986. "Greek Rhetoric and the Transition from Orality." *Philosophy and Rhetoric* 19, 38–65.

Coulter, James A. 1964. "The Relation of the *Apology* of Socrates to Gorgias' *Defense of Palamedes* and Plato's Critique of Gorgianic Rhetoric." *Harvard Studies in Classical Philology* 68, 269–303.

Croally, N. T. 1994. *Euripidean Polemic:* The Trojan Women *and the Function of Tragedy*. Cambridge.

Dale, A. M., ed. 1954. *Euripides Alcestis*. Oxford.

Davies, Malcolm, ed. 1991. *Poetarum Melicorum Graecorum Fragmenta*, vol. 1. Oxford.

De Lacy, Phillip. 1948. "Stoic Views of Poetry." *American Journal of Philology* 69, 141–71.

de Jong, Irene. 1987. *Narrators and Focalizers: The Presentation of the Story in the* Iliad. Amsterdam.

Denning-Bolle, Sara J. 1987. "Wisdom and Dialogue in the Ancient Near East." *Numen* 34, 214–34.

Denniston, J. D., and D. L. Page, eds. 1957. *Aeschylus:* Agamemnon. Oxford.

de Romilly, Jacqueline. 1975. *Magic and Rhetoric in Ancient Greece*. Cambridge, MA.

————. 1992. *The Great Sophists in Periclean Athens*, trans. Janet Lloyd. Oxford. Originally published as *Les Grands Sophistes dans l'Athènes de Périclès*. Paris, 1988.

Detienne, Marcel. 1996. *The Masters of Truth in Archaic Greece*, trans. Janet Lloyd. New York. Originally published as *Les maîtres de vérité dans la Grèce archaïque*. Paris, 1967.

de Vries, G. J. 1969. *A Commentary on the Phaedrus of Plato*. Amsterdam.

Dickson, Keith. 1995. *Nestor: Poetic Memory in Greek Epic*. New York.

Diels, Hermann, and Walther Kranz, eds. 1952. *Die Fragmente der Vorsokratiker* II. 6th ed. Berlin.

Diggle, J., ed. 1984. *Euripidis Fabulae*, vol. 1. Oxford.

Dillon, John, and Tania Gergel, trans. 2003. *The Greek Sophists*. London.

Dodds, E. R. 1951. *The Greeks and the Irrational*. Berkeley.

Duke, E. A., W. F. Hicken, W. S. M. Nicoll, D. B. Robinson, and J. C. G. Strachan, eds. 1995. *Platonis Opera*, vol. 1. Oxford.

Easterling, Pat, and Edith Hall, eds. 2002. *Greek and Roman Actors: Aspects of an Ancient Profession*. Cambridge.

Edwards, Mark. 1970. "Homeric Speech Introductions." *Harvard Studies in Classical Philology* 74, 1–36.

————. 1991. *The Iliad: A Commentary, Volume V: Books 17–20*. Cambridge.

————. 2005. "Homer's *Iliad*." In *A Companion to Ancient Epic*, edited by J. Foley, 302–14. Oxford.

Erbse, Hartmut, ed. 1969–83. *Scholia Graeca in Homeri Iliadem*, vols. 1–7. Berlin.

Faraone, Christopher A. 2006. "Stanzaic Structure and Responsion on Tyrtaeus." *Mnemosyne* ser. IV, 59, 19–52.

Farenga, Vincent. 1979. "Periphrasis on the Origin of Rhetoric." *MLN* 94, 1033–55.

Faulkner, Andrew. 2008. *The Homeric Hymn to Aphrodite: Introduction, Text, and Commentary*. Oxford.

Ferrari, G. R. F. 1987. *Listening to the Cicadas: A Study of Plato's Phaedrus*. Cambridge.

Fingerle, Anton. 1939. *Typik der homerischen Reden*. Diss., Munich.

Fletcher, Judith. 2008. "A Trickster's Oaths in the *Homeric Hymn to Hermes*." *American Journal of Philology* 129, 19–46.

Focardi, G. 1987. "Antistene Declamatore: *L'Aiace* e *L'Ulisse*, alle Origini della Retorica Greca." *Sileno* 13, 147–73.

Foley, John M., ed. 2005. *A Companion to Ancient Epic*. Oxford.

Ford, Andrew. 2002. *The Origins of Criticism: Literary Culture and Poetic Theory in Classical Greece*. Princeton.

Fox, Michael V. 1983. "Ancient Egyptian Rhetoric." *Rhetorica* 1, 9–22.

Friedländer, P. 1913. "ΥΠΟΘΗΚΑΙ." *Hermes* 48, 558–616.

Friedrich, Paul, and James Redfield. 1978. "Speech as a Personality Symbol: The Case of Achilles." *Language* 54, 263–88.

Frobish, Todd. 2003. "An Origin of a Theory: A Comparison of Ethos in the Homeric *Iliad* with that Found in Aristotle's *Rhetoric*." *Rhetoric Review* 22, 16–30.

Furley, David J., and Alexander Nehamas, eds. 1994. *Aristotle's Rhetoric: Philosophical Essays*. Princeton.

Fyfe, W. Hamilton, ed. and trans. 1927. *Aristotle: The Poetics; "Longinus": On the Sublime; Demetrius: On Style*. Cambridge, MA.

Gagarin, Michael. 1994. "Probability and Persuasion: Plato and Early Greek Rhetoric." In *Persuasion: Greek Rhetoric in Action*, edited by I. Worthington, 46–68. London.

———. 2002. *Antiphon the Athenian: Oratory, Law, and Justice in the Age of the Sophists*. Austin.

———. 2007a. "Background and Origins: Oratory and Rhetoric before the Sophists." In *A Companion to Greek Rhetoric*, edited by I. Worthington, 27–36. Oxford.

———. 2007b. "Litigant's Oaths in Athenian Law." In *Horkos: The Oath in Greek Society*, edited by A. Sommerstein and J. Fletcher, 39–47. Exeter.

Gagarin, Michael, and Douglas M. MacDowell, trans. 1998. *Antiphon and Andocides*. Austin.

Garner, R. Scott. 2005. "Epic and Other Genres in the Ancient Greek World." In *A Companion to Ancient Epic*, edited by J. Foley, 387–96. Oxford.

Garrett, Mary M. 1993. "*Pathos* Reconsidered from the Perspective of Classical Chinese Rhetorical Theories." *Quarterly Journal of Speech* 79, 19–39.

George, Andrew, trans. 1999. *The Epic of Gilgamesh*. London.

Gerber, Douglas E., ed. 1997. *A Companion to the Greek Lyric Poets*. Leiden.

———, ed. and trans. 1999. *Greek Elegiac Poetry*. Cambridge, MA.

Giannantoni, Gabriele, ed. 1990. *Socratis et Socraticorum Reliquiae*, vols. 1–4. Naples.

Giles, Herbert A. 1967. *A History of Chinese Literature*. Suppl. ed. New York.

Gill, Christopher. 1990. "The Character-Personality Distinction." In *Characterization and Individuality in Greek Literature*, edited by C. Pelling, 1–31. Oxford.

Goebel, George. 1989. "Probability in the Earliest Rhetorical Theory." *Mnemosyne* 42, 41–53.

Görgemanns, Herwig. 1976. "Rhetorik und Poetik im homerischen Hermeshymnus." In *Studien zum antiken Epos*, edited by H. Görgemanns and E. Schmidt, 113–28. Meisenheim am Glan.

Goldhill, Simon. 1986. *Reading Greek Tragedy*. Cambridge.

———. 1990. "The Great Dionysia and Civic Ideology." In *Nothing to Do with Dionysos? Athenian Drama in Its Social Context*, edited by J. Winkler and F. Zeitlin, 97–129. Princeton.

———. 1997. "The Language of Tragedy: Rhetoric and Communication." In *The Cambridge Companion to Greek Tragedy*, edited by P. Easterling, 127–50. Cambridge.

———. 2002. *The Invention of Prose*. Oxford.

Griffin, Jasper. 1986. "Homeric Words and Speakers." *Journal of Hellenic Studies* 106, 36–57.

Griffith, Mark. 1990. "Contest and Contradiction in Early Greek Poetry." In *Cabinet of the Muses: Essays on Classical and Comparative Literature in Honor of Thomas G. Rosenmeyer*, edited by M. Griffith and D. Mastronarde, 185–207. Atlanta.

Grimaldi, William. 1980. *Aristotle, Rhetoric: A Commentary*, vols. 1–2. New York.

Guthrie, W. K. C. 1971. *The Sophists*. Cambridge.

Gutzwiller, Kathryn. 2007. *A Guide to Hellenistic Literature*. Malden, MA.

Hainsworth, Bryan. 1993. *The Iliad: A Commentary, Volume III: Books 9–12*. Cambridge.

Halliwell, Stephen. 1990. "Traditional Greek Conceptions of Character." In *Characterization and Individuality in Greek Literature*, edited by C. Pelling, 32–59. Oxford.

Halverson, John. 1992. "Havelock on Greek Orality and Literacy." *Journal of the History of Ideas* 53, 148–63.

Haslam, Michael W. 1978. "The Versification of the New Stesichorus (*P.Lille* 76abc)." *Greek, Roman, and Byzantine Studies* 19, 29–57.

Havelock, Eric. 1957. *The Liberal Temper in Greek Politics*. New Haven.

———. 1986. *The Muse Learns to Write: Reflections on Orality and Literacy from Antiquity to the Present*. New Haven.

Heath, John. 2005. *The Talking Greeks: Speech, Animals, and the Other in Homer, Aeschylus, and Plato*. Cambridge.

Held, George F. 1987. "Phoinix, Agamemnon and Achilleus: Parables and Paradeigmata." *Classical Quarterly* 37 (ii), 245–61.

Hendrickson, G. L., ed. and trans. 1971. *Cicero: Brutus*. Cambridge, MA.

Hesk, Jon. 2007. "The Socio-Political Dimension of Ancient Tragedy." In *The Cambridge Companion to Greek and Roman Theatre*, edited by M. McDonald and M. Walton, 72–91. Cambridge.

Hett, W. S., ed. and trans. 1957. *Aristotle: Problems II, Rhetorica ad Alexandrum*. Cambridge, MA.

Hutchinson, G. O. 2001. *Greek Lyric Poetry: A Commentary on Selected Larger Pieces*. Oxford.

Innes, Doreen C. 1989. " 'Longinus' and Others." In *The Cambridge History of Classical Literature Volume I Part 4: The Hellenistic Period and the Empire*, edited by P. Easterling and B. Knox, 86–89. Cambridge.

———. 1995. "Longinus: Structure and Unity." In *Greek Literary Theory after Aristotle*, edited by J. Abbenes, S. Slings, and I. Sluiter, 111–24. Amsterdam.

Jakobson, Roman. 1960. "Linguistics and Poetics." In *Style and Language*, edited by T. Sebeok, 350–77. Cambridge, MA.

Janko, Richard. 1982. *Homer, Hesiod and the Hymns: Diachronic Development in Epic Diction*. Cambridge.

———. 2007. "Glenn W. Most (ed.), *Hesiod: Theogony, Works and Days, Testimonia*. Loeb Classical Library 57." *Bryn Mawr Classical Review* 2007.3.31.

Jeffreys, Elizabeth, ed. 2003. *Rhetoric in Byzantium*. Aldershot.

Johansen, Thomas K. 1999. "Myth and *Logos* in Aristotle." In *From Myth to Reason? Studies in the Development of Greek Thought*, edited by R. Buxton, 279–91. Oxford.

Jones, Henry Stuart, and John Enoch Powell, eds. 1942. *Thucydidis Historiae*. Oxford.

Kakridis, Johannes. 1949. *Homeric Researches*. Lund.

Karp, Andrew J. 1977. "Homeric Origins of Ancient Rhetoric." *Arethusa* 10, 237–58.

Kassel, Rudolf, ed. 1976. *Aristotelis Ars Rhetorica*. Berlin.

Keaney, J. J., and Robert Lamberton, eds. 1996. *[Plutarch]: Essay on the Life and Poetry of Homer*. Atlanta.

Kennedy, George. 1957. "The Ancient Dispute Over Rhetoric in Homer." *American Journal of Philology* 78, 23–35.

———. 1959. "The Earliest Rhetorical Handbooks." *American Journal of Philology* 80, 169–78.

———. 1963. *The Art of Persuasion in Greece*. Princeton.

———. 1992. "A Hoot in the Dark: The Evolution of General Rhetoric." *Philosophy and Rhetoric* 25, 1–21.

———. 1994. *A New History of Classical Rhetoric*. Princeton.

———. 1998. *Comparative Rhetoric: An Historical and Cross-Cultural Introduction*. Oxford.

————, trans. 2007a. *Aristotle on Rhetoric: A Theory of Civic Discourse*. 2nd ed. Oxford.

————. 2007b. "The Earliest Rhetorical Handbooks." In *Aristotle on Rhetoric: A Theory of Civic Discourse*, translated by Kennedy, 293–306. Rev. from 1959. Oxford.

Kerferd, G. B. 1981. *The Sophistic Movement*. Cambridge.

Kibédi-Varga, A. 1985. "L'histoire de la Rhétorique et la Rhétorique des Genres." *Rhetorica* 3, 201–21.

Kim, Lawrence Young. 2001. *Supplementing Homer: Creativity and Conjecture in Ancient Homeric Criticism*. Diss., Princeton University.

Kindstrand, Jan Fredrik, ed. 1990. *[Plutarchus] De Homero*. Leipzig.

————. 1973. *Homer in der Zweiten Sophistik*. Uppsala.

Kirby, John T. 1990. "The 'Great Triangle' in Early Greek Rhetoric and Poetics." *Rhetorica* 8, 213–28.

Kirk, G. S., et al., eds. 1985–93. *The Iliad: A Commentary*, vols. 1–6. Cambridge.

Knox, Ronald, and Joseph Russo. 1989. "Agamemnon's Test: *Iliad* 2.73–75." *Classical Antiquity* 8, 351–58.

Knudsen, Rachel Ahern. 2012a. "Poetic Speakers, Sophistic Words." *American Journal of Philology* 133, 31–60.

————. 2012b. "'I Was(n't) Born Yesterday': Sophistic Argumentation in the *Homeric Hymn to Hermes*." *Classical Philology* 107, 341–48.

Kurke, Leslie. 1990. "Pindar's Sixth *Pythian* and the Tradition of Advice Poetry." *Transactions of the American Philological Association* 120, 85–107.

Laird, Andrew, ed. 2006. *Ancient Literary Criticism*. Oxford.

Lamberton, Robert. 1986. *Homer the Theologian: Neoplatonist Allegorical Reading and the Growth of the Epic Tradition*. Berkeley.

————. 1997. "Homer in Antiquity." In *A New Companion to Homer*, edited by I. Morris and B. Powell, 33–54. Leiden.

————. 2002. "Homeric Allegory and Homeric Rhetoric in Ancient Pedagogy." In *Omero tremila anni dopo: Atti del congresso di Genova 6–8 luglio 2000. Con la collaborazione di Paola Ascheri. Storia e Letteratura 210*, edited by F. Montanari, 185–205. Rome.

Lamberton, Robert, and John J. Keaney, eds. 1992. *Homer's Ancient Readers: The Hermeneutics of Greek Epic's Earliest Exegetes*. Princeton.

Larrain, Carlos J. 1987. *Struktur der Reden in der Odyssee 1–8*. Hildesheim.

Latacz, Joachim. 1977. *Kampfparänese, Kampfdarstellung und Kampfwirklichkeit in der Ilias, bei Kallinos und Tyrtaios*. Munich.

Lattimore, Richmond, trans. 1951. *The Iliad of Homer*. Chicago.

Ledbetter, Grace. 2003. *Poetics before Plato: Interpretation and Authority in Early Greek Theories of Poetry*. Princeton.

Legge, James, trans. 1865. *The Shoo-King (Shu ching)*, vol. 3, pts. 1–2 of *The Chinese Classics*. London.

Lloyd, G. E. R. 1979. *Magic, Reason, and Experience: Studies in the Origins and Development of Greek Science*. Cambridge.

Lloyd-Jones, Hugh. 1973. "Modern Interpretation of Pindar: The Second Pythian and Seventh Nemean Odes." *Journal of Hellenic Studies* 93, 109–37.

————, trans. 1979. *Aeschylus: The Oresteia*. Berkeley.

Lloyd-Jones, H., and N. G. Wilson, eds. 1990. *Sophoclis Fabulae*. Oxford.

Lohmann, Dieter. 1970. *Die Komposition der Reden in der Ilias*. Berlin.

Lulofs, H. J. 1900. *De Antisthenis studiis rhetoricis*. Diss., Amsterdam.

Mackie, Hilary. 1996. *Talking Trojan: Speech and Community in the* Iliad. Lanham, MD.

Macleod, Colin W., ed. 1982. *Homer:* Iliad *Book XXIV*. Cambridge.

Maehler, Herwig, ed. 2004. *Bacchylides: A Selection*. Cambridge.

Malcovati, Enrica, ed. 1970. *M. Tullius Cicero Scripta Quae Manserunt Omnia fasc. 4: Brutus*. Leipzig.

Martin, Richard P. 1989. *The Language of Heroes: Speech and Performance in the* Iliad. Ithaca.

———. 2000. "Wrapping Homer Up: Cohesion, Discourse, and Deviation in the *Iliad*." In *Intratextuality: Greek and Roman Textual Relations*, edited by A. Sharrock and H. Morales, 43–65. Oxford.

———. 2004. "Hesiod and the Didactic Double." *Synthesis* 11, 1–22.

———. 2005. "Epic as Genre." In *A Companion to Ancient Epic*, edited by J. Foley, 9–19. Oxford.

———. 2007. "Ancient Theatre and Performance Culture." In *The Cambridge Companion to Greek and Roman Theatre*, edited by M. McDonald and M. Walton, 36–54. Cambridge.

Mastronarde, Donald J., ed. 2002. *Euripides: Medea*. Cambridge.

McCoy, Marina. 2007. *Plato on the Rhetoric of Philosophers and Sophists*. Cambridge.

McDonald, Marianne, and Michael Walton, eds. 2007. *The Cambridge Companion to Greek and Roman Theatre*. Cambridge.

McGrath, Kevin. 2004. *The Sanskrit Hero: Karna in Epic Mahābhārata*. Leiden.

Meineke, A., ed. 1877. *Strabonis geographica*, vols. 1–3. Repr. 1969. Leipzig.

Miller, Andrew M. 1986. *From Delos to Delphi: A Literary Study of the Homeric Hymn to Apollo*. Leiden.

Morgan, Kathryn A. 1993. "Pindar the Professional and the Rhetoric of the ΚΩΜΟΣ." *Classical Philology* 88, 1–15.

———. 2000. *Myth and Philosophy from the Pre-Socratics to Plato*. Cambridge.

Morris, Ian, and Barry Powell, eds. 1997. *A New Companion to Homer*. Leiden.

Morwood, James, trans. 1997. *Euripides: Medea, Hippolytus, Electra, Helen*. Oxford.

Most, Glenn W. 1999. "From Logos to Mythos." In *From Myth to Reason? Studies in the Development of Greek Thought*, edited by R. Buxton, 25–47.

———, ed. and trans. 2006. *Hesiod: Theogony, Works and Days, Testimonia*. Cambridge, MA.

Moulton, Carroll. 1981. "The Speech of Glaukos in *Iliad* 17." *Hermes* 109, 1–8.

Nagy, Gregory. 1990a. *Pindar's Homer: The Lyric Possession of an Epic Past*. Baltimore.

———. 1990b. *Greek Mythology and Poetics*. Ithaca.

———. 1996. *Homeric Questions*. Austin.

———. 1999. *The Best of the Achaeans: Concepts of the Hero in Archaic Greek Poetry*. 1st ed. 1979. Baltimore.

———. 2003. *Homeric Responses*. Austin.

Navia, Luis. 2001. *Antisthenes of Athens: Seeing the World Aright*. Westport, CT.

Nehamas, Alexander, and Paul Woodruff, trans. 1995. *Phaedrus*. Indianapolis.

Nicholson, Graeme. 1999. *Plato's* Phaedrus: *The Philosophy of Love*. West Lafayette, IN.

Nienkamp, Jean, ed. 1999. *Plato on Rhetoric and Language: Four Key Dialogues*. Mahwah, NJ.

Nightingale, Andrea. 1995. *Genres in Dialogue: Plato and the Construct of Philosophy*. Cambridge.

North, Helen. 1952. "The Use of Poetry in the Training of the Ancient Orator." *Traditio* 8, 1–33.

Obbink, Dirk, ed. 1995. *Philodemus and Poetry: Poetic Theory and Practice in Lucretius, Philodemus, and Horace*. Oxford.

Ober, Josiah. 1989. *Mass and Elite in Democratic Athens: Rhetoric, Ideology, and the Power of the People*. Princeton.

Ober, Josiah, and Barry Strauss. 1990. "Drama, Political Rhetoric, and the Discourse of Athenian Democracy." In *Nothing to Do with Dionysos? Athenian Drama in Its Social Context*, edited by J. Winkler and F. Zeitlin, 237–70. Princeton.

O'Sullivan, Neil. 1992. *Alcidamas, Aristophanes and the Beginnings of Greek Stylistic Theory (Hermes Einzelschriften 60)*. Stuttgart.

Page, Denys, ed. 1972. *Aeschyli Septem Quae Supersunt Tragoedias*. Oxford.

Parks, Ward. 1986. "Flyting and Fighting: Pathways in the Realization of the Epic Contest." *Neophilologus* 70, 292–306.

Parry, Adam. 1956. "The Language of Achilles." *Transactions of the American Philological Association* 87, 1–7.

———, ed. 1987. *The Making of Homeric Verse: The Collected Papers of Milman Parry*. Oxford.

Parry, Milman. 1930. "Studies in the Epic Technique of Oral Verse-Making. I. Homer and Homeric Style." *Harvard Studies in Classical Philology* 41, 73–147.

———. 1937. "About Winged Words." *Classical Philology* 32, 59–63.

Parsons, P. J. 1977. "The Lille 'Stesichorus.'" *Zeitschrift für Papyrologie und Epigraphik* 26, 7–36.

Pelliccia, Hayden. 1995. *Mind, Body, and Speech in Homer and Pindar*. Göttingen.

Pelling, Christopher, ed. 1990. *Characterization and Individuality in Greek Literature*. Oxford.

———. 2005. "Tragedy, Rhetoric, and Performance Culture." In *A Companion to Greek Tragedy*, edited by J. Gregory, 83–102. Oxford.

Pépin, Jean. 1993. "Aspects de la Lecture Antisthénienne d'Homère." In *Le Cynisme Ancien et ses Prolongements*, edited by M. Goulet-Cazé and R. Goulet, 1–13. Paris.

Pernot, Laurent. 2005. *Rhetoric in Antiquity*, trans. W. E. Higgins. Washington, DC. Originally published as *La Rhétorique dans l'Antiquité*. Paris, 2000.

Phillips, Carl, trans. 2003. *Sophocles: Philoctetes*. Oxford.

Plett, Henrich. 1985. "Rhetoric." In *Discourse and Literature*, edited by T. van Dijk, 59–84. Philadelphia.

Powell, Barry. 1991. *Homer and the Origin of the Greek Alphabet*. Cambridge.

Pratt, Louise H. 1993. *Lying and Poetry from Homer to Pindar: Falsehood and Deception in Archaic Greek Poetics*. Ann Arbor.

Prince, Cashman Kerr. 2002. *The Rhetoric of Instruction in Archaic Greek Didactic Poetry*. Diss., Stanford University.

Rabe, Hugo, ed. 1892–93. *Syriani in Hermogenem Commentaria*, vols. 1–2. Leipzig.

———, ed. 1913. *Hermogenis Opera*. Repr. 1969. Stuttgart.

———, ed. 1931. *Prolegomenon Sylloge*. Leipzig.

Race, William H. 1990. *Style and Rhetoric in Pindar's Odes*. Atlanta.

———, ed. and trans. 1997. *Pindar: Olympian Odes, Pythian Odes; Pindar: Nemean Odes, Isthmian Odes, Fragments*. Cambridge, MA.

Radermacher, Ludvig. 1892. "Der Aias und Odysseus des Antisthenes." *Rheinisches Museum für Philologie* 74, 569–76.

———, ed. 1951. *Artium Scriptores: Reste der voraristotelischen Rhetorik*. Vienna.

Rankin, H. D. 1986. *Anthisthenes (sic) Sokratikos*. Amsterdam.

Redfield, James. 1994. *Nature and Culture in the* Iliad: *The Tragedy of Hector*. 1st ed. 1975. Durham.

Reeve, C. D. C., trans. 1998. *Plato: Cratylus*. Indianapolis.

Reinhardt, Tobias, and Michael Winterbottom, eds. 2006. *Quintilian:* Institutio Oratoria *Book 2*. Oxford.

Richardson, Nicholas J., ed. 1974. *The Homeric Hymn to Demeter*. Oxford.

———, ed. 2010. *Three Homeric Hymns: To Apollo, Hermes, and Aphrodite*. Cambridge.

Robbins, Emmet. 1997. "Public Poetry." In *A Companion to the Greek Lyric Poets*, edited by D. Gerber, 221–87. Leiden.

Roisman, Hanna. 2005. "Nestor the Good Counsellor." *Classical Quarterly* 55, 17–38.

———. 2007. "Right Rhetoric in Homer." In *A Companion to Greek Rhetoric*, edited by I. Worthington, 429–46. Oxford.

Rorty, Amélie, ed. 1996. *Essays on Aristotle's* Rhetoric. Berkeley.

Rosner, Judith. 1976. "The Speech of Phoenix: *Iliad* 9.434–605." *Phoenix* 30, 314–27.

Rowe, C. J. 1986. *Plato: Phaedrus*. Warminster.

Russell, D. A., ed. 1964. *"Longinus" On the Sublime*. Oxford.

———. 1981. *Criticism in Antiquity*. London.

———. 1990. "*Ethos* in Oratory and Rhetoric." In *Characterization and Individuality in Greek Literature*, edited by C. Pelling, 197–212. Oxford.

Rutherford, R. B. 1982. "Tragic Form and Feeling in the *Iliad*." *Journal of Hellenic Studies* 102, 145–60.

Schiappa, Edward. 1990. "Did Plato Coin *Rhētorikē*?" *American Journal of Philology* 111, 457–70.

———. 1999. *The Beginnings of Rhetorical Theory in Classical Greece*. New Haven.

———. 2003. *Protagoras and* Logos: *A Study in Greek Philosophy and Rhetoric*. Columbia, SC.

Schiappa, Edward, and Jim Hamm. 2007. "Rhetorical Questions." In *A Companion to Greek Rhetoric*, edited by I. Worthington, 3–15. Oxford.

Schiappa, Edward, and David M. Timmerman. 2010. *Classical Greek Rhetorical Theory and the Disciplining of Discourse*. Cambridge.

Scodel, Ruth. 1982. "The Autobiography of Phoenix: *Iliad* 9.444–95." *American Journal of Philology* 102, 214–23.

———. 2002. *Listening to Homer: Tradition, Narrative, and Audience*. Ann Arbor.

Searle, John R. 1975. "A Taxonomy of Illocutionary Acts." In *Language, Mind, and Knowledge. Minnesota Studies in the Philosophy of Science* VII, edited by K. Gunderson, 344–69. Repr. in Searle, 1975, *Experience and Meaning. Studies in the Theory of Speech Acts*, 1–29. Cambridge.

Sedley, David. 2003. *Plato's* Cratylus. Cambridge.

Segal, Charles. 1986. *Pindar's Mythmaking: The Fourth Pythian Ode*. Princeton.

Snell, Bruno, and Herwig Maehler, eds. 1970. *Bacchylidis Carmina cum Fragmentis*. 10th ed. Leipzig.

———, eds. 1987. *Pindari Carmina cum Fragmentis* I. 8th ed. Leipzig.

Solmsen, Friedrich. 1941. "The Aristotelian Tradition in Ancient Rhetoric." *American Journal of Philology* 62, 35–50 and 169–90.

———. 1954. "The 'Gift' of Speech in Homer and Hesiod." *Transactions of the American Philological Association* 85, 1–15.

Solmsen, Friedrich, R. Merkelbach, and M. L. West, eds. 1970. *Hesiodi: Theogonia, Opera et Dies, Scutum; fragmenta selecta*. Oxford.

Struck, Peter. 2004. *Birth of the Symbol: Ancient Readers at the Limits of Their Texts*. Princeton.

Sudhaus, Siegfried, ed. 1892–1896. *Philodemi Volumina Rhetorica*, vols. 1–2. Leipzig.

Tigay, Jeffrey H. 1982. *The Evolution of the Gilgamesh Epic*. Philadelphia.

Toohey, Peter. 1994. "Epic and Rhetoric." In *Persuasion: Greek Rhetoric in Action*, edited by I. Worthington, 153–75. London.

Usher, Stephen. 1999. *Greek Oratory: Tradition and Originality*. Oxford.

van Buitenen, J. A. B., ed. and trans. 1973. *The Mahābhārata 1: The Book of the Beginning*. Chicago.

van der Valk, Marchinus, ed. 1971–87. *Eustathii Archiepiscopi Thessalonicensis Commentarii ad Homeri Iliadem Pertinentes*, vols. 1–4. Leiden.

Vickers, Brian. 1988. "The Atrophy of Modern Rhetoric, Vico to De Man." *Rhetorica* 6, 21–56.

Walcot, Peter. 1991. "The Homeric *Hymn to Aphrodite*: A Literary Appraisal." *Greece and Rome* 38, 137–55.

Walker, Jeffrey. 2000. *Rhetoric and Poetics in Antiquity*. Oxford.

Waltham, Clae. 1971. *Shu Ching: Book of History; A Modernized Edition of the Translations of James Legge*. Chicago.

Walz, Christian, ed. 1832–36. *Rhetores Graeci*, vols. 1–6. Repr. 1968. Stuttgart.

Watson, Burton. 1962. *Early Chinese Literature*. New York.

Welch, Kathleen E. 1990. *The Contemporary Reception of Classical Rhetoric: Appropriations of Ancient Discourse*. Hillsdale, NJ.

Wells, Cornelia. 2003. "Toward a Fragmatics, or Improvisionary Histories of Rhetoric, the Eternally Ad Hoc." *Philosophy and Rhetoric* 36, 277–300.

West, Martin L., ed. 1966. *Hesiod: Theogony*. Oxford.

———, ed. 1978a. *Hesiod: Works and Days*. Oxford.

———. 1978b. "Stesichorus at Lille." *Zeitschrift für Papyrologie und Epigraphik* 29, 1–4.

———. 1983. *The Orphic Poems*. Oxford.

———, trans. 1988. *Hesiod: Thoegony, Works and Days*. Oxford.

———, ed. 1989. *Iambi et Elegi Graeci ante Alexandrum Cantati*, vol. 1. Oxford.

———, ed. 1992. *Iambi et Elegi Graeci ante Alexandrum Cantati*, vol. 2. Oxford.

———, trans. 1993. *Greek Lyric Poetry*. Oxford.

———, ed. and trans. 2003. *Homeric Hymns, Homeric Apocrypha, Lives of Homer*. Cambridge, MA.

White, David A. 1993. *Rhetoric and Reality in Plato's* Phaedrus. Albany.

White, James Boyd. 1984. *When Words Lose Their Meaning: Constitutions and Reconstitutions of Language, Character, and Community*. Chicago.

Whitman, Cedric H. 1958. *Homer and the Heroic Tradition*. New York.

Willcock, M. M. 1964. "Mythological Paradeigma in the *Iliad*." *Classical Quarterly* 14, 141–54.

————, 1977. "Ad hoc Invention in the *Iliad*." *Harvard Studies in Classical Philology* 81, 41–53.

Wills, John W. 1970. "Speaking Arenas of Ancient Mesopotamia." *Quarterly Journal of Speech* 56, 398–405.

Winterbottom, Michael, ed. 1970. *M. Fabi Quintiliani: Institutionis Oratoriae Libri Duodecim*, vols. 1–2. Oxford.

Wooten, Cecil W., trans. 1987. *Hermogenes'* On Types of Style. Chapel Hill.

Worman, Nancy. 2002. *The Cast of Character: Style in Greek Literature*. Austin.

Worthington, Ian, ed. 1994. *Persuasion: Greek Rhetoric in Action*. London.

————, ed. 2007. *A Companion to Greek Rhetoric*. Oxford.

Zeyl, Donald J., trans. 1987. *Plato: Gorgias*. Indianapolis.

Index